# THE NURSE WHO BECAME A SPY

*For all women who have resisted Fascism*

# THE NURSE WHO BECAME A SPY

## MADGE ADDY'S WAR AGAINST FASCISM

CHRIS HALL

PEN & SWORD HISTORY

AN IMPRINT OF PEN & SWORD BOOKS LTD.
YORKSHIRE – PHILADELPHIA

First published in Great Britain in 2021 by
**PEN AND SWORD HISTORY**
An imprint of
Pen & Sword Books Ltd
Yorkshire – Philadelphia

Copyright © Chris Hall, 2021

ISBN 978 1 52677 958 8

The right of Chris Hall to be identified as Author of
this work has been asserted by him in accordance with the Copyright,
Designs and Patents Act 1988.

A CIP catalogue record for this book is available from the British Library.

All rights reserved. No part of this book may be reproduced or transmitted in
any form or by any means, electronic or mechanical including photocopying,
recording or by any information storage and retrieval system, without permission
from the Publisher in writing.

Typeset in Times New Roman 11.5/14 by
SJmagic DESIGN SERVICES, India.
Printed and bound by CPI Group (UK) Ltd, Croydon, CR0 4YY

Pen & Sword Books Limited incorporates the imprints of Atlas, Archaeology,
Aviation, Discovery, Family History, Fiction, History, Maritime, Military, Military
Classics, Politics, Select, Transport, True Crime, Air World, Frontline Publishing,
Leo Cooper, Remember When, Seaforth Publishing, The Praetorian Press,
Wharncliffe Local History, Wharncliffe Transport, Wharncliffe True Crime and
White Owl.

For a complete list of Pen & Sword titles please contact
PEN & SWORD BOOKS LIMITED
47 Church Street, Barnsley, South Yorkshire, S70 2AS, England
E-mail: enquiries@pen-and-sword.co.uk
Website: www.pen-and-sword.co.uk

Or
PEN AND SWORD BOOKS
1950 Lawrence Rd, Havertown, PA 19083, USA
E-mail: Uspen-and-sword@casematepublishers.com
Website: www.penandswordbooks.com

# Contents

*Acknowledgements* vi
*List of Illustrations* ix
*Abbreviations* xi
*Introduction* xiii

Chapter 1  Manchester Days: Early Life 1904–1937   1
Chapter 2  A War Far Away: Spanish Civil War 1936–1939   12
Chapter 3  From Apathy to Direct Action: British Responses to the Spanish Civil War   28
Chapter 4  Humanitarian Aid for Republican Spain: British Medical Volunteers   48
Chapter 5  Head Nurse at Uclés: Madge in Spain 1937–1939   69
Chapter 6  Europe 1933–1940: Spanish Republican Exiles, Events Leading to War and the Second World War to the Fall of France   102
Chapter 7  France 1940–1944: Vichy, the Resistance and British Support   121
Chapter 8  Resisting Fascism Again: Madge, Wilhelm and Thorkild: France 1940–1944   139

*Epilogue* 174
*Notes* 179
*Bibliography* 201
*Illustration Sources* 211
*Index* 212

# Acknowledgements

I was first interested in Madge Addy when I read a brief article by Angela Jackson about her life. In this article it mentioned that, as well as being a nurse in the Spanish Civil War (which I already knew), she also received an Officer of the Order of the British Empire medal for her Second World War activities. I had no idea she had a connection with Chorlton-cum-Hardy, where I have lived since 1995, or that she was involved in the Second World War. With these facts I decided to raise funds for a Manchester civic plaque in her honour if I could find a place of residence for her in Chorlton-cum-Hardy. This was duly found, and a plaque in her honour was unveiled in 2018. At the reception afterwards, many people came up to me and said her story must be told. My original intention was to have Madge Addy honoured by the city of Manchester and that would be the end of it; however, with so many people encouraging me to write her story, the seed was planted, and so I want to say a big 'thank you' to these people for their encouragement.

A big thanks goes to my wife Melanie Hall, who has been the chief editor throughout, frequently turning my ramblings into a structured piece of work. Her suggestions and patience have been key elements in completing the work. Thanks also to my two daughters; Alex provided essential IT advice and Rosa loaned her laptop until I possessed my own.

Thanks goes to my commissioning editor at Pen and Sword, Claire Hopkins, who championed Madge's story and trusted me to deliver it, and whose suggestions have turned this into the engaging book it has become. Her guidance and professionalism have helped to allay any fears I have had regarding the writing of this book.

An essential part of this book was the help and information provided by the very patient Ole Kleppe, the grandson of Wilhelm Holst, Madge's second husband. He answered my myriad emails, constant questions and requests, and supplied me with invaluable information about Madge and

## Acknowledgements

Wilhelm, as well as providing several key photographs and translating material from Norwegian.

Andrew Simpson, a much-published local historian, provided me with important information about Madge's family and sourced local photographs, despite being very ill during the time I was writing the book. His knowledge has been invaluable for material on Madge's time in Manchester.

I would like to thank the Addie family. Jackie Nixon got in touch with me after seeing a five-minute Granada Television broadcast about Madge. She organised and set up the interview with her father, Robert Addie, and her uncle, Geoffrey Addie (the different spelling of the surname is due, the family believe, to a mistake by the registrar when recording their births). Madge's nephews provided some very useful information on Madge's early life. The Addie family also kindly provided me with several family photographs.

Thanks go to Mike Arnott, who took pictures of Uclés Monastery, where Madge nursed wounded soldiers in Spain, and for putting me in touch with Máximo Molina Gutiérrez and the Cuenca Local History Group, who found the owner of the amazing photographs of Madge in Spain, as well as providing useful local history information. A very big thanks to Santiago Y Ángel García Langa, the owner of the photographs of Madge in Spain, who give me the rights to show these unique photographs of Madge and her medical colleagues at Uclés during the Spanish Civil War.

My thanks go to my work colleagues, who translated Spanish and French documents for me, and to Rachel Clarke who, like Madge, lived in Marseille for several years and used her language skills to translate some French documents for me.

A big thank you to Meirian Jump at the Marx Memorial Library, who give me permission to quote extensively from Madge's letters in their Spanish collection. Similarly, thanks to James King of Warwick University, who gave me permission to quote extensively from the Trades Union Congress archives, which included letters from Madge and Spanish Medical Aid Committee material. Without these permissions Madge's story in Spain would have lost the crucial human and personal dynamic. Anthony Grahame from Sussex Academic Press kindly allowed me to quote several extracts from Linda Palfreeman's book *Salud* on the Spanish Republican medical services in the Civil War.

The National Archives gave me permission me to use photographs in their collection of Madge and her third husband, Thorkild Hansen. The auctioneers Dominic Winter kindly allowed me to use a picture of Mr and Mrs Hansen's medals.

Every effort has been made to trace copyright holders and to obtain their permission for the use of copyright material, be they images or quotations. The publisher apologises for any errors or omissions in the above list and later credits, and would be grateful to be notified of any corrections that should be incorporated in future reprints or editions of this book.

# List of Illustrations

**Plate 1**   Madge Addy's father, Frederick William Addy (1). Madge's mother, Mary, with younger brother, Edward (2). Madge as a child with younger brother, Edward (3).

**Plate 2**   Madge, 1923; trainee nurse at Hope Hospital (right side) in concert party outfit (4). Madge with fellow trainee nurses and Miss Hayes, centre. Madge is fourth on the right, top row. Again in concert party clothes (5).

**Plate 3**   34 Manchester Road (on the right), Madge's home 1932–1937. Two of her brothers lived at what is now the dry cleaners (photo taken 2020) (6). Madge's pet dog 'Lion' (7).

**Plate 4**   Picture House Cinema, which was directly opposite 34 Manchester Road (8). Chorlton-cum-Hardy Public Library, across the road from 34 Manchester Road (9).

**Plate 5**   Uclés Monastery (photo taken 2019) (10). Entrance to Uclés, ornate door described by Madge in her letters (photo taken 2019) (11).

**Plate 6**   Madge giving the clenched fist anti-Fascist salute alongside British-supplied ambulance (12).

**Plate 7**   Madge posing with injured Republican soldiers (13). Madge outside the operating theatre with Spanish doctor (14).

**Plate 8**   Madge, centre, working in the X-ray department (15). Group picture of medical staff at Uclés; Madge is the woman on the left; last on the right on the front row is Wilhelm Holst (16).

**Plate 9**   Madge, third right, with medical colleagues in the 'Manchester Ward' (17). Teresa Martinez Garcia, a Spanish nurse at Uclés (18).

| | |
|---|---|
| **Plate 10** | Madge giving blood as part of a blood transfusion to a wounded patient (19). |
| **Plate 11** | Wilhelm Holst in the uniform of a Republican Army Major (20). Wilhelm's two sons, Per and Einar Andreas, in 1931. Later murdered by the Germans during the invasion of Norway in 1940 (21). |
| **Plate 12** | Madge and Wilhelm in Marseille around 1940 (22). |
| **Plate 13** | 'Mrs Oats', photo of Madge in Wilhelm Holst's SOE file (23). Thorkild Hansen, photo from his SOE file (24). |
| **Plate 14** | Photo taken of the front of Madge and Wilhelm's house in Marseille, 48 Rue Boudouresque (photo taken in 2020) (25). Rear of 48 Rue Boudouresque, showing the small harbour (photo taken 2020) (26). Back of the house in Marseille, Madge with little boy. Wilhelm is standing on the steps (27). |
| **Plate 15** | Group picture taken during the war. Madge is seated far left, front row. Wilhelm is standing on the far left (28). Group picture taken during the war. Madge is standing far right and Wilhelm second left (29). |
| **Plate 16** | Top row, Thorkild Hansen's medals: Danish medal for serving in the Second World War, British King's Medal for Courage in the Cause of Freedom, French Legion of Honour, French *Croix de Guerre* and French Resistance medal. Second row, Madge's medals: OBE and French *Croix de Guerre* with bronze oakleaf (30). City of Manchester commemorative plaque in honour of Madge, located at 34 Manchester Road, Chorlton-cum-Hardy (photo taken 2019) (31). |

# Abbreviations

| | |
|---|---|
| AFSC | American Friends Service Committee |
| BCC | Basque Children's Committee |
| BUF | British Union of Fascists |
| CBE | Commander of the Order of the British Empire |
| CEDA | *Confederación Española de Derechas Autónomas* |
| CNT | *Confederación Nacional de Trabajo* |
| CPGB | Communist Party of Great Britain |
| CSI | *Central Sanitaria Internacional* |
| FAI | *Federacion Anarquista Iberica* |
| FFC | *Forces françaises combattantes* |
| FFI | *Forces françaises de l'intérieur* |
| IBMT | International Brigade Memorial Trust |
| IFTU | International Federation of Trades Unions |
| LCC | London County Council |
| MBE | Member of the Order of the British Empire |
| MML | Marx Memorial Library |
| MRD | Medical Repatriation Board |
| NJCSR | National Joint Committee for Spanish Relief |
| OBE | Officer of the Order of the British Empire |
| PCE | *Partido Comunista de Espana* |
| POUM | *Partido Obrero de Unificación Marxista* |
| PSOE | *Partido Socialista Obrero Español* |
| PSUC | *Partido Socialista Unificado de Catalunya* |
| RAMC | Royal Army Medical Corps |
| SHD | *Service Historique de la Défense* |
| SIS | Secret Intelligence Service |
| SMA | Socialist Medical Association |
| SMAC | Spanish Medical Aid Committee |
| SOE | Special Operations Executive |

| | |
|---|---|
| SRN | State Registered Nurse |
| TNA | The National Archives |
| TUC | Trade Union Congress |
| UGT | *Unión General de Trabajadores* |
| UN | United Nations |
| WPSU | Women's Social and Political Union |
| YCL | Young Communist League |

# Introduction

The life of Marguerite Nuttall Lightfoot up to 1937 had been very conventional and could easily be described as ordinary. She is better known as Madge Addy and will be called this throughout this book. Madge spent her childhood, adolescence and adult life in various districts of Manchester. She had a normal childhood, although life would have been hard, as her father died when she was still a child. She trained as a nurse and married a local man. The marriage was childless, and this might have been the catalyst for Madge's transformation from a chiropodist in Manchester to a Spanish Civil War nurse, and later to a secret agent in the Second World War. The only sign of her adventurous spirit in her early life was that she learned to ride a motorcycle. Madge is the perfect example of how someone with no wartime, military or espionage experience and little training can become an important and, in some cases, essential part of an organisation.

Once Madge volunteered to nurse in Republican Spain she served to the bitter end, and became a PoW of the enemy forces, the Nationalists. She spent several months in Fascist Spain before she was able to return to Britain. During her time in Spain she became Head Nurse at Uclés Hospital and was the last British nurse to leave Spain. In Spain, Madge was wounded, and fell in love with a Norwegian volunteer called Wilhelm Holst. On her return from Spain, she stayed in Britain only a few months before leaving to live in Paris with Holst.

When the Second World War broke out Madge and Wilhelm lived in Paris until the German invasion of France in 1940, when it soon became obvious that the defeat of the French armed forces was only a matter of time. Madge and Wilhelm left Paris for Marseille, where there were many trapped British soldiers. Both Madge and Wilhelm would soon become involved in resisting both the puppet French Vichy government and the German occupation forces. Madge was involved in the setting up of the Garrow escape line, which later became the Garrow-O'Leary line, which helped to get Allied soldiers and airmen out of France and into neutral Spain. Later, she helped to set up the Pierre-Jacques escape line, helping compromised Allied agents escape from France. She also volunteered to be a courier, travelling to Portugal with secret messages. Madge became a full time agent with the rank of lieutenant and was deputy leader, and later the leader, of two Resistance groups: Billet and Alexandre. For her services in the Second World War she was awarded the OBE and was honoured by the French with the *Croix de Guerre* medal. Again, there was romance in dangerous and dark times, as Madge fell in love with a Danish special agent called Thorkild Hansen, who became her third husband.

Madge's life was full of encounters with strong women and men, and in several cases some exceptional ones. Madge's mother had strong left-wing views and brought up a large family as a single mother for most of Madge's childhood and teenage years. Not an easy thing to do in the 1910s and 1920s, and her mother's independent spirit and political views were certainly mirrored by Madge. Madge had an elder sister called Florence, whom she looked up to, and who also worked in the health services as a midwife. When Madge was training at Hope Hospital, her supervisor was an older nurse called Miss Hayes. In Spain, Madge met other British nurses and administrators and forged strong friendships with the Spanish trainee nurses. One nurse called Mercedes became her best friend. On her periods of leave in Britain she met members of the SMAC, including Leah Manning MP. In France, Madge met many ordinary, but incredibly brave, French women who willingly hid British and Allied military personnel, knowing that the penalty if they were caught was execution or slow death in a concentration camp. The most exceptional woman Madge knew in France was Nancy Fiocca, better known as Nancy Wake, who became one of the most famous female Resistance leaders in the Second World War.

During her lifetime, Madge came across some outstanding and brave men. In Spain she is full of praise for the Spanish doctors. A Dr Malimson in Manchester was her contact for fundraising activities for Spain. He is one of the few men who got Madge to relate how she was actually feeling. Madge's letters usually contained information about her colleagues, conditions in wartime Spain and making appeals and lists of medical equipment needed. Dr Malimson and his supporters

## Introduction

were able to raise enough money to equip a ward in Uclés Hospital, where Madge was based. The ward was called the Manchester Ward. In Marseille and during her Second World War exploits, Madge met ordinary Frenchmen who were willing to house and hide Allied military personnel, despite the risks they knew that they were running. Madge met three remarkable men during her Second World War activities: Ian Garrow, Patrick O'Leary (whose real name was Albert Guérisse) and Pierre Lalande (whose real name was Guido Zembsch-Schreve).

Two without doubt remarkable men in her life were her second and third husbands: Wilhelm Holst and Thorkild Hansen. Wilhelm was a Norwegian Quaker and an international volunteer in the medical services in the Spanish Civil War. He rose to become a major in the Spanish government medical services and became the conduit for medical aid from abroad entering Spain. In the Second World War he became a member of the British secret services and head of the Resistance groups Billet and Alexandre. There is a possibility that he and Madge were never actually married. Thorkild Hansen volunteered to fight in the French army and after the defeat of France he fled to Marseille. There he became one of the early group of volunteers, along with Madge, in assisting Ian Garrow to get British military personnel out of France and across the border to Spain. Thorkild became a British special agent and set up an escape route by sea. He was also the joint leader of the Pierre-Jacques line. Both Wilhelm and Thorkild were highly decorated for their wartime exploits. Thorkild and Madge were married in London in 1955.

Another theme throughout the book is the tragic and heroic story of the Spanish Republicans (supporters of the Spanish government in the Civil War). The Spanish Republican government, armies, medical services and its supporters feature heavily in the chapters about the Spanish Civil War. After the end of the Civil War they appear as refugees in France. In the Second World War many Spanish Republicans worked in the Resistance movement as fighters, couriers and mountain guides helping Allied military personnel over the Pyrenees into Spain. Others served in the French army and later the Free French Army of de Gaulle. The first unit of the Free French Army to enter Paris at its liberation were Spanish Republicans. Their story ends with their betrayal by the Allied powers, who allowed General Franco's Spanish Fascist regime to stay in power till his death in 1975.

Pulling together Madge's story was a complex process, involving several individuals, and records and photographs in different countries. Many Spanish Civil War veterans have been interviewed by academics in more recent years; however, Madge died in 1970, before the first groups of veterans began to be interviewed. Madge herself wrote an account of her experiences in the Spanish Civil War during the summer of 1939. Hers and Thorkild's (he died in 1966) medals have been sold in three auctions since her death; in the most recent sale all ephemera and written documents had disappeared and only the medals were sold. Madge's account of her time in Spain is currently lost to posterity along with letters of thanks regarding her Second World War activity and correspondence between medal collector Ron Penhall and Madge's wartime boss, Donald Darling. Madge wrote a mass of letters during her time in Spain, some of which have survived and are available, and they give a great glimpse into her wartime nursing experience in Spain. They also help to paint a picture of Madge herself. Madge is mentioned in several newspapers of the time; she also wrote for the SMAC bulletin and is mentioned in minutes of their meetings on several occasions. However, it proved much more difficult to find information about Madge's Second World War activities. Both her husbands have files in TNA in Kew, but she is only mentioned in Wilhelm Holst's files. She is mentioned a few times in books about the escape activities in Marseille. Donald Darling, a senior intelligence officer in Lisbon during the war, gives more details about Madge and, in particular, her activities as a courier. The letter recommending Madge for an OBE gives a brief account of her wartime activities. In the French Resistance archives in Vincennes, just outside Paris, there is a small file on Madge, outlining her wartime activities.

Madge left no diary or written account of her life; she had no children so there were no direct descendants to be interviewed or to have inherited her papers. Yet a combination of detailed researching, luck and different people pulling together has enabled enough material to be amassed to paint a picture of this remarkable woman's life. A television appearance by the author was seen by Madge's great-niece, who got in touch. This led to a meeting with Madge's nephews, both of whom are over 90 years old. They were interviewed and supplied some useful information about her Manchester days, and provided invaluable family photographs. Local Manchester historian Andrew Simpson further added to the story of her

*Introduction*

early life with genealogical information and some very helpful nursing documents.

A chance email led to the discovery of the amazing photographs of Madge in Uclés during the Spanish Civil War. I asked a fellow International Brigade Memorial Trust member, Mike Arnot, who was visiting Uclés, to take some photographs for me. After the trip he sent me his photographs and the photographs of Madge in Uclés. These were sent to him by Máximo Molina Gutiérrez of the Cuenca local history group. These photographs had been secretly hidden throughout the era of Franco's dictatorship in Spain (1939–1975) by the Uclés village doctor; his grandson, Ángel y Santiago García Langa, gave me permission to use these never-seen images, which further bring to life Madge's experiences in the Civil War.

Another email arrived out of the blue from Ole Kleppe, the grandson of Wilhelm Holst. Throughout the project he has sent and translated documents from Norway, Spain and France about Wilhelm and Madge, and supplied family photographs that included Madge. These portray a much more sophisticated, older, glamorous and confident woman than the ones in the Uclés photographs.

Madge lived through an eight-year period when the world changed forever. From 1936 to 1945, Madge was a committed anti-Fascist, who, from 1937 onwards (definitely through to 1944), was willing to risk her life to oppose Fascism. It did not matter which country was opposing Fascism; Madge was willing to do all she could to support those men and women who would not stand by and do nothing or turn a blind eye.

The book begins with Madge's life up to 1937 and first looks at her family, what is known about Madge in this period, and the Manchester in which she grew up and lived. It moves on to Madge's involvement in the Spanish Civil War. We will cover three aspects of the Spanish Civil War in some depth, to give the reader some understanding of Madge's activities in Spain. The first chapter is a general narrative about the Spanish Civil War, so that readers can understand why Madge made the decision to go to Spain. The next chapter looks at the reaction of Britain to the Spanish Civil War, the British government's view of the conflict and its actions, and the general public's views about Spain and the Civil War. The British government and the vast majority of the British people had little interest in the Spanish Civil War, but for a sizeable minority the war in Spain was a major event in their lives. For this reason, we will focus on the ways that these people helped the Spanish government during this time. Finally, before we get on to Madge's activities in Spain, we will look at medical aid to Spain, and the experiences of the British medical volunteers there.

Before we get on to Madge's activities in the Second World War, there are two linking chapters. The first describes events elsewhere in Europe while Madge was in Spain, and what happened to the defeated Spanish Republican refugees and ex-soldiers who fled to France at the end of the Civil War. It also looks at the early years of the Second World War, ending with the fall of France in 1940. The next chapter will look at occupied France, Vichy France and the French Resistance, and also the various British secret service agencies and their role in the Second World War.

Madge's story ends with a brief epilogue covering her last years, and the successful campaign within the city of Manchester to honour her life and work with a plaque.[1]

# Chapter 1

# Manchester Days: Early Life 1904–1937

In was a pleasant spring day in 1937 and two young boys were excited to be visiting their Aunty Daisy. She had promised that she would take them to an exciting open-air meeting to do with the war in Spain, which was in all the newspapers and appearing in newsreels at the local cinema. Robert and Geoffrey were dropped off by their father, Francis (Frank) Addy, at 34 Manchester Road, Chorlton-cum-Hardy, in Manchester. Aunty Daisy was Francis' younger sister, Marguerite, a married woman in her early thirties. The three of them left 34 Manchester Road. As they walked along, they could see across the road the local cinema and a billiard hall, and, as they crossed the road, they passed the Chorlton public library. Aunty Daisy took them past their junior school, Oswald Road, and then they turned right to walk from Chorlton-cum-Hardy towards Stretford, the home of Lancashire County Cricket Club and Manchester United football club. As they walked towards the meeting, they passed a mass of newly-built houses and finally arrived at their destination at Greatstone Road.

Here, a few hundred people had gathered in the open area surrounded by roads with new houses and a small branch public library on one side, and shops and a new large public house with mock Tudor decoration on the other. The boys were very excited as they and their aunt joined the waiting crowd. There were people selling newspapers and pamphlets, and some had banners with 'Arms for Spain' crudely written on a bedsheet between two poles. Other people went around collecting money in tins for the relief of the victims of war in government-controlled Spain and for medical aid. The meeting was brought to order and individuals from various organisations addressed the crowd. All the speakers had differing messages, from a local clergyman wishing for a peaceful solution, to a local Communist activist demanding that the British government sell arms to the Spanish Republican government. All the speakers, though, implored the crowd to give generously to support Republican Spain, and especially to give for humanitarian aid. A small group of people wearing little badges with a flash insignia did not stay quiet, and heckled the Communist speaker. They were the local Fascists and members of the British Union of Fascists, followers of the charismatic Sir Oswald Mosley.[1] The boys did not really understand what had gone on or what the speakers were saying, but they noticed on the way home that Aunty Daisy was much quieter than normal and deep in thought after the 'Aid Spain' meeting.

This and other 'Aid Spain' meetings attended by Madge Addy were part of the first steps that would change her life for ever. Up to this point Madge had led a conventional life; this was to change dramatically during a truly remarkable seven to eight-year period.

Madge's father was Frederick William Addy. He was born in Macclesfield in Cheshire in 1857; his father was born in Ireland and by occupation was a silk dyer. Frederick Addy's occupation was as a reed maker and finisher, a highly skilled profession a little like a modern precision instrument maker. Reed makers were an essential part of the cotton and textile industry, and their skill was needed to make the looms work effectively. By 1891 he and the family had moved to Bingley in Yorkshire, where he continued doing his skilled work. By 1901, he was living in Bolton as a boarder with his 11-year-old son Henry, still working as a reed maker. It is not known why he and his son were living separately from the rest of the family; it was possibly necessary in order to find skilled work. The rest of the family were living in Great Harwood near Blackburn in Lancashire. Frederick had married Madge's mother, Mary Costello, in Macclesfield in 1882.[2]

Like her husband, Mary Costello was born in Macclesfield in 1866. She was a dressmaker, which was a highly skilled job that could be done from home, but often involved long hours of toil, and intricate and painstaking work for often very low pay. It is possible that Mary had strong political views – there is a family story that she was known as 'Red Mary' for her extreme left-wing views. Maybe her mother's views were to have a significant impact on Madge's personal development and later strong anti-Fascist opinions and actions. Frederick William Addy died around 1909–1910, as in the census of 1911 Mary is recorded as a widow and the youngest child is aged 2. In a nursing report on Madge in 1929, her father is recorded as deceased. Mary Addy was effectively a single mother for most of Madge's childhood and was not to live to see Madge married, dying in 1924 in Manchester.[3]

The family had lived for a time in Yorkshire, so it is possible that the family members developed a Yorkshire accent during this time. Although she never lived in Yorkshire herself, Madge's accent may have sounded like the other members of the family, so that when she is mentioned during the Second World War the writers believed she was from Yorkshire. However, this could just as equally be the writers supposing that, because Madge had a northern accent, she was from Yorkshire. Since she spent all her life in Manchester and Salford before going to Spain, it is most likely that she had a Mancunian accent.[4]

There is a family tradition that the Addy family was linked to the famous Mark Addy. Mark Addy was born in Salford in 1838, and was a boatman, skilled oarsman and innkeeper. During his life he rescued over fifty people from the River Irwell. His first rescue was when he was aged 13 and he could not even swim; he later became a proficient swimmer. Mark Addy became a licensee of a public house called the Old Boathouse, located on the side of the Irwell river. In 1878 he was given 200 guineas by the people of Salford for his rescuing exploits and was thanked publicly by the mayor. His bravery was recognised nationally, and Queen Victoria presented him with the then highest award for civilian bravery, the Albert Medal. But his rescues from the river ultimately led to his death in 1890, when he swallowed water from the heavily polluted Irwell and developed tuberculosis. After his death, the people of Salford erected a large 4m-high memorial in his honour in Weaste Cemetery. A public house on the River Irwell bore his name for many years. There is no definitive link between Mark Addy and Madge's family, but Madge's future actions showed enormous courage which just maybe was inherited from this very distant relative.[5]

Marguerite Nuttall Addy was born on 16 February 1904; throughout her life she was known as Madge. Like most children at that time she was born at home, which was 13 Moreton Street in the registration district of Chorlton-upon-Medlock in south Manchester. Madge was the sixth child of Frederick William and Mary Addy, and the second girl. She had five older siblings; the eldest being Joseph, followed by Florence, Henry, Thomas and Francis. Madge would later have a younger brother called Edward. The religion of the family was Roman Catholic, although it was by no means strictly enforced, since in adulthood Madge had no religious beliefs. By 1911, the family had moved to Rusholme in Manchester and Mary, now a widow, lived with all her children except for 21-year-old Henry. The family was living at 58 Rusholme Grove in Rusholme, close to the city centre of Manchester.[6]

Rusholme started off as a separate village in the parish of Manchester. Its name described its early features of mossy land with reedy pools of water. In 1655 there were a mere fourteen ratepayers in Rusholme; by 1801 there were over 700 people in the village. In the 1870s many new houses were built there, which attracted both working-class and middle-class families. In 1885 Rusholme became part of the city of Manchester. This led to dramatic improvements in the state of its roads, street lighting, the introduction of three large municipal parks (Birch Fields, Platt Fields and Whitworth Park), and a public library. By the time that Madge was living in Rusholme in 1914, its population had grown to 20,000. The pre-Great War Rusholme in which Madge spent her childhood was a busy and bustling suburb of the city of Manchester, with many shops, a theatre, a tram service to and from the city centre, and parks with boating lakes and a paddling pool, which she almost certainly would have visited.[7]

Madge's eldest brother, Joseph, was born in Macclesfield and by 1911 he was working in Manchester as an iron turner, which was a metal machinist. Florence, Madge's only sister, was born in Bingley and at the 1911 census she was recorded as working as a dressmaker like her mother, although later she became a midwife. Her family name was Florrie. When Madge married for the first time her mother was no longer alive, and Florence was one of the two witnesses who signed the marriage certificate. After the Second World War, Florence made several trips to Canada to help chaperone war brides on the journey by sea from Britain to Canada. It seems that both Addy sisters had a desire to help people less fortunate than themselves, coupled with a wanderlust. Henry Addy was born in Bingley and was boarding with his father in Bolton in 1901. He was probably living with his father in order to learn the reed-making trade, and he may have stayed working in the cotton industry in Lancashire. He is the forgotten member of the Addy family; her nephews remember only four brothers and two sisters.[8]

Two more of Madge's brothers were born in Great Harwood near Blackburn; Thomas and Francis, or Frank, as he was called by the family.

## Manchester Days: Early Life 1904–1937

In the 1930s Thomas lived just two doors away from Madge in Chorlton-cum-Hardy in Manchester, renting the house with his younger brother, James Edward, and two women. By 1938–1939 they were still living together at 50 Nell Lane in Chorlton, which Madge used as a correspondence address when she was serving as a nurse in Spain. Frank Addy was the father of Madge's two nephews, Robert Francis and Geoffrey Michael, and was married to a woman called Mabel. During the Great War he served in the Royal Flying Corps. His profession was an engineer and he worked at local firms Metro Vickers and Ford. Like many of the family in the 1930s he also lived in Chorlton-cum-Hardy, at 13 Vincent Avenue. Madge's younger brother, Edward, was born in Manchester. He was referred to as James Edward, and as we have seen lived in Chorlton-cum-Hardy in the 1930s with his elder brother, Thomas. It was this younger brother who was named as the executor of Madge's will, which she organised before returning to Spain in early 1938.[9]

After living in Rusholme, the family moved to Moss Side, another inner-city suburb of Manchester. Here, Madge attended the Princess Road school and made the decision to become a nurse. She began her training in January 1923 at Salford Union Infirmary, which was known as Hope Hospital. The hospital began as a Poor Law infirmary; its role was to take the pressure off the local workhouse by looking after the destitute infirm and sick. For most of Madge's training there, her patients would have been these destitute, sick people. The hospital foundation stone was laid in March 1880 and it was formally opened in October 1882 with capacity for 1,000 patients. It was named Hope Hospital to hide its link to the workhouse. Widows were used to clean the hospital and they were paid a small wage, and a bath man was employed to bathe the patients once a week. Facilities were quite spartan and, although it had an operating theatre, few operations ever took place. Leadership was provided by a medical superintendent, a matron, a chaplain and a dispenser. Nurses were paid £5 a year and had to purchase their own medical instruments. A typical day for a nurse involved reporting at the hospital at 5.45 am and going on duty at 6.30 am. There were stories of a woman in a white robe haunting the hospital at night, who went around offering and giving help to patients. A night sister may have been one of the first pioneers in perfecting the art of 'being on call'. The hospital had one perfectly straight main corridor with wards on either side; the night sister would place an oil lamp in the corridor outside the ward she was attending so that lamp was easily spotted anywhere along the corridor. This made it easy for other staff to find her. By the time the Great War was taking place, nurses' wages had increased to £40 a year with an additional wartime bonus food ration. Besides continuing to look after destitute sick and infirm patients, the hospital also accommodated and cared for wounded soldiers returning from France. In 1925, Hope Hospital became a general infirmary, looking after the local residents as well as the destitute. This led to a dramatic increase in the number of operations (500) and births (366) at the hospital per year. Madge was doing her nurse training during these big changes at Hope Hospital and left the hospital as a trained nurse in February 1926.[10]

During her first Christmas at the hospital, Madge took part in two revues to entertain the staff and patients on 25 and 29 December 1923, and was pictured with other trainee nurses in costume surrounding a rather austere senior nurse known as Miss Hayes. She sent a postcard of the picture to the family, signed Daisy, which was what the family called her. Madge's first job after leaving Hope Hospital saw her working at a private nursing home at York Place in Manchester from April to July 1926. Later, in 1929, she worked as a private nurse in the Whalley Range area of Manchester. In April 1927 she gained her district nursing qualifications after attending lectures at the Manchester and Salford District Health Authority from September 1926 to March 1927. Madge attended the compulsory lectures plus optional ones on tuberculosis and ophthalmia. In her end exam she scored forty-six out of sixty. The superintendent called Madge 'a good and well-trained nurse' and the inspector stated: 'a good nurse, has adapted herself well to district work'. Under 'Other Qualifications and Remarks' the report lists cycling and motor cycling; knowing Madge's future activities, this comes as no surprise. Being a motor cyclist was not something many young women would have accomplished in the 1920s! Madge almost certainly would have utilised her cycling skills while carrying out Resistance activities in the Second World War. Throughout the period 1927–1931 Madge was a State Registered Nurse, with registration number 42223. It is hard to tell whether she worked as a district nurse from 1927–1929, or whether she left the nursing profession for a time, returning to it again in January 1929. As a volunteer nurse in Spain, Madge worked as a masseuse, general nurse, in the X-ray department and as a theatre nurse.

She learned many new things in Spain as medicine took major steps forward during the Civil War. But her training at Hope Hospital and as a district nurse provided the foundation of Madge's effectiveness as a nurse in Spain. During Madge's medical training she worked as a theatre nurse and learned to be a masseuse besides doing general nursing.[11]

In the late 1920s Madge was living at 33 Ruskin Avenue in Moss Side. Living next door to her at number 31 was an older man called Arthur Wilson Lightfoot. His father's occupation was a joiner, a little like a carpenter but a less skilled occupation. Arthur himself was an electrician by trade; in time he became Madge's boyfriend, and eventually her first husband. They were married at a Registry Office in the district of south Manchester on 26 March 1930. Arthur was 29 years old and Madge 26. They left Moss Side in 1932 and moved to Chorlton-cum-Hardy, where they lived at 34 Manchester Road, along with two lodgers who lived with them at different times up to 1937. They were Barbara and Gwyneth Jackson. From 34 Manchester Road Madge ran a chiropody practice and possibly also did some work as a trained masseuse. From the same address, an 'Arthur Lightfoot' ran a joiner's business. Madge's father-in-law was a joiner, so perhaps he used his son's house as a business address. Alternatively, Madge's husband Arthur could have been running a joinery business with skills he learned from his father, even though he was an electrician by trade, and not a joiner. In 1939 Arthur was working as an electrician, so maybe the joinery business was a way of earning a little extra money on the side. The marriage was childless, and the two of them seem to have grown apart and eventually divorced; this decline in their relationship may have been a factor leading to Madge's decision to volunteer to serve as a nurse in Spain. In 1939 Arthur Lightfoot was living with his mother at 83 Ruskin Ave in Moss Side and working as an electrician for the Manchester Corporation.[12]

Chorlton-cum-Hardy, where Madge lived in the 1930s before she left for Spain, was a rapidly-growing south Manchester suburb. Its name may be derived from the Anglo-Saxon, meaning 'Ceorlfrith's settlement at Hearda's Island'. Chorlton and Hardy were two separate communities and the change of name to Chorlton-cum-Hardy may have been brought about purely to distinguish it from Chorlton-on-Medlock. Chorlton was part of the medieval manor of Withington and was a small settlement which grew very slowly from 1640 to 1851; the population only increased from 85 to just over 750. Chorlton-cum-Hardy expanded greatly in the nineteenth century with the improvement in communications. The building of Wilbraham Road linked Chorlton with its neighbouring district, Fallowfield, but the biggest factor in Chorlton's growth was the opening of a railway station in 1880. Chorlton, which had always been based around an area known as the 'Green', now centred on a crossroads at the convergence of two major roads, one of which was Wilbraham Road. In 1904, Chorlton-cum-Hardy was incorporated into the city of Manchester. This led to further transport links to the city with the introduction of a tram service. By the time Madge and Arthur moved to Chorlton-cum-Hardy it was a growing urban area, with great transport links to the city centre, cinemas, a library, swimming baths and many shops.[13]

Madge lived at 34 Manchester Road on a major road connected to the main crossroads in the town centre. Across the road from Madge's house was a large cinema built in 1920, known as the Picture House. Later it became the Savoy, and was finally called the Gaumont when it eventually closed down in 1962. It was perhaps in this cinema that Madge saw newsreels about Spain and the European dictators, which may have helped to influence her decision to volunteer as a nurse in Spain. Next door to the cinema was a temperance billiard hall which was opened in 1907. Next to the billiard hall was the public library. As part of the deal of joining the Manchester Corporation, the people of Chorlton were promised cheaper gas and water rates as well as a brand new library. The first library opened in 1908 in a rented house, and a purpose-built library was not forthcoming until six years later. The library on Manchester Road was built with a donation of £5,000 from the steel magnate and philanthropist Andrew Carnegie, and was officially opened on 4 November 1914. It was a white building built in a classical style with a columned entrance and could house over 10,000 books. Could this library have played a part in Madge's decision to go to Spain? Local and national newspapers would have been available to read about current affairs, there would have been encyclopaedias and books to consult that would have given Madge background information about this exotic country so far away that was fighting back against the Fascist dictators and its own generals. The original plans of the library were lost when they went down with the *Titanic*! Around the corner from the library was Oswald Road school which Madge's young nephews, Robert and Geoffrey, attended. Farther up Manchester Road on Madge's side of the road were the local swimming baths. These had been promised by the Manchester Corporation and it took them over twenty years to fulfil this promise. The swimming baths were opened in September 1929; there was one pool for men and one for women, and also wash baths and a suite of Turkish baths. The Turkish baths were seen as being a bit of luxury where, for half-a-crown, Chorlton residents could lie for half an hour in a pale blue room, with blue sofas and curtains. Madge would probably have visited or frequented all these establishments with the likely exception of the temperance billiard hall, as she was not teetotal.[14]

At the same time as Madge was living in Chorlton-cum-Hardy, a young man called Bernard McKenna had agreed to go with his friend and join the Chorlton army cadet force. Like Madge, Bernard was to volunteer to fight in both the Spanish Civil War and the Second World War. In Spain he served in the transmission unit, which had the hazardous job of maintaining telephone communications between the frontline positions and the headquarters staff. Bernard was wounded twice in Spain, was captured and became a PoW. When the Second World War broke out, he volunteered for the RAF straight away and served throughout the war. After the war he married, had children, became a teacher and, in his retirement, lived on Egerton Road North in Chorlton.[15]

Today, 34 Manchester Road still has a business run from it and is now a popular hairdressers. The large cinema was where the Bee Gees made their debut (performing as the Rattlesnakes) in 1957[16] and is now a funeral parlour, although it may in the future become a local arts centre. The temperance billiard hall has now become a public house called the Sedge Lynn which is the name of a house which previously stood there. The public library has changed little on the outside and would be instantly recognisable to Madge if she were alive today. Oswald Road school is still there but has expanded greatly since the 1930s with extensions and new buildings to cope with the growing population of modern Chorlton. Chorlton's swimming baths and recreation centre sadly closed in 2015.[17]

Life for Madge at 34 Manchester Road would not have been quiet. Most of her siblings lived nearby, some only two doors away. So, visits from family members would most likely have occurred regularly. Besides Madge and Arthur and the two lodgers in the house, there was also a pet Alsatian dog called 'Lion' and a cat called 'Tiger'. Madge ran her chiropody business from the house, wearing a doctor's style white coat when she was on duty. Her nephew, Robert, remembers seeing Madge wearing her white coat and remarking 'Daisy hurt me' as he had recently had an injection at school administered by a nurse in a white coat. He further recalls that Madge was slim with dark hair and had a serious demeanour. He recalls Madge's husband, 'Uncle Arthur', who was a plump man who was going bald. Politically, the family and Madge seemed to have had left-wing views; Madge's brother Francis (Frank) was a member of the Left Book Club.[18] This was set up in May 1936 by the left-wing publisher Victor Gollancz as a way to distribute cheap and left-wing books, with many titles condemning Fascism. One of their early publications covered the Civil War in Spain and was called *Spain in Revolt*; possibly her brother's membership of the Left Book Club brought Madge into contact with literature that made her question what she was doing with her life. Madge's nephew, Robert, remembers Madge's political views as 'extreme left'; maybe she had inherited her mother Mary's views or more likely she was in the process of making a major decision that would change her life forever; that of volunteering to serve as a nurse in the Spanish Civil War.[19]

The Civil War in Spain broke out in July 1936. From the early months of the war, volunteers from Manchester and the surrounding area left to fight in Spain for the government forces, or to serve as medical personnel. The early volunteers from Manchester and the surrounding area included Arnold Jeans and Clem Beckett. Jeans was killed in action at Boadilla del Monte in December 1936, fighting in a small group of British volunteers that included Churchill's nephew, Esmond Romilly, serving in a German anti-Fascist unit. Beckett was a renowned speedway rider and died two months later at the Battle of Jarama. The first organised group of volunteers from the Manchester area left in November 1936, and included Bill Benson, Eddie Swindells, Ralph Cantor, Jud Colman, George Westfield and Maurice Levine. Only three returned from Spain alive. Around 200 men and women from Manchester and its surrounding area served in the Spanish Civil War as soldiers, nurses, doctors and medical staff, and over a quarter were killed in Spain. Madge would have known what was happening in the Civil War by reading the newspapers of the day, seeing newsreels at the local cinemas and attending 'Aid Spain' events locally and in Manchester city centre.[20]

The local 'Medical Aid' for Spain in Manchester had an office located at 42 Deansgate; it was run by volunteers and had local groups

*Manchester Days: Early Life 1904–1937*

throughout Manchester and the surrounding area. From this office leaflets were distributed, and fundraising events were planned. Next door to this office at 40 Deansgate was the office of the Manchester Food Ship Committee, which organised food shipments to the Spanish government ports. By August 1937, three food ships had gone to Spain. During the Civil War, Manchester and its surrounding area raised funds to buy ambulances and medical supplies for government Spain and supported around 250 child refugees from voluntary donations. In 1939, a car showroom even displayed Picasso's famous picture *Guernica* for a couple of weeks to raise funds for the Spanish government! Early medical volunteers from Manchester and its surrounding area who went to Spain included ambulance driver Leslie Praeger, and nurses Molly Murphy and Mary Slater. It is likely Madge would have visited the office at Deansgate to find out about volunteering for Spain.[21]

Madge would have written to the SMAC in London and, on receiving a positive reply from them, would have left Manchester for London. Here she would have been interviewed and then given details on how to get to Spain, with whom she would be travelling, and any contacts who would meet them in France and Spain. Madge was embarking on a journey that was to change her life forever. She was a woman who had only ever known the Manchester area; in the next few years she was to live in Spain and France, learn new languages, work with and love people of many different nationalities, and was to put her life in danger on many occasions. Her remarkable story starts with the outbreak of the Spanish Civil War.

## Chapter 2

# A War Far Away: Spanish Civil War 1936–1939

Four hundred years ago Spain was the most powerful country in Europe, with a vast empire, a large powerful army and navy, and huge amounts of gold entering the country every year. It controlled lands in Central and South America, the Caribbean, the Far East, North Africa, the Netherlands, Austria and Hungary, and its fleets controlled the seas. From the seventeenth century onwards, the power of Spain began to decline slowly but surely until, in 1898, the last of its empire was lost in a disastrous war with the United States of America. Defeat in this war led to the loss of Cuba and the Philippines, leaving Spain with only the Canary Islands and a small enclave in North Africa as the territories it controlled outside Spain. The defeat in 1898 had a profound effect on the Spanish military, who blamed the politicians. Without any major overseas duties, the Spanish army began to see itself as the 'guardian' of Spain, whose duty it was to intervene and overthrow any government they saw as being in any way 'non-Spanish'. This usually equated to a government with liberal or left-wing views and policies.[1]

After the disaster of 1898 Spain had a series of Liberal and Conservative governments, who took it in turn to govern and whose policies were roughly similar. This cosy situation was upset in 1921 when a Spanish army consisting mainly of conscripts was defeated with heavy losses by Rif tribesmen in Spanish Morocco. This campaign had been strongly promoted by the Spanish King Alfonso XIII who, fearing he might be blamed for the disaster, then supported a bloodless coup in 1923 by General Miguel Primo de Rivera. This coup was known in Spanish as a *pronunciamiento*, and Primo de Rivera became dictator of Spain until 1930. Although he banned all political parties and ruled with only a few advisers, de Rivera's rule was generally more benign than repressive, and he was responsible for the partial modernisation of the railways, roads and hydro-electric power. In foreign affairs, he defeated the Rif tribesmen in Morocco in a joint campaign with the French. But by 1930 his rule was unravelling, and many leading Spaniards wanted a return to democracy. The King sacked Primo de Rivera and appointed General Berenguer to replace him. In response to this there was an uprising in favour of forming a Republic, but this was crushed. Elections were held in the hope that they would show support for the monarch. In the countryside, monarchist candidates won easily because of *caciquismo*, the practice of the local magnate or nobleman getting all his employees, tenants or local villagers to vote for the candidate of his choice. However, in the cities the Socialist and Republican candidates were victorious. When the King could find no one willing to support him, he and his family abdicated in 1931 and, with much popular rejoicing, the Second Spanish Republic was born.[2]

The first Republican government of 1931–1933 was a Liberal-Socialist alliance and it began to implement many radical reforms. The Catholic Church's control of education was replaced by secular control of schools. The many landless peasants were given hope that the land that was not farmed by large landowners, who were mainly noblemen, would be distributed in small plots to them. Fairer labour laws were introduced which improved wages, reduced hours of work (which were traditionally very long), and improved job security. The Spanish army had been very top-heavy with one officer per ten men, so the government retired many senior officers early on full pay. But the land redistribution moved slowly; employers often ignored the labour laws and the policies on the Catholic Church and the army led to animosity towards the Republican constitution from these quarters. Opposition to the Republican constitution ranged from verbal criticism and ignoring some of its laws to the extreme of planning open rebellion. In 1932, in Seville, General Sanjurjo launched a coup against the Republican government which failed to gain any support and was easily defeated, but already it was clear that the Republic was under attack.

The Republican government was the first Spanish ruling body to introduce measures that positively affected women. For the first time, women in Spain were given rights that were embedded in the constitution. In article forty-six, women's rights at work and maternity rights were regulated. Article twenty-five of the constitution established that there were to be no advantages in law based on your sex. Laws regarding divorce and abortion were made far less restrictive and both were now more accessible to women. Most significantly, women were given the vote for the first time, although, interestingly, women could become members of the Spanish parliament, or *Cortes*, before they were entitled to vote.[3]

Several women entered the *Cortes* and became major parliamentary figures, a previously unthinkable situation in pre-1931 Spain. One of the first female *Cortes* members was Margarita Nelken (1894–1968). Born in Málaga to German Jewish parents and educated in France, she was a member of the Socialist Party and was elected for Badajoz in 1931. Her Spanish citizenship had to be rushed through so that she could sit in the *Cortes*. She soon became disillusioned with the slow progress of reform, particularly regarding agriculture, and, because of this, she joined the left wing of the Socialist Party. During the Civil War she joined the Communist Party, and, when the war ended, she fled to France and then Mexico where she spent her last years.[4]

Almost certainly the most famous woman to serve in the *Cortes* was the Communist deputy elected in 1936, Dolores Ibárruri (1895–1989), who was nicknamed *La Pasionaria* because of her fiery speeches during the Civil War. In a radio broadcast to the Republican defenders of Madrid in 1936 she ended with the slogan '*no pasaran*' – 'they shall not pass' – which became the anti-Fascist battle cry of the war. When the Civil War ended, she went to the Soviet Union to live in exile. Her only son was killed at Stalingrad during the Second World War. During the long period of her exile, she became the leader of the Spanish Communist Party for a time. In 1977 she was once again elected to the *Cortes* as a Communist deputy when democracy returned to Spain.[5]

The Spanish woman who held the highest office in the Republican government was an Anarchist! Federica Montseny (1905–1994) was born into a family of Spanish Anarchist intellectuals. In 1928 she joined the *Federación Anarquista Ibérica* (FAI) which consisted of small groups of intellectuals that formed the leadership of the Anarchist movement, particularly the trade union organisation. Federica was a major figure in the Spanish Anarchist movement, and a leading theoretician on the relationship between the sexes. During the Civil War she supported Anarchist involvement in government and became the health minister in the Spanish Republican cabinet of 1936–1937. In this role, she increased the number of childcare centres and improved the levels of hygiene in the hospitals. After the Civil War she lived in exile in France and did not return to Spain until the late 1970s, when Spain was a democracy once again.[6]

By 1933 the Republican Liberal parties and the Socialists were no longer willing to work together, and fought the election of 1933 as separate parties. Under Spanish Republican electoral rules, it was far more beneficial to fight an election as a coalition than to fight as separate parties. So, the Socialist vote increased, but they lost many seats and a victorious right-wing coalition formed the new government. Another reason for the left's loss of seats was the large organised Anarchist movement, which was unique to Spain,[7] whose members traditionally never voted. The Anarchist mass movement was centred on its revolutionary trade union, the *Confederación Nacional de Trabajo*. The leadership of the Anarchist movement tended to come from the FAI, a secretive organisation. In 1931, many of its members voted for Republican candidates; however, in the 1933 election, Anarchist leaders had strongly encouraged its supporters not to vote, and hence this led to a reduction in the left-wing vote.

The 1933–1935 right-wing coalition government began to repeal the legislation of the previous regime. This led to a huge strike by farm workers, which was defeated. Part of the coalition, but not actually in government, was a semi-Fascist party known as *Confederación Española de Derechas Autónomas* (CEDA), a collection of right-wing Catholic groups. The Socialist view was that if this party were invited into government then the Socialists would oppose this with an armed uprising and a general strike. When four members of CEDA were invited into the government in 1934, the Catalan separatists proclaimed an independent Catalonia, but they were defeated in one night because the Anarchists had no interest in supporting them. The call by the Socialists for a general strike was only taken up in a few isolated places and was easily crushed, but in Asturias a major uprising erupted. Here the left-wing parties – the Socialists and Communists – united together with the Anarchists and controlled the mining areas of Asturias for two weeks before the government brought in professional troops from Spanish Morocco under a general called Francisco Franco[8] (who would later lead the rebellion against the Spanish Republican government and become dictator of Spain until 1975) to crush the rebellion. Many rebels were killed and thousands were imprisoned, many being tortured. Having overcome this challenge to its authority, the right-wing government became embroiled in a series of corruption scandals, which, at the end of 1935, led the president of the Republic eventually to order a new election.

For the election of 1936, the Republican parties and the left-wing parties, the Socialists (*Partido Socialista Obrero Español*),[9] the Communists (*Partido Comunista de España*),[10] Catalan and Basque Nationalist parties[11] and various minor parties united to form a Popular Front.[12] Since the Popular Front was campaigning to free the political prisoners of the Asturian uprising, this time the Anarchists were eager to vote for them. After a bitter election campaign, the Popular Front won a narrow victory. The liberal Republicans formed the government with the left-wing parties merely voting with them as allies. The political prisoners were released. However, the extreme elements of the right-wing coalition began to plot with members of the armed forces to overthrow the new government.[13]

The right-wing plotters mostly comprised junior officers in the army, but also a significant number of high-ranking generals. The plotters were actively supported by the Spanish Fascist party, the *Falange*,[14] and by the ultra-Catholic party, the Carlists,[15] who believed the descendants of Don Carlos should be King. Other monarchist groups and powerful individuals like businessman Juan March were also supporters. In the *Cortes*, both sides spoke violently towards one another; armed battles on city streets between the *Falange* and Socialist youth supporters and a wave of strikes and illegal land seizures by peasants were sending the country into chaos. Right-wing and left-wing parties had their own armed militias, which were marching and training mainly in secret, but in some cases openly. The situation was ready to ignite; it just needed a spark to set it off.[16]

A popular captain, called Castillo, in the Republican Assault Guards was assassinated by a *Falange* hit squad. His colleagues in the Assault Guards were looking for revenge, and seized the right-wing parliamentary deputy Calvo Sotelo and murdered him. The plotters took this incident as the excuse they needed to launch a rebellion against a government that had lost control of the country. The organiser of the coup was General Emilio Mola, the military governor of Pamplona, an area with a very strong Carlist movement. Other generals of doubtful loyalty to the Republic had been sent away to obscure postings to make it

## A War Far Away: Spanish Civil War 1936–1939

difficult for them to support any uprising; Franco, for example, was in the Canary Islands. The plan was for Franco to fly from the Canary Islands to Spanish Morocco and take charge of the Army of Africa, Spain's best fighting force. This army included the Spanish Foreign Legion and Moroccan mercenaries, battle-hardened troops used to fighting against the local Rif tribesmen. Aeroplanes supplied by Germany and Italy would airlift this army to the mainland.

In Spanish Morocco the rising broke out in July 1936 and was successful. Mola, the only general in a right-wing supporting area, easily gained control of Pamplona. The rebels also gained control of Seville, and Galicia in northern Spain. The rising failed in Madrid, Barcelona and Valencia. Around a third of Spain fell to the rebels in the first few days, but what was intended as a quick coup had now turned into a Civil War. From the beginning the Nationalists, or Insurgents as they became known, received military aid from Nazi Germany and Fascist Italy. At first this numbered a few transport planes, but by the end of the Civil War this had multiplied into massive support in aircraft, tanks, rifles and machine guns and artillery pieces.[17] None of this was paid for in advance. From mid-1937 this military aid gave the Nationalists weapons superiority over the Republicans until the end of the war. Germany also had its own air force in Spain, known as the Condor Legion.[18] The Italians supplied their own land forces, the *Corpo Truppe Volontarie*, and air force, the *Aviazione Legionaria*.[19] Just as important to the Nationalists was the oil they received on credit from Texaco throughout the war; this enabled them to keep their aeroplanes and motor vehicles in action.[20]

At first the Republican prime minister did not believe that the uprising was taking place; thus, inaction by Republican governors led to the loss of cities such as Seville, Zaragoza and Oviedo to the rebels. Within a day, a new prime minister took office to try to negotiate with the rebels. When these negotiations failed, a third prime minister in two days was appointed. The new premier made the momentous decision to arm the workers, so that they could actively oppose the uprising. This meant that the Anarchists in Barcelona and Socialists in Madrid now had weapons and were able to assist the loyal armed police forces to crush the uprising in most of the major cities. After this, a social revolution erupted, particularly in Barcelona, Catalonia and Aragón, where the Anarchists and dissident revolutionary Communists, the *Partido Obrero de Unificación Marxista* (POUM), were strongest.[21] Workers took over the industries, militia columns were formed and for a time the revolutionaries were in control. This is the situation that George Orwell, author of *Animal Farm* and *Nineteen Eighty-Four*, found when he arrived in Barcelona in December 1936. He discovered that all the major buildings of Barcelona had been seized by the workers' organisations and the red and black flag of the Anarchists was predominant. Every small business had been collectivised, even down to the bootblacks. Private transport had disappeared and trams were painted in the Anarchist colours. Revolutionary posters were everywhere in vibrant colours. Orwell saw a city dominated by the working-class and where all other classes seemed to have disappeared:

> Practically everyone wore rough working-class clothes, or blue overalls, or some variant of the militia uniform .... There was much in it that I did not understand, in some ways I did not even like it, but I recognised it immediately as a state of affairs worth fighting for.[22]

Orwell fought in the POUM revolutionary militia with a small group of British and Irish volunteers and was wounded in Spain.[23] During this revolutionary period of July 1936 to June 1937, many women became involved in committees that were running villages, factories and police patrols. But the most striking image of the revolutionary period was women fighting in the militias as *miliciana*. Posters encouraging women to join the militias appeared in Barcelona on every street corner. Foreign journalists took pictures of militia women dressed in a mono (a dungaree-like garment), usually wearing a hat (side cap) in the Anarchist colours of red and black and carrying a rifle. Maybe no more than around 1,000 women fought at the front, but many more were involved in the medical services and support services, such as cooking and laundry. But early in the Civil War the *milicianas* were a symbolic image of the revolution and the resistance to the uprising. From January 1937, women were banned from serving in the militias, although a few managed to stay on until mid-1937 when the militias were fully militarised.[24]

Some militia women became prominent figures. Lina Odena, a Communist, became leader of a militia unit on the Granada front in southern Spain. She became famous, and, when she was surrounded and cut off, she used her last bullet to commit suicide. She was very likely aware that she would have faced multiple rapes and possibly torture if she were captured. Another Communist militia woman who rose to prominence was Rosario Sánchez, nicknamed 'Rosie the Dynamiter'. She first served in a militia unit in Aragón and Catalonia and, after several months, was transferred to a bomb-making unit. Here she lost a hand holding on to her bomb when she realised that, if she threw it, she would injure her fellow soldiers. Her heroic action led her to be paraded around the country; songs and poems were written extolling her bravery. Mika de Etchebéhère, an Argentine militant, came to Spain with her husband and took over a POUM militia column on his death. She led it in the defence of Sigüenza, where the majority of the column were wiped out. She continued to serve as a captain in the Republican army until mid-1937.[25]

There was revolutionary upheaval in the Republican areas, including the murder of right-wing supporters; however, in the newly controlled Nationalist areas, military rule was instituted, and any Republican or left-wing individuals were imprisoned or even executed. Although the Republicans controlled the bulk of Spanish territory, including the major centres of population and the biggest cities, the Nationalists controlled the major agricultural areas. As the war continued, the people in the Republican areas slowly became hungrier and weaker and were near starvation by the end of the war.

The initial campaigns achieved little; the Nationalists captured Irun in the Basque country, and cut off northern Spain's border links with France. Mola secured the Somosierra pass to the north of Madrid. The main Republican success was in Catalonia and Aragón, where mainly Anarchist militia columns advanced towards the rebel-held city of Zaragoza, but were stopped short of their goal near Huesca. This led to both sides digging in and holding on to what they had gained. With the front in Catalonia and Aragón mostly quiet, the Republicans launched a major invasion of the rebel-held island of Majorca in August 1936. This failed and was repulsed in early September. Around Madrid the only major action was the siege of the Alcazar, a medieval military academy in Toledo. Here a group of rebels were besieged by Republican militia from the first days of the war until they were relieved by Franco's forces in late September.

One force that did make rapid progress, however, was Franco's Army of Africa. This army was landed on the mainland by a combination of air lifts and a sea landing protected by the aircraft. Officers in the Spanish navy tried to join with the Nationalist rebels, but the sailors resisted, killing several of them and imprisoning the rest. From Seville, the elite Army of Africa began its march north, destroying anything in its path. A combination of professionalism and brutality led to them pushing aside any Republican force in their way. By September the Army of Africa reached the town of Badajoz, storming it using bayonets and knives. The Nationalists' attack on Badajoz had led them to suffer heavy losses, so they had no mercy on the defeated: anyone with a bruised shoulder – a sign that you had fired a rifle – was taken to the bullring to join the thousands of prisoners who were butchered by machine guns. From Badajoz, with Madrid within striking distance, Franco made a political decision to relieve the Alcazar. This further enhanced Franco's reputation as the leader of the Nationalist forces. In October he was formally made both head of state and Commander-in-Chief of the army. But this detour to save the Alcazar had given the people of Madrid valuable time to prepare to defend their city.

The new left-wing Republican government under the Socialist Francisco Largo Caballero had replaced the previous Republican administration in early September. Largo wanted to include all workers' organisations in this government; remarkably, this government included four Anarchist members! Despite their high morale, the workers' militias performed poorly. They were untrained, very disorganised and had little discipline, leading to many defeats and routs. The poor performance of the militias led to a re-organisation of Republican armed forces, laying the foundations of what became the 'People's Army'. Firstly, mixed brigades were formed, where militia columns were mixed with regular soldiers and officers, thus improving their efficiency, equipment and discipline. Nevertheless, the Republican government left Madrid for Valencia, believing that Madrid was likely to fall to Franco's forces, whose attack on the city began in November 1936. The attack was to be launched by four columns of his Army of Africa with a so-called 'fifth column' of right-wing supporters inside Madrid who were supposedly ready to rise in support of Franco's attack. A significant boost to the mixed brigades fighting in defence of Madrid was the arrival of the first organised units of foreign volunteers, known as the International Brigades.[26]

The International Brigades were foreign anti-Fascist volunteers from around the world; probably over half of them were Communists. The raising of these volunteers was organised by the international Communist organisation, the *Comintern*. Volunteers were processed in Paris and then sent by rail to Spain. In later years the France–Spain border was closed, and so, in order to enter Spain, the volunteers secretly crossed the Pyrenees at night. During the Civil War, around 40,000 volunteers from fifty-three different nations served in the International Brigades; at least a quarter of the volunteers were killed and most of the rest were wounded. The International Brigades became the shock troops of the Spanish Republic. In time, the number of volunteers decreased, and Spanish volunteers made up for losses. The International Brigades who helped defend Madrid in November numbered only a few thousand, but gave the city's defenders a professional core and, in showing the people of Madrid that they were not alone, gave a massive boost to their forces' morale.

Around this time the Republic received the first of its military aid from the Soviet Union. At the outbreak of the Civil War, the Spanish Republic was keen to buy arms from other countries, especially from France. Britain feared that the Civil War in Spain could lead to another world war, and pressurised France into accepting what was called the Non-Intervention Agreement, whereby the major countries of Europe and the Americans agreed to supply neither side in the Civil War. At first view this appeared to be a good compromise; but this constantly worked against the legitimate government of Spain as they were not allowed to buy arms, while the Nationalists were openly being supplied arms by Italy and Germany. In desperation for a supply of arms, the Republic turned to the Soviet Union, who agreed to supply them. However, these were not obtained on credit, but were paid for by shipping the Spanish gold reserve – one of the biggest reserves in the world – to the Soviet Union. The Republicans were also supplied with weapons by the friendly Mexican government and bought arms from wherever they could find them. This often meant buying very poor-quality arms at exorbitant prices. The Republicans were supplied with a variety of weapons by the Soviet Union, from state-of-the-art weaponry to obsolete equipment that the Soviets simply wanted to get rid of. At least up to the middle of 1937, arms were shipped from the Soviet Union in large quantities; however, the number of arms decreased as the war dragged on. The Soviet Union supplied a mass of planes, tanks, artillery guns and rifles, but never enough to give the Republic a decisive advantage against the better-supplied Nationalists.[27]

The attack on Madrid lasted around three weeks and both the International Brigades and Franco's Army of Africa sustained heavy losses as they fought among the ruins of Madrid's university buildings, often with one side holding one floor and the other side another. An Anarchist force from Aragón also came to support the defence of Madrid. This was called the 'Durruti Column', named after its charismatic leader Buenaventura Durruti, who was killed in mysterious circumstances during the battle for Madrid.[28] The people of Madrid and its defenders were exhorted to resist by the fiery Communist parliamentary deputy Dolores Ibárruri. After three weeks of bitter street fighting, although they had gained some ground, the Nationalists abandoned their frontal assault on Madrid for a new form of warfare. For the first time, the systematic bombing and shelling of a European city was carried out, at first extensively and then on a regular basis until the end of the war.[29]

Having dug in outside Madrid, the Nationalists looked to cut Madrid's supply lines with the interior, and in particular with Valencia. In December 1936, the Nationalists launched an attack towards the Corunna Road. The battle lasted into January 1937, but after heavy losses on both sides the Nationalists were left with only 11km of captured territory, and Madrid's supply lines were still intact.

In 1937, both sides made the government more politically centralised in areas under their control. In the Nationalist zone, Franco, already the acknowledged leader of both the Nationalist government and its armed forces, forcibly combined the two main political groupings in the Nationalist zone – the Fascist *Falange* and the Carlists – into one political party, any dissenters being imprisoned and threatened with execution; the new party had the incredibly long name of *Falange Española Tradicionalista y de las Junta de Ofensiva Nacional-Sindicalista*.[30] In the Republican zone, 1937 was the year when the Republican government took back control from the revolutionaries. In December 1936 the revolutionary POUM representative in the Catalan government, Andrés Nin, was removed from his post of justice minister at the insistence of the Communist Party. The Communists believed they needed a centralised government and conventional army to win the war, and so supported the national Republican government against the revolutionaries. Things came to a head in May 1937 in Barcelona, where the regional government was undermining the power of the revolutionaries little by little. The attempt by the government-backed security forces to occupy the telephone exchange in Barcelona, which was then controlled by the Anarchists, was the spark that led to an open rebellion against the Republican authorities, which lasted for several days. The fallout led to the replacement of the prime minister, Largo Caballero, by another, more right-wing Socialist, Juan Negrín, who was the Republican prime minister to the end of the Civil War.[31] In June 1937, the POUM was declared an illegal political party and its leader, Nin, was murdered. The Anarchists lost representation in the both the Catalan regional and national governments. The Council of Aragón, an Anarchist-dominated revolutionary body, was forcibly dissolved and the collectivised farms were broken up. Revolutionary control of industry and agriculture was ended, and revolutionary militia columns were integrated into the 'People's Army' by threatening to refuse them weapons.[32]

In late January 1937, the Nationalists launched an offensive towards Málaga in the south of Spain. The poorly led and poorly armed militias were no match for the Nationalist forces, which included a contingent of allied Italians. Málaga fell in early February 1937. In the same month the Nationalists launched a second attempt to cut the supply lines to Madrid. They launched a fierce attack in the Jarama Valley, and in the subsequent two-week battle the Nationalists drove a salient into the Republican lines, but they were again unable to cut off Madrid from its supply lines.

In March 1937 the Italian dictator, Benito Mussolini, demanded that his Italian troops carry out an offensive on their own. Buoyed by their easy success at Málaga, he believed they would achieve another easy victory. A Spanish column and an Italian column launched the attack near Guadalajara, north-east of Madrid; the plan was to cut off the city from the rest of Republican Spain. At first, progress was easy and the inexperienced Republican troops were pushed back. But resistance stiffened, particularly against the Italian forces. The Republic quickly sent reinforcements to the area; these included Soviet tanks, more experienced troops and Italian International Brigaders. The motorised Italian Nationalist force was strung out along the local roads; when the weather turned dreadful, they became bogged down in the wet conditions. Italian planes could not take off from their temporary runways, whereas the Republic's Soviet planes were able to take off from their permanent runways. A combination of Soviet tanks and planes, and more experienced Republican troops, drove the Italians back. As a result of this, the other Nationalist force abandoned its attack. Although the battle was trumpeted as a great Republican victory and Italian PoWs were paraded for the world press, the Nationalists still gained some territory; however, they had again failed in their strategic aim of cutting off Madrid.[33]

After the failure at Guadalajara, and on the advice of his German allies, Franco decided to change tactics. He abandoned any attempt to cut off Madrid from its interior. The Republic had concentrated its best units and equipment around Madrid, so Franco decided to attack isolated Republican areas, which were poorly armed and badly organised. He selected the Republican northern coastal strip of the Basque lands, Santander and Asturias for his assault, since these regions had three separate armies and governments. The Basque lands were mountainous and highly-wooded, and good for defence; around the main city of Bilbao was the so-called 'Ring of Iron'. This was a series of extensive trenches and concrete gun emplacements, but these were not designed by military engineers and had many weaknesses. To make matters worse, the chief architect of the 'Ring of Iron' deserted to the Nationalists and told them its weakest spots. The Basques fought doggedly, but were heavily outgunned and had virtually no aeroplanes. Franco's Basque campaign was notorious for two terror bombing raids: one on Durango and the other one on the town sacred to the Basques, Guernica.[34] Here the intention was to terrorise the civilian population using mainly fire bombs by the German Condor Legion to destroy the two towns. The 'Ring of Iron' was breached and Bilbao fell to Nationalist forces in June 1937.

In August the campaign was resumed and Santander, a mainly flat area of Spain, was overrun in less than two weeks. The Asturians, cut off from the rest of Republican Spain, resisted in their mountain strongholds for almost two months till they were defeated, and the main city of the area, Gijon, was captured in October 1937.

While the campaign in the north was taking place, the Republicans attempted to stop this offensive by attacking Nationalist forces around Madrid. In scorching temperatures in July 1937, the Republicans surprised the Nationalists by launching a large offensive at Brunete. The plan was to cut off the Nationalist forces that were besieging Madrid from the rest of their forces, and force them to withdraw troops from northern Spain. The initial attack drove an 8km salient into the Nationalist lines, and several defended villages were captured. However, the slow advance of the Republican forces enabled the Nationalists to occupy the high ground and halt the advance. Once the Nationalists were reinforced, they went on the offensive and drove the Republicans almost back to their starting position. The battle ended in a draw, but the Republican attack was only able to temporarily delay the Nationalist northern offensive.[35]

A second Republican offensive was launched in August 1937 and was aimed at capturing Huesca and Zaragoza on the Aragón. The Republicans were able to capture the towns of Quinto and Belchite, along with some territory, from the Nationalists, but they failed either to capture Huesca or Zaragoza or stop the northern Nationalist offensive. In November 1937, the Republican government moved from Valencia to Barcelona. It was discovered that the Nationalists were planning to launch an offensive against Madrid; to pre-empt this, the Republicans decided to launch a surprise offensive of their own. They chose Teruel, a major provincial city located in a salient of Nationalist territory that was surrounded by Republican land.[36]

The attack was launched in December 1937 and was fought in arctic conditions. In the sub-zero temperatures, many soldiers on both sides froze to death, and more suffered frostbite. Oil froze, and aeroplanes could not fly. The city of Teruel was surrounded, but was not finally captured until January 1938, when the last of the defenders surrendered. Franco then ordered the Nationalist troops to recapture the city. By February 1938 the Republicans in Teruel were now the besieged force. On 20 February 1938, the last of the Republican units had escaped from Teruel, and the town was recaptured by Nationalist forces.[37]

After the recapture of Teruel, the Nationalists launched a devastating offensive on the Aragón and Levante in March 1938, with overwhelming numbers of aeroplanes and military equipment. In the first week the Republicans were forced back nearly 100km. By April 1938, Lérida in Catalonia had fallen to the Nationalists, and less than a month after the start of the offensive, the Nationalists reached the sea at Vinaroz on 3 April. This cut the Republican zone in half. The Nationalists continued to widen the coastal territory that they had captured, but with Republican resistance increasing, they halted the offensive in June. Franco then decided to launch his next attack towards Valencia. This appeared to be a surprising choice, since Republican forces in Catalonia were disorganised. Moreover, many were survivors from the last Nationalist offensive who had been forced to flee across the River Ebro, in many cases swimming across it, to avoid capture.

While Franco's forces were fighting near Valencia, the Republican forces in Catalonia had time to re-group, rest, re-train and most importantly, re-arm. On the night of 24 July, the Republican forces crossed the Ebro and launched a successful surprise assault across the river. The plan was to force Franco to abandon his Valencia campaign and try to reunite Republican territory, thus showing the world that they were still capable of renewed resistance. The attacking Republican forces advanced up to 40km in places, only being halted before the town of Gandesa. As the Nationalist reinforcements poured in, the Republicans dug in to hold on to what they had gained. In the next three months the Nationalists drove back the Republicans, little by little, by a combination of their air superiority, their large concentrations of guns and their ability to follow up air attacks with constant infantry attacks. Often stationed in mountain defences, the Republicans were blasted off each defensive position, one after the other. The last Republican force retreated across the Ebro on 18 November 1938. The loss to the Republic of so much military equipment and so many experienced soldiers could never be replaced.[38]

During the Ebro campaign the Republican prime minister, Negrín, tried to broker a peace deal by withdrawing the International Brigades in September 1938, hoping that the Nationalists would also withdraw their foreign volunteers. This they did, but mostly non-frontline troops and wounded men. In Barcelona, in late October 1938, the Republican government gave the International Brigades an emotional farewell parade. The men were garlanded with flowers and hugged by the people of Barcelona. The Communist parliamentary deputy, *La Pasionaria*, addressed them in one of history's iconic speeches. She described the International Brigaders as 'history' and 'legend' and spoke of how they had gladly given their lives for Spain fighting Fascism; she exhorted the Spanish to remember them, and invited the volunteers to return to Spain when the war was over.[39]

Franco's attack on Valencia had been abandoned after fierce resistance, but the Republic's prospects going into 1939 were bleak.

In late December 1938, the Nationalists began their offensive in Catalonia. Six armies attacked across the Ebro and, except in isolated places, they quickly overran the now exhausted Republican resistance.

## A War Far Away: Spanish Civil War 1936–1939

In desperation, the Republicans even conscripted 16-year-olds to fight in the army. But, like a steamroller, the Nationalists captured strongpoint after strongpoint and by mid-January 1939, they had captured Catalonia's second city, Tarragona. Any hope that Barcelona might successfully resist, as Madrid had done, proved illusory, and on 26 January 1939, the Nationalists entered Barcelona unopposed. What followed was a mass exodus of civilians and soldiers to the French border. Here the soldiers were disarmed, and soldiers and civilians alike were interned in concentration camps, where many died from malnutrition and exposure. By the end of February, all of Catalonia was in Nationalist hands.

Republican prime minister Negrín, who had fled to France, decided to return to the remaining Republican territory in southern Spain. He hoped either to broker a peace deal or continue resistance until a European war broke out, with the chance that the Republic would receive outside help. In Madrid, on 4 March, a coup was launched against Negrín's government by a group of army officers led by Colonel Casado and supported by leading Socialists such as Julián Besteiro, and Anarchists like Cipriano Mera. This led to a mini civil war between supporters of Casado and Negrín on the streets of Madrid. Casado's forces were victorious and formed a junta, leading Negrín and his supporters to flee Spain. Casado believed that, as a fellow army officer, he might be able to broker a peace deal with Franco; however, attempts by Casado to negotiate an agreement were unsuccessful. His failure to organise any proper evacuation from Spain led to many Republicans falling into Nationalist hands, where they were imprisoned, and many were executed. In late March the Nationalist offensive on the Republican zone was unopposed and the Nationalists entered Madrid on 28 March, reaching the coast on the following day. The war was officially classed as over on 1 April 1939.[40]

## Chapter 3

# From Apathy to Direct Action: British Responses to the Spanish Civil War

Britain in the 1930s was a country in the middle of an economic depression, but was still a major power that controlled a large overseas colonial empire. Unemployment was high but it was concentrated in areas where traditional manufacturing was in sharp decline, for example South Wales and north-east England. In many other places, standards of living were actually rising. The country was ruled by a Conservative-dominated coalition government called the National Government, which had won the 1935 General Election with a large majority over the Labour Party. The horrors of the Great War still dictated actions in foreign affairs, leading to a desire to avoid a foreign war at all costs and a policy of appeasing aggressive military powers like Japan, Italy and Germany – a policy supported by the majority of the British people. The trade union movement had still not recovered from its defeat in the General Strike of 1926 and had a cautious policy regarding the support of any militant action. On the fringes of politics were various minor political parties, one of which – the Communist Party of Great Britain – was to make support for the Spanish Republic its number one political goal and was the driving force for aid to Spain.

All of these different groups, as well as the press, various Christian groups, intellectuals and artists, had views on the Spanish Civil War. For many Britons, the war in Spain was the most important thing to them for a time, and in some cases became the most significant event of their lives. But the reaction of most Britons to the war was one of passing interest at best, or indifference to what was happening in Spain.[1]

Britain's involvement in the Spanish Civil War can be divided into diplomatic action, humanitarian efforts and the participation of volunteers in the war in Spain. The National Government's main aim was to avoid the Civil War turning into a European war; so, because of this, its policies were detrimental to the Spanish Republican government. The main diplomatic efforts by Britain during the Civil War centred on its policy of appeasement and in ensuring that its colony of Gibraltar was not in danger. In Britain, the 'Aid Spain' movement raised large amounts of money throughout the war, which was used to send humanitarian aid to Republican Spain and to help to look after around 4,000 Basque refugee children who were evacuated from northern Spain due to the bombing of Bilbao (see Chapter 4). Over 2,000 men from Britain and Ireland fought in the British Battalion of the International Brigades, and over 500 of them were killed. On top of this, around 200 men and women served in the various medical units in Republican Spain. Money was also raised (particularly by Catholic organisations) to support humanitarian efforts for Nationalist Spain, and a handful of volunteers served as soldiers and, in one case, as a nurse on the Nationalist side. But the amount of money raised, the number of volunteers and the support for Nationalist Spain were tiny compared to the efforts to support the Republicans.[2]

What did British people know about Spain in the 1930s? Most people had a stereotypical image of the country and its people; Spain was seen as an exotic and romantic land, with flamenco dancers, matadors, flickering fans, long robes, religious possessions and medieval art.[3] The Spanish people were viewed as individualistic, lazy, incompetent and cruel. Unfortunately, by criticising the other side in terms of 'backwardness' or 'barbarism', the supporters of both sides merely reinforced the stereotypical views of Spain held by many British people at the time. Those people who had visited Spain or who lived there saw the Spanish as inferior to the British, on a par with colonials in the British Empire. To many British people, the Civil War was an alien war that we should stay out of:

> ... most people continued to regard Spain as the land of Carmen and the Inquisition, and commentaries did little to change that view. For most, the Spanish political scene remained comic and incomprehensible, a landscape inhabited by bomb-throwing anarchists and pistol-waving generals all readily disposed to revolution.[4]

Randolph Churchill, a cousin of Winston Churchill, stated crudely what many members of the establishment thought of the Spanish Civil War. It was a war that only a few Catholics and Socialists cared about; the vast majority of the British general public had little interest in the war and saw it as a conflict involving 'bloody dagoes'.[5] Although they may have been uninterested in the conflict in Spain, many of those people contributed food or money to the various humanitarian efforts in support of the Spanish Republic. But thousands and thousands of British people did become involved in the war in Spain on a one-off basis, or as fundraisers, taking part in demonstrations, serving on an 'Aid Spain' committee or serving in Spain as soldiers or as medical personnel.[6]

Most British support in the Civil War was for the Republican side. In a poll carried out by the British Institute of Public Opinion in March 1938, fifty-seven per cent of those polled supported the Republic, rising to seventy-two per cent in January 1939. The pro-Franco figures were always less than ten per cent.[7] Although a minority of the British public were involved in supporting the Spanish Republic, it was one of the largest ever protest and charitable movements in British history:

> During the next three years it was to become the most widespread and representative mass movement in Britain since the mid-nineteenth century days of Chartism and the Anti-Corn League, and the most outstanding example of international solidarity in British history.[8]

The support for Republican Spain in Britain was characterised by the diversity of political support for humanitarian efforts, with Conservative voters serving on the same committee or speaking at events alongside Communist supporters. Many working-class households and areas regularly gave support to the 'Aid Spain' initiatives in their areas.

The many committees set up throughout the country to support humanitarian aid to Republican Spain could only run effectively with the active support of many women, who often worked behind the scenes. Not all women, though, were hidden away, and many committees at both the local and national level were led by women, or had women playing a major role in them. A myriad of women-only organisations, meetings and activities at national and local levels helped to provide humanitarian aid for Spain. A very small sample of some of those groups and activities included:

- Women's World Committee Against War and Fascism
- Labour Party Women's Sections
- Co-operative Women's Guilds
- All Party, All Women's Meeting
- Manchester Housewives Day and Manchester Women's Food Ship Committee
- All London Women's Meeting, and
- Women's Committee to Help Spain.

While many women did not support the Spanish Republic's policies or its right to buy arms, this did not stop a lot of those same women being involved in humanitarian efforts to support the victims of the Civil War in Republican Spain. Women played a key role in the 'Spanish Aid' movement, knocking on doors asking for donations and taking part in a plethora of different fundraising events, from taking part in amateur dramatics performances to knitting socks for war orphans.[9]

The rise of Fascism in Italy and Germany, and in Britain of Oswald Mosley's 'Blackshirts',[10] had politicised many people, especially the young. The Civil War became a symbol of a democracy that was resisting Fascist aggression and led thousands to demonstrate on its behalf, to raise money for aid to Republican Spain and to actually volunteer to fight in Spain or serve in the medical services. Although the majority of British people may have been indifferent to the Spanish Civil War, most of them knew it was going on through newspapers and newsreels at the cinema. At least one historian has claimed that the effects on Britain of the Spanish Civil War were greater than any other foreign war in the twentieth century:

> Indeed, of all the foreign conflicts of the twentieth century in which Britain was not directly involved, the war in Spain made by the far the greatest impact on British political, social and cultural life.[11]

When the Spanish Civil War broke out in July 1936, Britain was governed by the National Government, and an alliance of Conservative (mainly),

Liberal and Labour MPs with a large majority over the opposition, which was the Labour Party. During the Civil War period of 1936–1939, Britain had two prime ministers; firstly Stanley Baldwin (1935–1937), and secondly Neville Chamberlain (1937 to the end of the Civil War). Both were Conservatives. The foreign secretary for most of the period 1936–1938 was Anthony Eden.[12]

The British government's greatest desire was to prevent the Spanish War turning into a European war and to have a stable government in Spain; whether that was the legally elected government or the Nationalist rebels did not seem to concern them. British business interests in Spain were to be protected, although attacks on British merchant shipping were, on many occasions, openly ignored.

Britain saw the Mediterranean Sea as a strategic area in terms of access to its empire. In line with this policy they wanted to reach an agreement with Italy that would acknowledge this, trying to draw them away from any alliance with Nazi Germany. If this meant turning a blind eye to Italian involvement in Spain, this was not a problem, as long as British strategic needs were met. Any hostile action towards the British colony of Gibraltar was not to be tolerated. The policies of the colony's authorities in the early months of the Civil War were strongly supportive of the Nationalists.

Finally, many National Government MPs had limited knowledge of Spain, and what they did know was often coloured by stereotypical views of Spain as a backward country on the edge of Europe. Newspaper stories of chaos (church burnings and armed fighting in the streets) after the Popular Front election victory, and again when the Civil War erupted, meant that many Conservative MPs were pro-Nationalist. They feared that the disorder in Spain meant that the Republican government was Communist, or that Spain was turning Communist.[13]

The British government's fear of the escalation of the war in Spain into a European war was encapsulated in its policy of non-intervention and the setting up of the Non-Intervention Committee. This was probably the most controversial aspect of British foreign policy towards the Spanish Civil War. The policy of non-intervention denied both sides in the Civil War the right to buy arms abroad. However, this meant the democratically elected government of Spain and the armed rebels were treated as equals. Professor Tom Buchanan firmly believes that the non-intervention policy of the British Government contributed to the defeat of the Spanish Republic.[14]

*From Apathy to Direct Action*

In the first few weeks of the war the Spanish ambassador requested arms for his government, but this was opposed by the British foreign secretary. France, which had a Popular Front government like the one in Spain, was willing to supply arms to the Spanish Republicans and had signed an agreement in 1935 to supply them with arms. Britain pressured the French Socialist prime minister, Léon Blum, telling him that if France was to supply arms to Spain, then Britain would not support it in any future war. Blum, who had problems with allies in his government and vocal and violent right-wing opposition groups, proposed non-intervention in Spain, which was keenly supported by the British government.

The first meeting of the Non-Intervention Committee took place in September 1936 in London and included representatives from all over Europe, including Nazi Germany and Fascist Italy, and also, from October 1936, the Soviet Union. At first this approach was supported by the Labour Party, trade unions, the majority of the British population who had any interest in the Civil War and even the CPGB. It was chaired by the British junior minister Lord Plymouth, and it became a device to ignore illicit arms being sent to both sides in Spain, but particularly to the Nationalists by Italy and Germany. Any reports or evidence of illegal arms supply or bombings of civilians were moth-balled using bureaucratic delays. One diplomat described the Non-Intervention Committee thus: 'I had thought it was generally admitted to be largely a piece of humbug. Where humbug is the alternative to war it is impossible to place too high a value on it.'[15]

From March to June 1937 Britain took part in naval patrols to prevent illegal arms reaching Spain. This broke down when the Republicans attacked a German warship. During the summer of 1937, British shipping and other countries' ships were being sunk by unknown submarines, which turned out to be Italian ones. In November 1937 at Nyon, an anti-submarine patrol was set up and Italy ceased its submarine attacks. However, the new British prime minister, Chamberlain, was eager to make a deal with Italy and saw Nyon as a potential stumbling block. Disagreements over foreign policy led to Eden's resignation in February 1938. In November 1938 an Italo-British treaty was signed, whereby Britain recognised Italy's conquest of Abyssinia (modern Ethiopia) and in return Italy agreed to reduce its troop numbers in Spain and agreed to Britain's sea dominance in the Mediterranean.[16]

British trade with Spain was a tiny part of its world market, but Britain controlled around forty per cent of foreign capital in Spain. British representatives in Spain dealt with both sides in the Civil War to protect Britain's business interests and assets there. Commercial ships travelling to Spain received little protection from the Royal Navy and many were sunk trying to reach Republican ports. The British government's response tended to be to advise merchant ships not to travel to Spain, rather than make any formal complaint or take any naval action.[17]

The British colony of Gibraltar played a significant role in the early months of the Civil War. The British naval officers at Gibraltar had been appalled by the mutiny in the Republican fleet whereby the rank-and-file sailors had prevented the officers joining the rebellion. In the early months of the Civil War, Nationalist rebel forces (including ships and planes) were supplied with food, fuel and ammunition. They were also allowed to use telecommunications on the colony and were passed military intelligence about the Republican fleet, whereas the Republican fleet was denied access to Gibraltar to refuel. This led to the Nationalists gaining control of the Strait of Gibraltar, thus enabling them to bring the elite Army of Africa from Spanish Morocco to the mainland, which led to the conquest of much of southern Spain.[18]

The British government's bias against the Spanish Republican government was shown in many ways. As mentioned earlier, in July 1936 the legitimate request from one government to another to buy arms was rejected. The British ambassador in Spain, Sir Henry Chilton, was himself a critic of Republican Spain and left the country as soon as the war began, basing himself in the French border town of Hendaye. When it looked like the war might end quickly with the capture of Madrid in October 1936, the British Cabinet agreed to give the Nationalists belligerent rights if Madrid fell, which would put both sides in the Civil War on an equal footing.

In November 1936, Britain began the process of legitimising its links with the rebel Nationalist regime. In that month it suspended its payment agreement with the Spanish Republic. This agreement had meant that exports from rebel territory to Britain led to payment to the Spanish Republican government. Also, around this time minor trade and diplomatic agents were sent to Nationalist Spain to make contact with the Nationalist authorities. This culminated in November 1937 when Sir Robert Hodgson was sent to Nationalist Spain. He had only commercial accreditation but it was seen as the de facto recognition of the Nationalist rebel regime.

As the defeat of the Republic looked ever more likely, British government support for the Nationalists increased. During the summer of 1938 the number of British ships damaged or destroyed by aerial attack in Republican harbours led to heated exchanges in Parliament, but nothing was done to prevent the attacks. Jill Edwards believes that the British government's policy in late 1938 of deliberately not protecting its merchant shipping was done to hasten the end of the Civil War by starving the civilian population of Barcelona into submission.[19] On 27 February 1939, with the Civil War still ongoing but a Franco victory appearing certain, the British government officially recognised the Nationalist regime as the legitimate government of Spain. In the same month a Royal Navy vessel helped to organise the Balearic island of Minorca's surrender to the Nationalists.[20]

The British trade union movement in the 1930s was the strongest part of the labour movement, as the Labour Party was struggling to recover from a catastrophic General Election defeat in 1931. In the 1930s the British trade union movement was a cautious organisation that tended to avoid strike action if at all possible and was strongly anti-Communist. By 1936, membership had grown to around 4 million members, a steady increase of ten percent from 1931. During the period of the Spanish Civil War the movement was dominated by two trade union leaders: Walter Citrine and Ernest Bevin. Internationally, the Trades Union Congress, the lead body of the trade union movement, was affiliated to the International Federation of Trades Unions. The Spanish Socialist trade union, the *Unión General de Trabajadores*, was one of the foreign trade union bodies also affiliated to this group. The trade union leaders acted like a brake on support for the Republic in their opposition to providing any major aid to Republican Spain, often going against much of their more left-leaning membership. Yet it is safe to say that the majority of union members were more interested in workplace 'bread and butter' issues than what was happening in a country they regarded as being on the fringes of Europe.[21]

At first, British trade union movement leaders embraced and supported the government policy of non-intervention, in part because of the Republican government's loss of control in many areas to the revolutionaries. In fact, in August 1936, Citrine even stated that the greatest danger to Republican Spain was not the Fascists, but its internal divisions and extreme groups like the Anarchists. It was further believed that, by starving both sides of arms, non-intervention would benefit the Spanish Republic with its greater industrial centres and more of the population; therefore, this policy would help to shorten the war in the Republic's favour. Protests and arguments from UGT members of the IFTU that non-intervention was working against the Spanish Republic were ignored. In 1936, Bevin believed there was no popular desire from his union's members for intervention in Spain:

> He had a very large union and the only resolutions were from Communist sources and he might say they had a stereotyped resolution from 38 branches, and everyone could have said where it had come from.[22]

At the 1936 Labour Party Congress, the block vote system (each trade union cast its vote, not as one union, but by the size of its membership) carried the vote for non-intervention by a large majority. But two days later the passionate pleas of two Spanish delegates led the Congress to reconsider its decision on non-intervention. As a result, two leading Labour Party members conferred with Chamberlain, and, on their return, Congress passed a resolution which stated that, if non-intervention proved ineffective, then the British and French governments should allow the Republican government to buy arms openly. Bevin then made the exaggerated promise that TUC officers would lobby the government every day in support of the Spanish Republic's right to buy arms on the open market.[23]

By the time of the TUC Congress in the autumn of 1937, non-intervention had been totally rejected and support for Republican Spain was almost total. Yet many of the rank-and-file initiatives were undertaken without support by the TUC, so, besides lobbying the government, what were the trade union leaders actually willing to do to support Republican Spain?

When it was suggested there should be a blockade of ships heading for Nationalist ports, Bevin refused to support this on the grounds that it might lead to workers being locked out of their place of work, the loss of wages and breaking of agreements. In March 1937, Citrine and Bevin had a meeting with the foreign secretary, Eden, where they demanded non-intervention be tightened up and argued that minerals going from the British-owned Rio Tinto mines in Spain to Germany undermined Britain's security.[24] However, supporting direct involvement in the Spanish Civil War on behalf of the Spanish government was rigorously rejected. George Gibson, head of the Mental Health Workers' Union, stated at their union conference in June 1937 that he rejected any policy that would support intervention in Spain and lead to the death of any of his members.[25]

The trade union movement tried to help Republican Spain in four ways:

- Lobbying the government to allow the Spanish Republican government to buy arms freely.
- Humanitarian aid, in which around £200,000 of aid was sent to Republican Spain.
- The maintenance of a hospital in Spain.
- Helping to look after around 4,000 Basque refugee children in Britain.

The performance of the trade union leadership during the Spanish Civil War, compared to the volunteers who went to Spain, or the rank-and-file activists involved in 'Aid Spain' initiatives, was anything but heroic. Non-intervention was too easily accepted and only grudgingly abandoned. No major trade union leader visited Spain, unlike leaders of the Labour Party and Communist Party. The TUC was happy lobbying for Spain and organising humanitarian aid, but it had no desire to support British military involvement in the Spanish Civil War.[26]

While the trade union leaders were happy with their role, and believed they had done all that was legally possible, their role in the war, and that of the Labour Party, was savaged at the Labour Party Congress in May 1939 by Sybil Wingate, who had been a volunteer in Spain. Firstly, she compared funds raised by the Labour Party and TUC during the war with the far larger sums raised by unofficial bodies. Then she delivered this indictment:

> ... our National Executive, who by their obstinate refusal to take any effective action worthy of the situation afterwards, have cost us the key position in the fight against Fascism and sacrificed the lives of so many of our best and bravest comrades.[27]

In 1924 and 1929–1931 the Labour Party had formed the government of the day, although in both cases they had no overall majority. In 1931, with the worldwide depression hitting Britain, and unemployment rising rapidly, the Labour government broke up over the decision to implement cuts in benefits for the unemployed. Ramsay MacDonald – the Labour prime minister – and a small core of Labour MPs joined with the Conservative Party and some of the Liberals to form a National Government.[28] The result of this was the near-annihilation of the Labour Party at the 1931 General Election, when only fifty-two of its MPs were returned to Parliament. At the 1935 General Election the Labour Party recovered a little with the election of 154 MPs, but the National Government during the Spanish Civil War (1936–1939) had a huge majority over the Labour Party. The weakness of the Labour Party in Parliament in the 1930s meant it had little power to influence government decisions and the party was strongly influenced by the trade union leadership. Like the trade unions, Labour Party policy tended to be conservative during this period, since they were trying to show the British people that they were a future government in waiting. At the same time, they were also trying to control their own left-wing supporters.[29]

The policy of the Labour Party leadership during the Civil War mirrored that of the trade union leadership. The National Council of Labour was the lead body in deciding the policy of the labour movement towards Spain. The Council included both trade union and Labour Party leaders, with the trade union leaders having a majority of seats on this committee. The Labour Party's initial reaction to the outbreak of the Civil War was to declare support for the Republic; this lasted until the late summer of 1936, when it changed to supporting non-intervention. Like the trade union leadership, Labour leaders believed non-intervention would both avoid a European war and help the Republic to win the Civil War. This position also fitted with the party's support for pacifism in the early and mid-1930s. The Labour Party also had to be seen to be supporting the policy of Léon Blum, the leader of their fellow socialists in France. During the summer of 1937 the policy of non-intervention started to crumble as it became ever more obvious that Germany and Italy were openly ignoring non-intervention, and by autumn 1937 the Labour Party were demanding that the Republican government be able to buy arms on the open market. The Party set up a Spain Campaign Committee, led by prominent left-wingers Stafford Cripps and Ellen Wilkinson. Its high point was a rally at the Royal Albert Hall in December 1937; after that its focus changed from lobbying the British government to change its policy on Spain, to one of supplying humanitarian aid.[30]

All requests from other left-wing parties to unite with them on Spain were rejected, particularly any from the CPGB. In 1937 Labour Party members who were also members of the Stafford Cripps-led Socialist League were threatened with expulsion from the party if they continued to work and lobby with other left-wing parties such as the CPGB. Only one major Labour Party politician visited Spain and that was its leader, Clement Attlee[31] (later to be prime minister from 1945 to 1951). In Spain he visited the British volunteers in the International Brigades and even allowed one of its companies to be called the Major Attlee Company in his honour. In a handful of by-elections during the Civil War, the Labour Party withdrew its candidate to allow Popular Front pro-Republican candidates to run instead. In one by-election they withdrew in favour of a pro-Republican Conservative, Katherine, Duchess of Atholl, who was one of only a handful of Conservatives who supported Republican Spain. Pamphlets on Spain were also published by the party, with titles such as *We Saw in Spain* and *What Spanish Democracy is fighting for*.[32]

Throughout the Civil War the Labour Party was keen to avoid a European war and was strongly anti-Communist. At Labour Party conferences, attempts by the CPGB to affiliate to the Labour Party were rejected, and any attempts to get the Labour Party to join other left-wing parties in any sort of alliance in support of the Spanish Republic were heavily defeated. Labour politicians and members were ordered not to work with other political parties in any activities relating to aid for Spain, or to share platforms with their speakers, particularly those from the CPGB. Yet many of its rank-and-file members ignored this and were strongly involved in activities in support of Republican Spain, with the highest level of involvement in the Civil War being fighting as a member of the International Brigades. The Labour Party did not openly support the International Brigades, although 115 known Labour Party members or youth members fought in Spain, including four councillors. One of these was Jack Jones, who became a commissar (political officer), and later became the general secretary of the Transport and General Workers' Union.[33]

At a lower level, many rank-and-file Labour Party members, along with MPs and high-profile figures attempted to influence the leadership's policies on Spain. In March 1937, some party members formed an unofficial Labour Spain Committee in order to lobby the leadership to change its policy on Spain. In April 1938, a cross-party National Emergency Conference was held, which included many Labour Party members and trade unionists. This was boycotted by the Labour leadership. Labour branches like Battersea raised money and sent an ambulance to Spain. Other members worked tirelessly with church groups, humanitarian organisations and known Communists to raise money for aid. Other Labour Party members took part in demonstrations supporting 'Arms for Spain'. Many Labour Party members openly ignored what the leadership said on Spain, and some activists were so disgusted at the leadership's inaction that they joined other political parties, in particular, the CPGB, which was the party most involved in supporting Republican Spain.[34]

Many Labour Party members and trade unionists were also members of the Co-operative Movement, but many Co-op members belonged to no political party at all. The Co-operative Movement was a massive organisation with thousands of shops and wholesale outlets based on the principles of its Rochdale founding fathers, and allowed anyone to become a paid member and have a say in its business strategy. The Co-operative Movement was by far the largest civic organisation in Britain; in 1938, it had around 8.5 million members. This organisation was strongly involved in humanitarian efforts supporting the Spanish Republic and refugees from the Civil War. Its most successful humanitarian campaign was 'Milk for Spain' (the Co-op was Britain's main supplier of milk) where Co-op members could buy tokens at 6d or 3d. Money raised by the buying of milk tokens was used to supply powdered milk for Republican Spain. It was a very successful campaign and was seen as non-political in that it provided food aid to the victims of war. Children and women were often portrayed as the recipients of the milk.[35]

One small political party in Britain threw all its efforts into supporting Republican Spain. This party was the CPGB. For a very brief moment at the beginning of the war, the CPGB supported non-intervention; however, once the Soviet leader Joseph Stalin had instructed the international Communist movement to support the Spanish Republic, the CPGB put all its meagre resources into becoming the Spanish Republic's number one support organisation in Britain. In 1936, the CPGB was a small political party; it had one MP and a small number of local councillors, who were concentrated mainly in London, South Wales and the Scottish coalfields of Fife. Its membership stood at around 11,500 and it was looked upon unfavourably by trade union and Labour Party leaders. Yet this small political party – its leaders and rank-and-file members – was the driving force in supplying political, humanitarian and military aid to Republican Spain.[36]

Throughout the war the Communists were at the forefront of lobbying for the ability of the Spanish Republic to buy arms openly. They were constantly bringing forward evidence of occasions when the Fascist powers, Italy and Germany, had broken the Non-Intervention Agreement. Demonstrations demanding 'Arms for Spain' always involved Communists holding placards, carrying mock coffins to show that inaction only led to more deaths in Spain, or carrying effigies of political figures who were either pro-Fascist or who did nothing to support the Spanish Republic. Many demonstrations were organised by Communists, and usually at least one speaker was a member of the party. Throughout the Civil War the CPGB sold a mass of pamphlets on the war with titles such as *Arms for Spain*, *Save Spain from Fascism* and *Spain Organises for Victory*. In addition, the Left Book Club produced many titles on Spain, quite often written by Communists, or people sympathetic to their position on Spain. It published one book a month, as well as special editions from a left-wing point of view, and was very popular across the country. Their books were especially widely read by people in the labour movement.[37] Left Book Club titles on Spain included *Civil War in Spain*, *Spanish Testament*, *Spain in Revolt* and *Catholic in Republican Spain*. Communist Party leaders, such as its general secretary Harry Pollitt and its MP Willie Gallagher, spoke at countless rallies and visited British volunteers in Spain on several occasions.[38] The Communist newspaper, the *Daily Worker*, gave the Civil War in Spain constant coverage in its pages, often on its front pages. The paper regularly featured local initiatives to support the Spanish Republic and also the volunteers out in Spain.[39]

The Communist rank-and-file could be found in almost every committee set up to send aid to Spain. Money was raised to send food, medical supplies and ambulances. The CPGB supported the sending of doctors, nurses and ambulance drivers, and many of the most dedicated nurses and doctors in Spain from Britain were Communists. (The next chapter will cover Medical Aid to Spain in detail.) Communists often worked with religious organisations and non-political people, as well as people from other parties, and were the backbone of many committees, doing much of the most laborious work such as knocking on doors asking for food or money. Communist Party members also helped to support the upkeep of refugees from Spain, particularly in 1937, when around 4,000 Spanish children from the Basque region were evacuated to Britain because of the dangers from aerial bombing (see Chapter 4). Some leading Communists spoke at several meetings a day; one of them, Lewis Jones[40] – a South Wales councillor – literally killed himself working for Spain when he died of a heart attack after addressing thirty meetings in one day. At the first Labour Party Conference after the end of the Civil War, Sybil Wingate stated in her speech how the tiny CPGB with its dedicated membership had raised more money for Republican Spain than both the Labour Party and the TUC organisations, who had vastly greater memberships.[41]

The Communist Party's most significant contribution was the organisation, recruitment and leadership of the British Battalion of the International Brigades, which served in Spain from January 1937 until September 1938. Around 2,500 British and Irish volunteers served in the International Brigades; 526 were killed in action, while the majority of the rest were wounded. The volunteers fought in all the major military actions of the Civil War. It is estimated that around sixty per cent of the British and Irish volunteers were Communists, if this percentage is reflected in the number of volunteers killed, it means that a small political party like the CPGB must have lost over 300 of its best young members – a huge sacrifice for a minor political party. The Moscow archives contain statements from 1,107 British and Irish volunteers who were members of the CPGB or the Young Communist League, although many volunteers gave their political party as 'Anti-Fascist'. Most volunteers were working-class men who had often been involved in clashes with Oswald Mosley's Fascist BUF before they went to Spain. A significant number of volunteers were of Jewish heritage.[42]

The majority of the British Battalion volunteers who had still been in Spain arrived home in December 1938 at Victoria Station in London, where they were greeted by thousands of well-wishers. Still in Spain were some British nurses, and those British and Irish volunteers who were PoWs. British and Irish volunteers had been captured by the Nationalists at Jarama, Calaceite and in the Ebro campaign. Conditions in the PoW camps were similar to those in concentration camps: a starvation diet, regular beatings, poor sanitation, freezing cold accommodation and occasional executions. Most British and Irish PoWs were returned to Britain during 1939, although a handful remained after this date.[43]

The Communist Party filled most of the leadership positions in the British Battalion, particularly the office of commissar. The British Battalion had twelve commissars, of whom three were killed in action, including a couple of leading Communists: Harry Dobson from South Wales and Walter Tapsell from London.[44] In the British Battalion, unlike more traditional armies, there was a distinct possibility of being killed, wounded or suffering from battle fatigue, even for the Battalion commanders. There were twelve commanders during the British Battalion's time in Spain: two were killed in action and several others were wounded, or were relieved of command due to stress-related factors.

More than any other political party, the CPGB had supported the Spanish Republic to the maximum of its ability. The Party provided soldiers and medical staff and organised the recruitment and leadership of the British Battalion of the International Brigades. Its members were at the forefront of demonstrations in support of Spain and a dedicated party member would be involved in almost any 'Aid Spain' committee. The Party leadership spoke constantly on behalf of the Spanish Republic and visited Spain many times. Its constant activities in support of the Spanish Republic during the Civil War led to an increase in Party membership to nearly 18,000, and the readership of its newspaper, the *Daily Worker*, increased to over 40,000 during the week and reached 80,000 at the weekends.[45]

Compared with the number of men who fought in the Republican armed forces or who served in their medical forces, the number of those who fought on the side of Franco's Nationalists in the Civil War was very small. From Ireland, around 600–700 volunteers went to fight as a unit in the Nationalist army. They were led by Eoin O'Duffy, the leader of the 'Blueshirts' movement, Ireland's equivalent of the BUF.[46] This force remained in Spain for a few months and returned home after a rather inglorious stay. There was no such equivalent force from Britain; a handful of individuals served in the Nationalists' armed forces. Former Cambridge University student, Peter Kemp, went to Spain and served in both the Spanish Foreign Legion and the Carlist forces. Frank Thomas from South Wales also served in the Spanish Foreign Legion. The wealthy socialite Priscilla Scott-Ellis was the only British woman who served as a nurse in Nationalist Spain.[47] Probably the most important contribution to the Nationalist war effort by an English person was by a Captain Bebb, who flew Franco in a British privately hired plane from the Canary Islands to Spanish Morocco, where he took over the Army of Africa, beginning his rise to eventually becoming dictator of Spain.[48]

The mass media in Britain were divided in their support for the Republican and Nationalist sides in the Spanish Civil War. The left-wing and liberal press tended to support the Republican side. The *Daily Herald*, which supported the Labour Party, faithfully supported the policy of the Labour Party; so it was pro-Republican but also in favour of non-intervention. The Liberal newspapers – the *Manchester Guardian*, *News Chronicle* and *Reynolds News* – were pro-Republican and more critical of non-intervention than the *Daily Herald*. Left-wing magazines like the *New Statesman* were, unsurprisingly, pro-Republican. The British Broadcasting Corporation aimed for an impartial view on the conflict and featured reports from both sides in the Civil War. Newsreels of the day shown in cinemas tended to be simplistic and avoided any mention of the politics of the conflict. Some reporters, like George Steer, who worked for newspapers that supported the Nationalists, were still able to send stories favourable to the Republic. In Steer's case he was the first journalist to enter Guernica after its destruction and his report swayed many people into supporting the Republic.[49]

As we have seen earlier in the chapter, the British establishment, including the government, favoured the Nationalists. The main newspapers of the day were also supportive of the rebels. The *Times* followed the government position of non-intervention in Spain. The *Daily Mail*, the *Morning Post* and the *Sunday Observer* were strongly pro-Franco, while the *Daily Express* was less strident in its support of the Nationalists. The *Daily Mail* published many exaggerated atrocity stories from Spain, describing in lurid details anti-clerical acts allegedly committed by revolutionaries on the Republican side. The *Daily Telegraph* supported government policy towards Spain, but was critical of its appeasement policy towards Germany.[50]

The leading British and Irish intellectuals, which included writers, poets and artists, were overwhelmingly in favour of the Republican side. Many of them viewed Fascism as a creed that crushed free will and artistic expression, which was reinforced when the leading Spanish playwright and poet Federico García Lorca was murdered by the Nationalists.[51]

A survey in June 1937 called *Authors take sides on the Spanish War* found that 127 authors supported the Republic, sixteen were neutral and five were against the Republic. The sample was biased in favour of pro-Republicans, although George Orwell was very critical of the survey, calling it, 'bloody rot' and refusing to respond. However, the survey does give us a very rough indication of the artistic community's position on the Civil War. Several intellectuals fought in Spain; four – all Communists – were killed: Ralph Fox, a leading Marxist scholar; John Cornford, a young Cambridge poet; Christopher Caudwell, a novelist; and David Haden-Guest, a scientist. During the Civil War, leading and aspiring British and Irish writers, poets and artists wrote politicised poetry, plays and books for the Left Book Club, they designed billboards and posters in support of 'Aid Spain', and sold art to raise money.[52]

The two main religious groups in Britain showed little support for Republican Spain; the Church of England was very conservative and tended to support the government's non-intervention policy. The Catholic Church was pro-Nationalist, portraying Franco as a Catholic crusader protecting the faith. In the early days of the Civil War, the Anarchists burned churches and murdered priests and nuns, and the Republican government was well aware of the worldwide bad publicity this gave them. To counter this view, they invited a delegation of Church of England and Free Church clergy to Spain in February 1937, followed by a second group of clergies in March. The clergy concluded that the Catholic Church was to blame for supporting the rebels and favouring the rich over the poor, and saw the Republican government as a progressive democratic regime. But, as individuals, the clergy were divided over which side they supported in the Civil War. Confusingly, some Catholic priests supported the Republicans, but the majority of working-class church-going Catholics would listen to their priest denounce the godless Republicans at Mass, and then still support the Republicans through their trade union or through the 'Aid Spain' movement. Many Christians of all denominations ignored the views of their faith leaders and actively supported campaigns to provide humanitarian aid to Republican Spain.[53]

One religious denomination remained neutral in the Spanish Civil War, while sending a significant amount of aid to Republican Spain. This denomination was the Society of Friends, or Quakers. They oppose all war, remaining neutral during conflicts, and are obliged to help people who are suffering. The bulk of aid from the Quakers went to Republican

Spain because they were seen as the people in the most need. Also, the Quakers were not welcomed by the Nationalists. Their main role in supplying aid was to raise money for relief, both within the Quaker movement and also as part of the 'Aid Spain' movement. In Spain, Quakers always had a small team in place that organised the feeding of thousands of children, set up colonies for orphans and set up children's hospitals. In all cases they worked closely with other organisations from Britain, Spain and other countries. After the Civil War ended, the Quakers tried to stay behind and organise relief for the starving civilians, but by June 1939 the Franco authorities had closed down all major Quaker relief efforts in Spain.[54]

The Catholic Church in Britain was strongly pro-Nationalist. Its leading papers *The Tablet* and the *Catholic Herald* were at first wary about supporting the Nationalists, but stories of Republican atrocities against the Catholic Church led it supporting the rebels. The leaders of the Catholic Church and most of its priests were openly pro-rebel and encouraged their congregations to support the Nationalists as protectors of the Catholic faith against the godless Republicans. The Catholic Church portrayed the Nationalists as anti-Communist and anti-secular forces, who were aiming to set up a new state based on Catholic values. The Catholic Church also raised money for medical aid to Nationalist Spain and sent ten or eleven ambulances to the rebels, although the amount of money raised was tiny compared to that raised by Republican supporters via the 'Aid Spain' movement. The Catholic Church also supported the upkeep of a large number of the Basque refugee children who came from Spain in 1937, since the majority of them were Catholics.[55]

As stated, most of the British population saw the situation as a war in a distant country that meant little to them and were happy to support the government's policy of non-intervention, although many of these people would have given money or food to an 'Aid Spain' activist. However, Spain became a very important part of the lives of a not insignificant section of the British people. Many were involved in raising money and collecting food. Politically, many people participated in demonstrations demanding 'Arms for Spain', or they lobbied politicians and trade union leaders. Many spoke at meetings or were involved as members of 'Aid Spain' committees. Almost 3,000 volunteers went to Spain as soldiers in the International Brigades or as part of the medical services. As we have seen, British people with any interest in the Civil War were mostly pro-Republican, but a small minority supported the Nationalist rebels, and their views were echoed by the Catholic Church and several leading newspapers.

In the next chapter we will look at how the 'Aid Spain' movement was organised and the role of the Spanish Medical Aid Committee, how the 'Aid Movement' with help from the Catholic Church looked after 4,000 Basque refugee children in Britain and the contribution of British volunteer medical staff to the Republican cause.

# Chapter 4

# Humanitarian Aid for Republican Spain: British Medical Volunteers

In the previous chapter we heard about the hundreds of thousands of ordinary people who helped to raise money to send medical and humanitarian aid to (mainly) Republican Spain, or who gave money or donated food to appeals for 'Aid for Spain'. The different organisations involved in organising aid included political parties, trade unions, religious groups, artists and intellectuals and, on occasions, some or all of these groups working together. In this chapter we will look at the impact of the 'Aid Spain' efforts in Britain and how this aid was coordinated. It will focus on medical aid and the involvement of British volunteers in the medical services of the Spanish Republic; but it will also look at the biggest domestic fundraising event during the Civil War, which was precipitated by the arrival of around 4,000 Basque refugee children into Britain.

When the Civil War broke out in Spain, the two main foreign relief bodies in Britain, the British Red Cross and the Save the Children Fund, were non-political groups; so, although they were willing to raise funds to help the people of Spain, they would not take sides in the war. In 1936, with neither the government or the main relief agencies favouring Republican Spain, a bewildering number of different groups were raising money, collecting food, and, in one case, making clothes in a disused factory for the people of Republican Spain. Thousands of 'Aid Spain' events took place in Britain during the Civil War. These ranged from jumble sales in village halls, film shows about Spain and fundraising meetings to mass demonstrations and selling out the Royal Albert Hall in London several times. At least fifty different organisations produced pamphlets about Spain, which sold in their hundreds of thousands, and millions of leaflets were produced between 1936 and 1939 requesting donations for Spain. During the Civil War, the various 'Aid Spain' groups and organisations raised nearly £2 million (around £130 million in present day value) of aid for Republican Spain. This multitude of disparate groups needed a body to coordinate them or, at the very least, to help them to cooperate efficiently.[1]

The coordinating group for the various 'Aid Spain' organisations, the National Joint Committee for Spanish Relief, was set up in November 1936 and held its first meeting at the House of Commons on 6 January 1937. The first meeting of the NJCSR included several MPs and representatives of fifteen organisations. The main instigator of the committee was the Liberal MP Wilfred Roberts, who was nicknamed the 'MP for Spain'. He invited the Duchess of Atholl, a Conservative MP, to be its chair. The committee's role was to try to prevent any overlapping of appeals, and to efficiently organise the raising of funds and the sending of material to Republican Spain. The committee's mission was to:

- Look after refugees.
- Remove civilians from war areas.
- Provide medical aid.[2]

The NJCSR was set up to be a non-sectarian and impartial committee. It included non-political organisations like the Quakers and 'Save the Children'. These groups saw the role of the NJCSR as a cooperative rather than a coordinator, and continued to pursue their own agendas regarding Spain. Although it claimed to be impartial, the NJCSR only ever sent relief to Republican Spain. During the Civil War it organised the evacuation of children from Madrid, it ran a colony for children at Puigcerda in Catalonia and sent several food ships to Spain. By the end of the Civil War the NJCSR was taking care of 8,000 Spanish children in central Spain and had spent heavily on feeding and accommodating large numbers of Basque refugee children who had arrived in Britain in 1937. In time, 150 organisations were cooperating within the NJCSR, which provided these organisations with advice, ideas, support and helped to set up local 'Aid Spain' committees where there had previously been none. Several national coordinating committees covering different aspects of relief were set up during the Civil War to coordinate fundraising or to increase cooperation between different organisations, and quite often the same people were on these various committees.[3] Three other major national committees were set up; one managed the care of the Basque refugee children, the International Brigade Dependents' Association raised money to support the families of men fighting in the British Battalion in Spain and to help care for the men who returned home wounded,[4] and the third coordinated medical aid.

The coordinating body for sending medical aid to Spain was known as the Spanish Medical Aid Committee (SMAC) and was formed in late July 1936 after an appeal by the Spanish Republican government for medical aid from overseas. Isabel Brown,[5] a leading Communist, had received an earlier appeal for medical aid from the International Red Aid. She was put in touch with a young left-wing trainee doctor, Dr Kenneth Sinclair-Loutit, who could advise on purchasing £100 (which quickly grew to £500) worth of medicines. They heard of the appeal from the Spanish government and contacted the medical adviser to the TUC, Hyacinth Morgan, about forming a SMAC. Morgan contacted Dr Charles Brook, a General Practitioner who was a member of the London County Council and the secretary of the Socialist Medical Association. Through a friend, Dr Brook organised a room for Brown and Sinclair-Loutit at the National Trades Union Club at 24 New Oxford Road in London. The first SMAC meeting was called for 31 July 1936, and Brook contacted the press and interested individuals. Brook became the SMAC secretary and Morgan the chair. Christopher Addison, a former Liberal health minister and now a member of the Labour Party, became the president. The first SMAC committee included Isabel Brown, several doctors, professors, nobility, trade union leaders like Leah Manning and MPs. Later, businesspeople and clergy also served on the committee.[6]

Two members of the SMAC – Leah Manning and Dr George Jeger – were to play a big role in the life of Madge Addy as people with whom she spoke and corresponded, and by whom she was interviewed when on leave in Britain.

Leah Manning was born in 1886 and was brought up by her grandparents. She trained as a teacher and joined the socialist Fabian Society. In 1913 she married Will Manning. She became Labour MP for East Islington in 1929 and the following year became president of the National Union of Teachers. She became an anti-Fascist in the early 1930s as secretary of the Coordinating Committee Against War and Fascism. In this role she visited Spain after the crushing of the Asturias uprising in 1934 and wrote a book about what she had discovered.

Manning became a key member of the SMAC, and made several trips to Spain to deliver medical supplies. She is best known, though, for her work with the Basque refugee children. Later she became Labour MP for Epping from 1945 to 1950. She was awarded an OBE in 1966 and died in 1977.[7]

Madge Addy wrote to Dr George Jeger, and met him while she was on leave, discussing the situation in Spain with him. Madge also sent aid requests to him. Jeger was mayor of Shoreditch in London and a Labour Party parliamentary candidate, later becoming a Labour MP. In December 1936 he took over the secretary duties of the SMAC from Dr Brook.[8]

Although the SMAC was strongly influenced by the CPGB and Socialist Medical Association, it always presented itself as a non-political committee. It met daily and had the cooperation of the Spanish embassy and the British government, who gave them permits to export goods to Spain.

The first public meeting of the SMAC was held in August 1936 in the Quaker Meeting House in Euston, London. An advertisement, signed by several eminent doctors, was placed asking for volunteer doctors, trainee doctors, nurses and assistants to serve in Spain. Not everybody was in favour of the SMAC aims; the British Medical Association, for example, refused to give its endorsement, but individual doctors could make up their own minds about volunteering. Within a very short time the SMAC were able to set up and organise the first British Medical Unit for dispatch to Spain.[9] Dr Brook was the driving force behind having a medical unit ready to leave for Spain by 23 August 1936, just three weeks after the first meeting of the SMAC.[10]

Before we look in detail at the role of British medical staff in the Spanish Civil War, let us first look at one of the greatest British humanitarian efforts of the Civil War period. When raising money for medical aid, Madge Addy also raised money for Basque refugee children and wrote letters to the press about their situation. In April 1937 the independent Basque government appealed to foreign countries to accept Basque refugees fleeing from the Civil War and daily bombings. The NJCSR asked the British government to allow up to 4,000 Basque children to enter Britain. The government agreed to accept them, with the understanding that the children were aged between 5 and 15, their welfare was to be funded by private donations only and they were to be returned to Spain as soon as possible.

Leah Manning of the SMAC and Edith Pye[11] from the Quakers went to Bilbao to organise the evacuation. A new committee called the Basque Children's Committee was formed to manage the fundraising and the organisation of the care of the children. It was chaired by the Duchess of Atholl, assisted by the Independent MP Eleanor Rathbone.[12] The Catholic Church agreed to look after 1,200 children and the Salvation Army another 400.[13] In May 1937 approximately 4,000 Basque refugee children arrived in Britain to be housed, fed and cared for.

Housing 4,000 children was a major headache until a farmer offered the use of a large field in North Stoneham, in Hampshire, where a makeshift camp was set up. On 23 May, the *Habana* docked at Southampton with 3,861 children, accompanied by 230 adult helpers, teachers and priests. Within days of their arrival, some of the children were moved from North Stoneham to various locations around Britain. Eventually, the refugees were housed in over seventy different buildings around Britain; roughly a third organised by the Catholic Church and most of the rest by the NJCSR and BCC. There were some cultural and language problems in looking after the children, many of whom had been traumatised by the Civil War. When Bilbao fell some of the older boys went on a so-called 'rampage', where the total cost of damage was around £10. Some right-wing newspapers demanded they be sent home.[14]

To help to raise funds the children performed concert parties, singing traditional songs and performing regional dances. The NJCSR was quite open in its advice to fundraisers that they were to use the children as a physical example of what 'Aid Spain' could achieve. As one young Basque boy related, playing and singing in tune seemed of secondary importance if the audience could see their 'sad little faces'.[15]

Concerts were held throughout Britain, including one at the Royal Albert Hall in London, where a Picasso sketch of his masterpiece *Guernica* was printed on the front of the programme. The original sketch was auctioned to raise money for the upkeep of the Basque children.[16]

As the Civil War drew to its conclusion the British government wanted the children to be returned to their families in Spain. The BCC was adamant they would only allow them to return to Spain if it was safe. By the outbreak of the Second World War in September 1939, around 1,000 Basque children were still in Britain. By the end of the Second World War in 1945, approximately 400 of the Basque child refugees were still in Britain and many of them made this country their home.[17]

The man appointed to lead the first British Medical Unit to Spain was 23-year-old medical student Kenneth Sinclair-Loutit.[18] On Sunday, 23 August 1936, thousands of people gathered in London, along with six mayors, to support the dispatch of the first British Medical Unit, which was the first medical unit from any country to go to Spain. It had been organised and equipped in just four weeks, thanks to the efforts of the SMAC and donations from the public and various organisations. The volunteers were interviewed, and a small group of medical personnel from differing backgrounds and politics were chosen to leave. The unit included four doctors, four medical students, four nurses, six drivers and six ambulances. Granen, on the Aragón front, was chosen as the base for the British Medical Unit as it was on a major road junction and close to the frontlines. An abandoned farmhouse became the hospital and, although it was filthy, with limited electric and no water supply except for a local stream, within a few days two operating theatres were set up and twenty-five beds were ready for occupation. The medical staff at Granen were not organised like a traditional British hospital. Drivers had also to be mechanics, cleaners and, on occasions, anaesthetists; nurses became administrators, prescribed treatments for patients and performed minor operations; doctors took on medical tasks outside their areas of expertise, drove ambulances, and became cleaners and hospital managers. Medical personnel at Granen did what was necessary to treat battlefield casualties.[19]

One member of the first British Medical Unit was a woman called Rosita Davson. Madge wrote to her, and met her in Spain, requesting food and medical supplies from her for Madge's hospital. Rosita was chosen to go with the first British Medical Unit because she had good language skills. She stayed in Barcelona at the SMAC office, and in time became the SMAC go-between with the Spanish government. From Barcelona she sent medical supplies to the various hospitals. She was praised by the Republican authorities, Leah Manning and the SMAC for her efforts in Barcelona, although it seems she was less liked by British medical personnel in Spain, who accused her of giving British medical supplies away too easily to the Spanish authorities and was suspected of being a British government spy. After the Civil War Davson became a member of the British diplomatic corps, which added weight to the suspicions, since anyone who had served in Spain would normally have had no chance of such a position.[20]

By November 1936 Sinclair-Loutit recorded that over 1,500 patients had been treated and the ambulances had travelled over 22,500km. The number of beds had increased to seventy and there were now surgical, medical and venereal disease wards and a reception. However, when military action took place the hospital had too few ambulances, too few staff and no X-ray facilities. Requests from Spain led to the dispatch of a second British Medical Unit to Granen. There were also requests for English food because all the members of the unit had upset stomachs from the unfamiliar Spanish food. Reading matter in English was also requested, as was suitable clothing, such as overalls for the women who also did manual work. The requests specified 'no ties' as they were of no use to anyone![21] Nurse Patience Darton was highly critical of the impractical clothing offered to the female members of the unit. This included overalls which meant that the wearer had virtually to strip off if they wished to go to the toilet and 'two silly little frocks'.[22]

The area around Granen was controlled by the Anarchists. Their local leader did not take kindly to the presence of the hospital, mainly because they had not asked his permission to set it up. His hostility ended after he seized a petrol lorry from the hospital and ended up getting burnt as he was a keen smoker! The hospital staff's excellent treatment of his burns ended his hostility.[23]

During the autumn of 1936 some of the medical staff left Spain for various reasons; one nurse had been wounded by machine gun fire while helping an injured militia fighter. In September 1936 two new doctors and six more nurses arrived to reinforce the unit. By the autumn of 1936, twenty-nine British medical staff were working at Granen, along with some Spaniards and other international volunteers. There were some tensions amongst the medical unit at Granen. Some of these were political – the Communists were resented because they met separately from the others – but there were also personality clashes and some romances. The key problem was that the Aragón front had become quiet, and boredom and inactivity were affecting morale. By January 1937 Granen was taken over by a wholly Spanish medical team. In the same month, the bulk of the British Medical Unit moved to Albacete to join the International Brigades, medical support team. Some of the nurses went to a hospital at Poleñino in Aragón instead.[24]

Two other British medical units went out to Spain in 1936 and early 1937. The first was the Scottish Ambulance Unit, the brainchild of wealthy

Glasgow businessman Sir Daniel Macaulay Stevenson. He refused to work with the SMAC and in September 1936 sent out a unit of twenty volunteers and six ambulances, led by the eccentric kilt-wearing Fernanda Jacobsen. The unit did good service near Madrid, dealing with over 2,500 wounded and evacuating thousands of refugees. Within a few months battle fatigue meant the unit was no longer functioning and it returned to Britain. A new unit went out to Spain in January 1937, but, when Jacobsen announced they were to give aid to both sides, several members of the unit left to join SMAC medical units. By the middle of 1937, the remnants of the unit were back in Britain. Another unit was in Spain in September 1937, and remained until July 1938, distributing food to the civilians of Madrid. Jacobsen led each unit that went to Spain and returned on her own in January 1939 to organise food distribution to the civilians in Madrid, staying on after the Civil War ended. The Scottish Ambulance Unit was dogged with controversy; some members of the unit were accused of looting, its ambulances evacuated Nationalist sympathisers from Madrid, and Jacobson's comments about giving aid to both sides caused the unit to lose support.[25]

The London University Ambulance Unit was the creation of Sir George Young, a former diplomat and Labour parliamentary candidate. In February 1937 it travelled to southern Spain to help the Quakers run their hospitals in this region. Young also helped to fund the housing of refugees, setting up colonies for children and his own hospital. Eventually the financial burden of these initiatives in Spain led him to hand over the management of these enterprises to the Quakers.[26]

Around a dozen members of the British Medical Unit became part of the medical staff of the International Brigades and were assigned to support the 14th Brigade, which was predominantly made up of French volunteers. Over the next few months, the SMAC sent more medical staff to Spain; some were sent to join the International Brigades, medical staff, including medical support for the British Battalion, some to support the original nurses from Granen and others to a variety of military units and hospitals. The impact of the expertise of foreign medical staff was shown at a couple of battles fought by the 14th International Brigade at Lopera, where twenty per cent of the wounded died in Spanish hospitals at Las Rozas de Madrid, but only five per cent of the wounded died in International Brigade hospitals. This was actually an improvement on the fatality statistics of the Great War. At the Battle of Jarama in February 1937, the nurses worked until they were exhausted, but further medical advancements reduced fatalities from wounds to a mere three and a half per cent. During the battle, the number of British volunteers was increased by reinforcements to about twenty. These volunteers were further reinforced by four men who had left the Scottish Ambulance Unit. By the summer of 1937, a SMAC report could boast of sending 126 medical staff to Spain, having people working in seven hospitals, and helping to support a further eighteen hospitals as well as sending a mass of trucks and ambulances.[27]

During the summer of 1937 the Republican government decided to organise the foreign medical staff in either the International Brigades (officially part of the Republican Army) or as part of the Republican Army. There were some misgivings in the SMAC about loss of independence and a fear that the volunteers would come under Communist control. In July 1937 the SMAC agreed that all medical personnel and supplies going to Spain were to be used by the Spanish medical services, *Sanidad*, as they saw fit. In addition, it was agreed that aid from the SMAC was to go through the *Centrale Sanitaire Internationale*, which was set up in Paris in January 1937 to be the conduit for foreign aid sent to Spain. Throughout 1937, British medical staff were involved in all the major battles, and some were also based at hospitals away from the military fronts. At the end of 1937, British medical staff serving in the International Brigades, medical services numbered eleven doctors, ten nurses and thirty-four other medical staff. After the Battle of Teruel and the collapse of the Aragón front in the spring of 1938 (which led to the Spanish Republic being cut in half), the vast majority of British medical staff retreated into Catalonia, along with the armed forces, who were defeated on the Aragón front. This disaster led to the setting up of the National Spanish Aid Committee which was to coordinate the distribution of all foreign aid through the CSI. In the south of Spain, at a former monastery called Uclés, the SMAC still had staff, including British volunteers; however, the hospital was for wounded Spanish soldiers only. This hospital became Madge Addy's major posting in Spain and I will cover her time at Uclés in detail in the next chapter.[28]

Thanks to the initiative of an ambulance driver called Max Colin, who was invalided home after the Battle of Brunete, the SMAC was able to significantly improve the reliability and quality of the ambulances available to the Republican medical services. Colin and two SMAC colleagues recommended the best type of vehicle, and when they returned to Spain in January 1938 they collected a mass of spare parts for the vehicles, got together a team of skilled mechanics and set up a giant workshop which could service 200 vehicles at a time during the Battle of the Ebro in the summer of 1938.

During this battle the British medical staff worked in a cave hospital at La Bisbal de Falset, while medical services near the front were based in a railway tunnel at Flix. Most British medical staff returned home during the autumn of 1938, with a smaller number returning in early 1939. A small handful of them retired into France with the Republican army and civilians, and were interned briefly in concentration camps. The last British medical volunteer to leave Spain was Madge Addy, who was still in Spain when the Civil War ended in April 1939 (there will be more on this in the next chapter).[29] In the autumn of 1938, SMAC claimed it had sent fifteen doctors, forty-four nurses and more than eighty other medical staff, including ambulance drivers, to Spain. Equipment-wise SMAC had sent eighty-two ambulances and trucks and three refrigeration units for the blood transfusion service and X-ray equipment. It had also set up nineteen hospitals as well as many temporary frontline hospitals.[30]

During the Spanish Civil War, great strides were made in treating the injured, which meant that recovery rates in Spanish Republican hospitals were far greater than in the Great War. Several of the new techniques used in the Civil War to treat wounded soldiers were to be used in the Second World War and the Korean War. Some of the leading Spanish Republican doctors and surgeons fled to the west after the Civil War and their wartime experiences were utilised – sometimes reluctantly – by Allied medical staff in the Second World War. The knowledge of British volunteer doctors and surgeons who returned from Spain was passed on to the heads of British armed forces medical services, who did not immediately see the advantages of this information. The four main areas of military medical advance during the Civil War were:

- Treatment of wounds, particularly fractures.
- Development of blood transfusion service and blood banks.
- Organisation of medical support services.
- Containment of infectious diseases.

British volunteer medical staff were to be involved in all areas of these medical advances.[31]

In the treatment of serious injuries, especially fractures, the leading Spanish surgeon was Josep Trueta Raspall, who was based in Barcelona. In the Great War, wounds were rapidly stitched up to reduce bleeding, and fractured limbs were encased in plaster straight away, with the injured soldier being sent to the base hospital to be operated on. This delay, coupled with foreign bodies in the wound, led to a high mortality rate from gas gangrene as the wound or wounds became infected. This resulted in many amputations and often death. Trueta devised the following system:

- Surgery was to take place as soon as possible, ideally within eight hours. The surgery included debridement, which was the removal of all dead and contaminated skin and muscle, conserving, where possible, skin and bone. After surgery, the wound was left exposed and unstitched.
- The wound was cleaned with soap and water and iodine, using a nailbrush.
- Wounds were packed with dry sterile gauze and provision was made for the wound to drain.
- Fractures were immobilised in plaster.

Some surgeons advocated the use of Kramer splints for fractures; here the patient was immobilised in a wire splint thickly packed with cotton wool and tightly bandaged. This proved impractical under wartime conditions and fractures were plastered instead. If a wound was sutured or stitched and then plastered, a window was left in the plaster so the wound was easily accessible. Trueta claimed that during the Civil War he treated 1,073 patients with war fractures and only six died. Trueta visited Britain in 1939, after the Civil War, and spoke to the Royal Society of Medicine. He lived in this country until 1967 and became a professor of Orthopaedic Surgery at Oxford University.[32]

In the Great War, many soldiers had bled to death from wounds before they could be taken to frontline clearing stations or to hospital to be operated on. Dr Norman Bethune, a Canadian doctor,[33] was the pioneer of mobile blood transfusion services at the front so that wounded soldiers could receive a blood transfusion as soon as possible. Specially converted lorries were used to carry the refrigerated blood. The Republican authorities set up a large-scale blood donor scheme and, in the summer of 1938, there were 14,000 blood donors in Barcelona alone. The leading organiser of the blood donor scheme was a Catalan doctor, Dr Frederico Duran-Jorda. Like Trueta, Duran-Jorda fled to Britain after the Civil War and helped to organise the London blood transfusion centre. Later he became a laboratory technician and eventually a pathologist. He died in 1957.[34]

In the Great War, medical clearing stations near the frontlines treated the wounded, and then ambulances took them away to the base hospitals for any operations. In the Spanish Civil War, it was recognised that injured soldiers should be treated as quickly as possible to give them the greatest chances of survival. Each Republican army unit had a First Aid post which evacuated the injured soldier to the frontline *hospital de sangre*, which was often a temporary tented affair. Here a doctor, sometimes a nurse, undertook triage, where they would decide who needed to be operated on straightaway, who was dying and needed to be made as comfortable as possible, and who could be sent to the rear-guard hospitals. By being operated on quickly or being given a blood transfusion, many injured soldiers lived who would otherwise have died on the journey to the rear-guard hospitals. A typical mobile hospital included at least some of the following: a triage team, a surgical team, an X-ray team, a blood transfusion unit, ambulance drivers, stretcher bearers and kitchen staff. The Republicans also had mobile operating vehicles known as *autochirs*, which were adapted lorries.[35]

For many young British doctors, surgeons and medical students, the lessons they learned and the experience they gained in Spain led them to become first-rate medical practitioners. Several served in the Royal Army Medical Corps in the Second World War, where they were able to use their knowledge and experiences. Some of the British doctors who served in Spain included Colin Bradsworth, C. F. Hill and Harry Bury, who each were at one time Battalion Medical Officer for the British Battalion of the International Brigades. Dorothy Collier worked with the eminent Catalan surgeon Trueta in Barcelona, and played a major role in arranging his residence in Britain after the Civil War. Richard Joseph and Thomas Ruys were attached to the 13th and 11th International Brigades. Len Crome, who became Chief Medical Officer of the 35th Division, was put in charge of the military hospital in Naples during the Second World War. One of the most famous British medical volunteers was Archie Cochrane, who was a medical student when he went to

Spain as part of the first British Medical Unit and was sent home after Brunete to complete his medical training. He was a medical officer in the Second World War; after the war he became a scientist, a professor and a major exponent of medical research with a database and research centres named after him. He was awarded both a Member of the Order of the British Empire (MBE) medal and Commander of the Order of the British Empire (CBE) medal for his contributions to medicine.[36]

Three doctors who made major contributions to medical aid in Spain and later had distinguished careers in medicine were Kenneth Sinclair-Loutit, Reg Saxton and Alexander Tudor-Hart. Sinclair-Loutit was expelled from public school but still studied medicine at Cambridge University. In Spain he led the first British Medical Unit and became a lieutenant in the 14th International Brigade. He served in Spain from August 1936 to December 1937. He completed his medical training on his return to Britain. During the Second World War Sinclair-Loutit played a significant role in air defence (for which he was awarded an MBE), and in the post-war period he worked abroad for the World Health Organisation. His first wife was fellow Civil War veteran Thora Silverthorne.[37] Reg Saxton also studied medicine at Cambridge and, before going to Spain, he practised as a GP in Reading. In Spain, he served in the first British Medical Unit and also in the 14th International Brigade, specialising in working with the blood transfusion service. In the Second World War he was a member of the British Army Blood Transfusion service, then continued practising as a GP after the war. After the death of his wife he married his Civil War love, nurse Rosaleen Ross.[38] Like Sinclair-Loutit, Alexander Tudor-Hart also studied medicine at Cambridge, and became a GP, but he became a surgeon for the 35th Division when he went to Spain. Here, he became a specialist in dealing with fractures. On his return to Britain he wrote articles in medical journals about his experiences and served in the RAMC in the Second World War. After the war he returned to being a GP.[39]

The standard of nursing in Spain before the outbreak of the Civil War was at a rudimentary level, except in a few modern hospitals in Madrid and Barcelona. Patients were cared for by nuns or poorly trained nurses, who were able to carry out only the most basic of tasks. In the smaller hospitals it was expected that the patient's family would take care of any nursing needs. Standards of hygiene were poor and generally the services provided in most Spanish hospitals were at the most elementary level.

The arrival of professionally trained nurses from Britain, Europe and America during the Civil War helped to turn Spanish medical services into a highly efficient life-saving service. They showed Spanish medical personnel how to care for patients in a professional way and helped to train Spanish women to become properly trained nurses.[40]

British nurses in Spain during the Civil War made an 'invaluable contribution'[41] to the success of the Republican medical services. British nurses were renowned for their insistence on high levels of hygiene, their high organisational ability, and exceptional levels of dedication to the welfare of their patients. When it was needed, they worked over several days with little or no sleep, carried out duties without question and worked under fire. During the Civil War, the number of deaths of wounded patients was greatly reduced from those in previous wars, not only by new techniques in surgery and blood transfusion, but also by very observant and careful nursing where the patient's condition and wounds were constantly checked. This is not to say that some British nurses did not fit this high ideal; some had to be sent home because they were unsuitable or were suffering with stress-related illnesses. But most British nurses gave themselves unflinchingly to the cause of the Spanish Republic, for humanitarian reasons, or anti-Fascist views, or by being a CPGB member, or a combination of these factors. One English nurse, Ada Hodson, showed how her personal safety came second to that of her patients (during the Civil War, Republican hospitals were regularly targeted by enemy planes). During the air raid she was wounded both near the eye and on her wrist. She refused to have her wounds treated until she had sedated all the patients in her care and attempted to protect the heads of all of them from shrapnel. A fellow nurse commented:

> … she picked up the tin soup plates and went around putting them on the heads of all the men. It sounds easy, but it really takes a great deal of courage to move around and do things while a raid is on, especially if a tent is the only protection.[42]

As well as using their nursing skills to help care for the patients and assist the doctors and surgeons, British volunteer nurses also played a significant part in the training of Spanish nurses. Particularly in rural areas, the volunteer Spanish women needed to be taught to read and write before they could be given elementary nursing training. Nurses were also used as a propaganda tool, featuring in newspaper articles and touring Britain when on leave, giving talks about the Civil War. People who were not necessarily supporters of the Spanish Republic or uninterested in what was going on in Spain were more likely to give money to support medical aid and British nurses than, say, to give money to an 'Arms for Spain' demonstration bucket collection.[43]

Many of the British volunteer nurses who went to Spain had given up paid positions to do so. Those nurses who served with the first medical unit in Spain received no pay at all and had to beg the local Communist Party *Partido Socialista Unificado de Cataluña* in Catalonia for everything: supplies, food and money. In the International Brigades, medical services, it was different; volunteer nurses were paid a basic salary and given the rank of private. American volunteer nurses were ranked as officers and paid more because of this! In the early days, the nurses were supplied with overalls (see earlier comments of Patience Darton), which were useful for doing physical tasks but very difficult if the nurse needed to relieve herself outside. Some volunteer nurses brought their own uniforms. Some New Zealand nurses arrived wearing large headdresses, but were formally requested to stop wearing them because they made them look like nuns, and some of the patients had been deliberately mistreated by pro-Fascist nuns in previous hospitals. The overalls were replaced in time by typical-looking nurses' uniforms of white dress and headdress.[44]

From the summer of 1937, SMAC appointed Winifred Bates as a sort of manager of the British nurses in Spain. She was living in Spain with her husband, the writer Ralph Bates, and early in the Civil War was a journalist and broadcaster with the PSUC. From July 1937 she was employed by SMAC as a courier, reporter, photographer and someone to manage the nurses. She looked after forty nurses and acted as a sort of mentor, listening to their concerns, giving advice and comforting them when necessary. Many nurses had seen horrific things for the first time and needed to talk to someone about them. The nurses also needed to confide in her about other nurses; some they criticised, and others they praised for their professionalism and personal bravery. Many requested through her a return to frontline nursing, while others begged to be allowed to stay at the front. The nurses under her charge were a mixed bag, but Winifred was 'in awe of their courage'.[45]

Some of the nurses became romantically involved with patients or other medical volunteers and some discovered their true sexuality.

Some doctors and nurses from the Civil War married and, as we will see in the next chapter, Madge Addy became romantically involved with a Norwegian volunteer.[46]

One of the medical advances during the Civil War was the reduction in the number of deaths by infectious diseases, such as typhoid. The death rate in SMAC and International Brigade hospitals was reduced to less than ten per cent. Nonetheless, four British nurses suffered from typhoid: Mary Slater, Joan Purser, Janet Robertson and Penny Phelps.[47] As we will see, Madge Addy contained an outbreak of typhoid at the hospital where she worked. In places in Republican Spain where medical services were more basic or non-existent, typhoid was a mass killer. Nurse Penny Phelps was sent to contain an outbreak at the hospital of the anti-Fascist Italian International Brigaders at Quintanar; she describes what she found and what instructions she gave to contain it:

> The troops' quarters were dirty, overcrowded two-storey barns. The bunks, eating and drinking utensils were all in a sorry state. I spoke to the cooks, explained how typhoid was carried from hand to mouth and that absolute cleanliness should be the watchword.[48]

As related, one of the major medical advances was the treatment and performance of surgery on injured soldiers as close to the front as possible. Lillian Urmston treated the sick and wounded at Caspe in improvised wigwams made from branches and constructed by local poachers and a Native American volunteer. They lived in these wigwams for three weeks; to keep warm she was taught how to keep the fire going, as well as how to hide the smoke from the fire so that planes could not spot them.[49]

It was important to hide smoke plumes to prevent enemy pilots from spotting your position from the air and bombing you. In a similar vein, Thora Silverthorne experienced how frontline medical units had to set up quickly anywhere and be ready for the battlefield casualties. Often travelling was done at night, and once a suitable room had been found all the medical equipment would be crammed into it. An operating theatre would be set up and surgical instruments sterilised. It was rare for staff to have a chance to sleep before the wounded arrived. As Nurse Silverthorne comments, 'always such a lot of confusion'.[50]

Nurse Phyllis Hibbert served in frontline mobile hospitals in the early months of 1938, when the Republican Aragón front was collapsing after the Battle of Teruel. She experienced similar conditions to Nurse Silverthorne; her unit was always close to the front and because of this it was regularly bombed and machine-gunned. Nurse Hibbert was in the mobile medical unit when the Aragón front collapsed in early 1938 and relates a story of regular retreats, finding a new building and setting up a new hospital and then being forced to move again. She remembered the freezing temperatures with no heating and sometimes having to deal with as many as 200 wounded a night. At times she was working for forty hours continuously in 'appalling conditions'.[51]

Nurse Penny Phelps served in the frontline hospitals under battlefield conditions at Brunete in July 1937; as was often the case, medical supplies ran low. Nurse Phelps was on duty almost continuously for five days and nights and stayed awake with the help of coffee and cigarettes. She was fed on bully-beef sandwiches. When the staff had a chance to have a brief sleep, the only thing available to lie on were 'blood-soaked stretchers' which had been used to carry the wounded. In Nurse Phelps' case, Brunete was fought in a Spanish summer, so extreme heat was the problem; flies were everywhere, the operating theatre was unbearably hot and the floors were awash with blood. Medical supplies and medical clothing ran out, so the staff wore sheets supplied by the local people. Once the electrical generator failed and operations had to be performed by shining several torches to provide light.[52]

As we will see, these shortages of medical supplies were to be mirrored at Uclés Hospital, where Madge Addy was to become Head Nurse.

The use of blood transfusions to save injured soldiers was revolutionised during the Civil War. Many British nurses were involved in blood transfusions and many gave their own blood to aid injured patients. Hospital administrator Nan Green relates her experience of this process:

> Many people don't know how lovely it is to lie down beside the man whose face has gone ghastly white and your blood goes into him and you see the colour come back into his face and you see him begin to breathe.[53]

Although Madge Addy was not directly involved in the medical delivery of blood transfusions, she freely gave her blood in direct blood transfusions to patients in similar circumstances to Nan Green and was pictured doing so on the front cover of the *Daily Worker*.

Nurses were often involved in the traumatic decision-making of triage, where they needed to decide who was fit to travel to the outlying hospitals, who needed treating straight away and who could not be saved but needed pain relief. Not surprisingly, having to make choices like this affected many nurses and, in some cases, an individual's death or an incident had a lasting haunting impact on the nurse. Nurse Margaret Powell described the trauma of having to make stark choices during the triage process. Two men were dying, and she could only help one at a time and she decided to help the older man; however, he persuaded her to leave him and treat a younger man instead, which she did:

> ... as I held up the container of blood for a transfusion, I saw the older man die. The young one screamed – they were brothers. The older was the regiment's commissar. I wanted to run away.[54]

Patience Darton experienced the impossibility of saving a group of wounded men. Eight or nine wounded Spanish soldiers had been abandoned for three days; their wounds had been operated on but a combination of inadequate post-operative care and being left untreated meant the men all suffered from gas gangrene. They were discovered by Nurse Darton and her medical team and taken to a hospital in a railway tunnel (for protection from aerial attack). Their wounds were cleaned and attempts to drain away the infection failed. Once they could not be saved, they were given morphia to numb the pain and all that could be done was to help them to die peacefully. But they lingered on for many days; Nurse Darton soberly calls them 'men who wouldn't die'.[55]

The scars of serving in Spain are reflected in the comments of Penny Phelps shortly after her return to Britain, possibly showing signs of post-traumatic stress disorder:

> 'But Spain is red,' a friend said to me. 'Yes,' I replied, 'It is red with blood. Blood is splashed over the streets and the gutters run with it. For weeks my fingernails were stained by the blood, and my arms were spattered up to the elbows with it.'[56]

*The Nurse Who Became a Spy*

Yet even when seeing so much suffering, and facing an enemy that bombed hospitals, attacked ambulances and injured and killed thousands of Republican soldiers, British nurses treated captured Nationalist soldiers who were injured in the same way as they treated any Republican – a remarkable humanitarian effort. Annie Murray cared for a seriously injured Nationalist officer; this was not favourably received by her Republican patients, who kept shouting, 'Let him die'.[57]

Nationalist Officers were particularly hated as they were portrayed – often correctly – as the most enthusiastic supporters of the military revolt, and the executioners of captured Republican troops and left-wing and liberal civilians.

By the autumn of 1938, most British nurses were back in Britain. A small number served after this period and were caught up in the fall of Catalonia in January and February 1939. One nurse caught up in the mass retreat to France was Margaret Powell. She lost her passport and was arrested by French police and sent to a makeshift camp for Spanish refugees which was no better than a concentration camp. She was rescued by the Quakers. Lillian Urmston served with the Republican Catalonian army to the bitter end, treating injured soldiers and civilians and describing the situation as 'utterly ghastly'. Lillian Urmston said that during the retreat to the French frontier she delivered many babies – often at the roadside – and treated many mules so that they could continue to carry household possessions or elderly people. At the frontier she was determined to hold on to her passport, hiding it in 'in my knickers' where it remained hidden to the French border authorities![58] Like Margaret Powell, Lilian Urmston was interned in a refugee camp and was returned to Britain after the intervention of the British consul.

Several medical volunteers from Spain formed the 'British Medical Unit from Spain' on their return to Britain. They travelled around the country with an old ambulance, holding meetings and raising money for food and medical supplies for Republican Spain. Nurses Mary Slater and Margaret Findlay were part of this group.[59]

To give a fuller picture of the sort of women who volunteered to nurse in Spain, I am going to look at the experiences of three British volunteer nurses in more detail.

Molly Murphy (whose real name was Ethel), one of seven children, was born in Leyland in Lancashire in 1890. Her father lost his manager's post over a pay dispute and they were forced to move to slum dwellings in Salford, near Manchester. They moved out of the slums after her mother obtained a manager's post. In 1908, Margaret became involved in the Suffragette movement with her mother, demanding votes for women and joining the Manchester Committee of the Women's Social and Political Union. In 1912 she became a full time organiser for the WPSU in Sheffield. She attended night classes to further her education and then moved to London and trained as a nurse in Hammersmith. In 1921 she married Communist activist Jack Murphy, and joined the CPGB. She went with Jack to the Soviet Union where she met the Communist leader, Lenin. On their return to Britain they had a son. In the 1930s both Jack and Molly became disillusioned with the CPGB and left it, later joining the Labour Party. Molly served in Spain as a volunteer nurse from January to July 1937, when she was forced to return to Britain because of ill-health. In the Second World War she served in a mobile medical unit in St Pancras, in London, but her poor health meant she could not continue her nursing career after the war.[60]

Penny Phelps was born in Tottenham, London, in 1909. She came from a working-class family of ten brothers and sisters; her father was a casual labourer and her mother a coal merchant's daughter. She received a basic education and left school at 13 to look after her younger siblings. She worked in factories and did some dressmaking. She joined the Plymouth Brethren, a strict religious sect, and began evening classes. In 1927 she began her training as a nurse in London, becoming an SRN. Phelps was nursing in Hertfordshire when the Spanish Civil War broke out, and she left for Spain in 1937. She worked with various units and helped to contain an outbreak of scarlet fever and typhoid in the Italian Garibaldi International Brigade unit of 600. For this she was given the honorary rank of medical officer. She contracted typhoid in Spain and was sent back to Britain to recover. In 1938 she returned to Spain, only to be badly injured by a bomb blast and sent home for surgery. During her recovery from her injuries she met Dr Michael Fyvel and they married in 1938. During the Second World War she served at a First Aid post and later as a social worker for children with physical disabilities. After the war she helped her husband run his private medical practice in Harley Street. She died in 2011, one of the last surviving British volunteers to have served in Spain in any capacity.[61]

Thora Silverthorne was born in South Wales in 1910. Her father was a miner, trade union activist and CPGB member. She had seven brothers and sisters and, tragically, her mother died when she was 15. She trained as a nurse in Oxford and London, where she became known as 'Red Silverthorne', and was involved with the Labour Party, YCL and the CPGB. She left for Spain in the first British Medical Unit in August 1936. She worked with the distinguished Catalan surgeon, Dr Broggi, who played a major role in the introduction of mobile operating theatres. On her return to Britain she married fellow volunteer Kenneth Sinclair-Loutit. She helped to set up the first nursing union and later became its general secretary. As secretary of the SMA she was involved in discussions with the Labour government regarding the setting up of the National Health Service. She later became a full time official with the Civil Service Union and retired in 1970. She had two daughters and was married for a second time to an architect. She died in London in 1999.[62]

The SMAC and the volunteers from Britain who went to Spain played a major part in saving lives in the Spanish Civil War. The SMAC helped to coordinate medical and food supplies going to Spain, and to recruit medical staff. Medical volunteers who went to Spain from Britain included doctors, trainee doctors, nurses, administrators, drivers and mechanics. They came from all walks of life, from the upper classes to the working classes (who formed the bulk of the volunteers). Their politics also varied; some were committed Communists, and some had no politics at all. But most of the medical volunteers seem to have been moved by the desire to give humanitarian aid to a country which had been attacked by its own military, who were supported by the Fascist powers. Like many men who served in the International Brigades, many medical volunteers saw their time in Spain as the most significant time of their life and had few doubts that serving over there was the right thing to do. As nurse Phyllis Hibbert comments: 'It was not until I served in the British Medical Unit in Spain that I learned the true meaning of the word comradeship.'[63]

We shall see that this respect and comradeship permeates Madge Addy's experiences in Spain, and her desire to do almost anything to support her medical colleagues and patients. A final word on medical and humanitarian aid to the Spanish Republic is rightly left to the leader of the first British medical unit to Spain, Kenneth Sinclair-Loutit:

> What was achieved in Spain? I believe that all those who went to Spain and those who made it possible for us to do so did something important to preserve human decency at a time of widespread moral decay.[64]

## Chapter 5

# Head Nurse at Uclés: Madge in Spain 1937–1939

Conflicting news and rumours were circulating among the staff and patients at Uclés Hospital. Madge and the medical staff decided to continue as normal, doing ward rounds and tending to the patients' needs until the victorious Fascist forces arrived. Eventually a dust cloud could be seen approaching Uclés. Ahead of the cloud were Republican soldiers, travelling in ones and twos. Unsure of what was going to happen, they had abandoned the frontlines to return home to their families, desperate to see them in case this was the last time they would ever be together. Nationalist forces were not known for their leniency; newly captured villages, towns and cities were ruthlessly purged of anyone with liberal or left-wing tendencies, regardless of whether they were the local mayor or merely a member of a trade union. As the dust cloud got nearer, Madge and many of the medical staff would have been apprehensive about what might happen in the next few hours. However, not all the staff were quite so fearful, since some of them had had Fascist sympathies which they had kept secret during the Civil War.

The Nationalist column of troops, medical staff and the Fascist women's relief organisation *Sección Femenina* arrived at Uclés. The Republican medical staff were interviewed and either replaced by Nationalists, or worked under the supervision of Nationalist doctors. In time, Uclés became a large concentration camp where many patients and medical staff were imprisoned, some even being executed alongside many other Republicans. The women of the Falangist *Sección Femenina* handed out food to the patients and local villagers. Madge was brought before an aristocratic woman in charge of this group. The woman wore a long skirt and the blue blouse of the Falange, with the red yoke and arrows emblem on her blouse. She was mystified by Madge's presence at Uclés and launched into a tirade about the 'heathen reds'; she could not comprehend why a woman like Madge – with an education – would want to help the 'Reds' in any capacity. For the time being Madge was under house arrest and was forbidden from leaving the hospital until they decided what to do with her.

This was just one of the remarkable incidents that Madge Addy was both to live through and deal with in her time in Spain. An experience that changed her forever.

She served in Spain as a nurse on the Aragón front and at the old monastery hospital at Uclés as a member of the British Medical Unit that was organised by the SMAC. While in Spain, she helped to train Spanish women in British nursing techniques, she taught English to Spanish medical staff and helped to transport refugees by sea from Barcelona to Valencia. In Spain, her arm was broken by a bomb splinter during a bombing raid and she also had a period of illness. Madge was the last British nurse to leave Spain, leaving several months after the war had ended. But her time there is lit up by the mass of letters she wrote; in one letter she says that this was the thirty-second letter she had written that day![1] These letters paint a detailed picture of the incredible woman that Madge was, and the way that she intended to serve her patients and the Spanish Republic to the bitter end: requesting aid, recounting her activities as a nurse, describing conditions at Uclés, writing about Spanish medical staff and other nurses, and even talking about a romance.

The chronology of Madge's time in Spain is problematic but the following timeline seems the most likely. She arrived there in the summer of 1937 and served on the Aragón front, possibly at Poleñino hospital.[2] After that she was posted to Uclés Hospital in central Spain in late 1937 or early 1938. She went on leave for the first time in February 1938 and returned to Spain in March 1938.[3] In June 1938 she suffered a broken arm during a bombing raid, and was sent back to Britain to recover, returning to Spain in August 1938. Madge was back on leave in England in November 1938 and, as in earlier periods of leave, she was involved in many 'Aid Spain' activities and organised medical supplies for Spain.[4] She returned to Spain in December 1938 and, in the same month, helped to get refugees out of Barcelona to Valencia by boat.[5] She fell ill in Uclés in January 1939 but was soon back on duty and continued to nurse until Uclés was captured by Fascist forces at the end of the war in March 1939.[6] During April 1939 Madge was not permitted to leave

## Head Nurse at Uclés: Madge in Spain 1937–1939

Uclés; however, when she was eventually allowed to depart, she went to Valencia to try to obtain exit papers to leave the country. She finally received them in June 1939 which allowed her to return to Britain.[7]

Why did Madge volunteer to serve in Spain as a nurse? We have no record of her giving her reasons for volunteering, and she says little about her political views in her letters except to end most of them with 'yours in the fight, Madge'. In one letter only does she really discuss politics, when relating a discussion with Spanish doctors. Madge comments:

> It really makes my heart ache, when perhaps we are discussing the war, and they say, 'Yes! But the fascists have got more material than we have'. How ashamed I feel when I think that England and France if they cared to, could give them such assistance. I mean officially of course. I am not criticising the help that comes from the workers, I mean official action! ... I feel the state this country has been reduced to is an everlasting disgrace to all nations who call themselves civilised, and I feel sure you agree. Really when I think of all the misery in China, Spain and Czechoslovakia, refugees from Germany and Italy, I wonder how much longer people are going to stand for it ...[8]

This was written in January 1939 after Madge had been in Spain for eighteen months and clearly demonstrates her anti-Fascism, humanitarianism and awareness of current events; however, rather than a definitive answer, this letter only gives us clues to why she decided to go to Spain.

The nurses who went to Spain, as we saw in the previous chapter, seem to be divided between those who were members of the CPGB and went to help the fight against Fascism, and those who were not necessarily politically inclined but went for humanitarian reasons.[9] One nurse even went to Spain to gain experience of nursing in a war.[10] Nottingham-born hospital administrator Nan Green recalls in her memoir that there was a disagreement about how British medical staff, including nurses, were to be deployed: should they support the International Brigades or be deployed in separate SMAC hospitals? Madge served for most of her time in Spain at the hospital in Uclés, which was a SMAC sponsored hospital and was viewed as being staffed by non-political British nurses.[11]

Madge's nephews were asked in an interview whether they knew anything about Madge's politics. They replied that she was 'extreme left' but were not sure if she was a member of any political party. They mentioned that Madge once took them to an 'Aid Spain' meeting in Manchester and that she was sympathetic to the Republican cause, which suggests she may have been involved in the 'Aid Spain' movement locally.[12] One of Madge's brothers was a member of the Left Book Club. It is also possible that at this time her marriage was in trouble, but whatever the case, when she reached Spain, she filed for divorce.[13] What evidence we have suggests Madge went to Spain for both political and humanitarian reasons and wished to use her nursing skills in a worthwhile cause at a time in her life when she was ready for significant change.

Madge Addy was never interviewed about her time in Spain, so we have no authoritative chronological account of her time there. But what we do have is a treasure-trove of Madge's correspondence, written mostly in Spain but some written in Britain when she was on leave. Unlike interviews recorded many years after the event, what Madge gives us in her letters is immediate and in real time. We have a mass of information about her time in Spain, and incredible insight into what it was like to work as a nurse during the Civil War and the conditions in the Spanish Republic in the last months of the war. We need to take care when reading these letters, since Madge freely admits that some were written for propaganda purposes to raise money in Britain. Also, only a few of her letters have survived, as they had to get past the Spanish censors before being allowed out of the country. Madge's surviving letters from Uclés Hospital begin in July 1938 and end in March 1939, a few weeks before the war ended. We also have a description of a bombing raid on Valencia for the SMAC bulletin and a letter to a provincial newspaper written by Madge.[14] SMAC meetings would have discussed her letters and made decisions concerning medical aid going to Spain.

She wrote to the SMAC in London, but the bulk of her letters were addressed to 'Dear Nat', who ran the North Manchester SMAC. Nat Malimson was a medical doctor and Labour Party member who, when approached to chair the local North Manchester SMAC, agreed to persuade other local doctors to become involved and to try and raise money for medical supplies for the Spanish Republic. The North Manchester SMAC had been formed by a local Communist, Issy Luft, who was the person who initially asked Dr Malimson to chair the committee. On the committee were a pharmacist, the head of Christie's Hospital, Labour Party members, CPGB members, trade unionists and those with non-political views. They carried out street collections and raised quite substantial amounts of money. In some instances, collectors were cautioned for begging by the police. In response, Dr Malimson gave the collectors a letter of authorisation, then wrote to the local police superintendent stating firmly that medical support for the police would be withdrawn if they continued to harass collectors. The police backed down. The North Manchester SMAC had its meetings at Malimson's surgery, and organised many fundraising activities such as film shows, dances and meetings that were addressed by politicians, writers and religious figures. One local Conservative gave the committee free billboard space to advertise its events. Money was raised to send several ambulances to Spain, as well as medical supplies and food.[15]

Madge is most remembered for the time she spent as Head Nurse at Uclés Hospital, near the Madrid-Valencia road in Cuenca province. Uclés was a former sixteenth-century monastery that had been converted into a hospital. It was financed by the SMAC and different wards were supported by donations from different areas: for example, Madge worked in the 'Manchester Ward'. The SMAC plan for Uclés was to supply it with medical equipment and drivers, and for British nurses to train Spanish nurses. The hospital was to include 500 beds for patients, a laboratory, a surgical area, transport depot, a nurse training school and a convalescent home. In the autumn of 1938, it was caring for 800 Spanish wounded. It was kitted out with a new drainage system, new toilets, bathrooms and water supply, all provided by SMAC donations.[16]

The early days at Uclés in the spring of 1938 were incredibly difficult for the first British nurses who served at the hospital. Nan Green, who arrived briefly as an administrator, describes the problems that the first British nurses had with rats and hygiene. Nan would try to raise the morale of the nurses by kind words and helping to delouse them when they came off duty, as many patients arrived at the hospital infested with lice. One poor British nurse was weeping because of the problems with rats. This nurse worked days only, she was forbidden from working nights. One patient was a paraplegic and had no sensation in his legs so, when the rats bit him, he felt nothing. So, the British nurse put the legs of his bed in tin cans full of disinfectant to repel the rats. During the night the Spanish nurses removed the tin cans full of disinfectant because they looked unsightly!

Nan Green mentions the horrific state of the outside of the hospital before it was cleaned up, and identifies the cause of the rat infestation: 'A dry moat round the whole building into which they had been throwing soiled dressings and bits of amputated limbs ...'[17]

Nan had been sent to Uclés to support a Communist railway worker called Frank Ayres, who had been sent there to try to improve the sanitation situation at the hospital. Nan Green was born in Beeston, Nottingham and got her first job as an office worker aged 15. She married George Green, and both became CPGB members. With George she had two children. George served in Spain as an ambulance driver and was killed in September 1938 at the Battle of the Ebro. Nan also went to Spain when the rich left-wing artist Wogan Phillips offered to pay for her two children to go to the progressive boarding school, Summerhill. Nan was an administrator at several hospitals in Spain, particularly Valdeganga, Huete and at the cave hospital at Bisbal de Falset. At Huete, purely by chance, she met her husband George for the last time. After the Civil War, Nan helped Spanish Republican refugees in the concentration camps in France and helped to organise the evacuation of Spanish Republican refugees to Mexico on board the *Sinaia*, where she looked after the children. During the Second World War she worked for Poplar Town Hall in London as an Invasion Defence Officer. After the war she became secretary of the International Brigade Association and in the 1950s became involved in the peace movement. She lived in China for several years, then on returning to Britain became Secretary of the IBA once again until her death in 1984. She may possibly have met Madge during her time at Uclés, but she makes no mention of Madge in her autobiography. She did, however, meet Madge in London in 1939 on Madge's return from Spain.[18]

Louise Jones, one of the first nurses at Uclés, described the conditions that the British nurses faced. The building was very cold with no heating, the 800 patients could not be washed for lack of towels and bowls (some had not been washed for weeks) and there were no clean sheets or pyjamas for the patients. As Nurse Jones comments: 'even with the best will in the world it is impossible to prevent the beds from becoming verminous and the discomfort of the patients is acute ...'[19]

Louise Jones arrived in Spain in early 1937 and, as well as performing all the duties of a trained nurse, she began the process of training the Spanish nursing assistants to become fully trained nurses, which was

## Head Nurse at Uclés: Madge in Spain 1937–1939

something that the SMAC viewed as a key role for British nurses at Uclés. Madge was very keen to continue with this process. Louise states:

> The *chicas* (young women) are very keen and anxious to learn all that I can teach them. They are having medical lectures and can already name all the bones of the body, and every spare moment I am pressed into giving them lessons in dressings, fomentations, bandaging etc ...[20]

On her return to London with four other nurses from Spain, she tried to present a letter to the prime minister's (Neville Chamberlain) wife, requesting that she ask her husband to tell Mussolini to stop using his Italian planes to bomb civilians in Barcelona. They went to 10 Downing Street and, when told that she was not there, they went to Chequers. Again, they were unable to deliver the letter, so in the end they posted it. The story gave the war in Spain some good publicity. It is possible Louise worked briefly with Madge at Uclés.[21]

During the time Madge worked at Uclés conditions improved but, as we will see, they worsened again as the end of the war drew closer. At its height, Uclés Hospital had the following staffing complement:

- twelve doctors, of which four were surgeons
- one radiologist
- two pharmacists
- sixteen *practicantes* (medical students)
- thirty-four nurses
- eleven kitchen staff
- nine *chicas* (trainee nurses)
- forty-three orderlies and male nurses
- eighty-nine maintenance staff

By February 1939 this complement of staff was down to seven doctors, twenty-four nurses and thirty ward maids or *chicas*.

Thanks to money from the SMAC, the number of operating theatres was increased to three and an X-ray department was added, along with further convalescent areas and more vehicles.[22]

In a letter written as a propaganda piece, Madge describes the monastery of Uclés. She describes it as a dignified old building which, since it was

75

built on a hill, dominated the countryside all around, including the village at its foot. Madge writes: 'I fell in love with it the moment I saw it …'

The monastery was entered through 'immense' iron studded doors. Through the doors were cloisters with a very decorative well in the centre. Up a giant staircase was a large religious painting which had a message hung from it asking the residents not to mock the painting but to respect the 'art of Spain'. The Catholic Church in Spain was viewed by many Republicans as supporters of the rich and the military rebellion. Many Republicans would have had little respect for anything religious.

A sign above the theatre block read 'From the Spanish Medical Aid Committee London'.

Madge mentions the wounded:

> Last but most important of all, meet some of our 800 wounded ranging from fifteen years and upwards, some with legs off, some with arms off, others with malaria and typhoid; one and all grateful of everything that is done for them.

Madge ends the letter with a plea:

> … double your efforts, winter is coming, at this hospital the winter is severe with a temperature of 10 degrees below zero … give generously, give us the means to heal some mother's son, somebody's father.[23]

While on leave in July 1938, Madge reported to the SMAC in London that conditions at Uclés were improving. Madge described the conditions at the hospital as 'very satisfactory'. A new Spanish director was now in charge of Uclés and Madge suggests that his management was improving conditions at the hospital. The hospital and its staff did very well when it received a large number of wounded from the battles around Valencia and, once they had made the patients comfortable, were able to move them on to other hospitals in the area. Madge lists the improvements to the hospital:

- bathhouse
- barber's shop

- addition of a third operating theatre
- dark room to support X-ray work
- shortage of clean linen, after many difficulties, had been resolved.

The British volunteers were getting on well with the Spanish staff, and each day at 4pm they met up for a chat and a cup of tea. There was also a games room, and a recreation room had been created in the cellar where the former monks were buried, which also doubled up as an air raid shelter! Supplies for the hospital were sent from Marseille in southern France and then by ship to Valencia and then onto to Uclés. Madge ended her report by requesting they needed scrubbing brushes and peroxide of hydrogen.[24]

As the war progressed and the defeat of the Republic became ever more likely, conditions at Uclés worsened. The lack of food was especially severe. In a letter of August 1938, written after she had returned from leave, Madge writes:

> We are short of Doctors and *practicantes* etc because every male who was fit and could possibly be spared has been sent to the front. All of the dear little boys out of the office are gone ...

She further comments:

> I was very grieved indeed to find everyone so much thinner than when I left; The Doctors and nurses look thin and pale, and food is terribly scarce ...[25]

In October 1938 Madge describes a typhoid outbreak at Uclés and the problems resulting from the inability to segregate those with typhoid from the rest of the patients, and the sufferings of these poor men:

> ... typhoid we had five cases, one died, it worries me terribly that they are with the other men, but we have nowhere else for them. I have got them all a piece of mosquito netting for their faces, but they are delirious more or less and keep tearing it off and oh if you could see the flies. Their mouths are black with flies and I am constantly urging the nurses to keep cleaning out their mouths ...[26]

Later, after a failed Republican offensive, Madge writes of the sorrowful state of the patients and the lack of available nourishment. Like previous nurses at Uclés, Madge and other medical staff are lousy:

> We are having a very bad time indeed here, and I am working every hour of the day at the hospital. Some of the doctors and a lot of the staff have been sent to the front, and consequently we are short-handed. A month ago, we had 1600 wounded in from the Estremadura front, and we got the lot in in two days. Dirty, hungry, lousy, war-weary men, never have I seen such a depressed filthy lot of men. We haven't clean clothes for them, there isn't enough to eat, it is impossible to procure any kind of nourishment for the very sick. We have one hypo syringe left in the hospital which is mine, and which I guard with my life. We are all lousy, we cannot get the men or the place clean because we haven't shirts, sheets or pillow slips. The clothes that the men arrived in, or a great many of them, have had to be destroyed, those who are up have no shoes of any kind (they arrived in this state from the front, where they have been fighting in bare feet.), Some of them have septic feet, others keep getting them cut on stones. I cannot adequately describe the utter hopelessness of everything.[27]

Nevertheless, among all the human suffering and lack of supplies and food, Madge was able to relate the odd humorous story. In one case the SMAC sent out a large quantity of Izal toilet rolls – a rather basic and rather tough toilet paper. She relates the new use for this toilet paper:

> Talking about paper, the committee sent out a gross of Izal toilet rolls, but they cannot be used for the purpose they were intended for. The Director said to me, 'Madge, we were very glad indeed for the paper'. I said, 'What paper?' and he said, 'Well it was really toilet paper, but we are using it in the office, come and see.' And at every desk, by each typewriter is a roll of Izal toilet paper, and the clerks are typing away on it! That will give some idea of the shortage of everything.[28]

## Head Nurse at Uclés: Madge in Spain 1937–1939

In Spain, Madge took on every nursing challenge that was thrown at her: she managed wards, specialist departments, assisted doctors and trained nurses, to name only a few activities. In a letter from October 1938 we have a timetable of a typical day at Uclés for Madge:

> I am working very hard at the moment and come home dog tired every night. I go on the 'Manchester Ward' prompt at 9 am. and do the temps and pulses (there are 33 of them) then the dressings and then toddle off to the *Fiero Therapia* where I have now got thirty patients for massage. Porta has lent me the *sanatorio* orderly of the ward to help me and he does most of the vapour massages. We work on until about 1.45 pm. and then I come up to the house to eat. Back at 4pm. to the 'Manchester Ward' where I again take all the temps and pulses, give the injections, subcutaneous, intravenous and intramuscular, odd jobs like passing catheters, flatus tubes etc, and that brings 8 pm. when I am only too glad to come to the house.[29]

Earlier in the same month she was asked to manage the X-ray and ultraviolet ray departments in return for no longer running the 'Manchester Ward' but, as we read in her previous letter, she was shortly combining all three jobs. Madge expresses her excitement about managing these two new departments:

> I have been happy there ('Manchester Ward') but we are the proud possessors of a small medical electricity and Ultra-Violet ray dept, and the director has asked me if I will take charge of the dept as they have no one else, and combine it with the X-ray theatre ... seriously though, this is a splendid step forward and many a man will regain the use of his limbs which before through lack of many things, have just gone useless.[30]

One aspect of her time in Uclés that was particularly picked up on by the press was Madge's bravery in giving her own blood to wounded soldiers. There is a dramatic picture in the *Daily Worker* of her giving blood via a tube in a rather primitive blood transfusion process (see photograph).[31] Although Madge gave blood several times, she was never involved in managing or developing blood transfusion services; however, she was also working nights later in the war due to lack of staff:

> I am at the moment staying on duty all night. Possibly you remember the photo of the blood transfusion. The same man is back here again, and when I arrived, he was having haemorrhages from his stomach. Three nights ago, I gave him another blood transfusion in preparation for his operation the next morning.[32]

As the war drifted to its inevitable conclusion Madge was asked to take on ever more responsibilities:

> I am back working in the hospital and of all places in the theatre, it is a bit difficult for me, as it is so many years since I did theatre work. However, Dr. Landa asked me if I would work in the theatre with him, and I told him it was years since I had done theatre work, but he said, 'No importa, you will soon get the hang of it again'. If help is needed in one of the wards I go there, so have a roving commission.[33]

Nevertheless, on occasions Madge was torn as to what her role at Uclés should be. The SMAC wanted British nurses to train Spanish nurses and use their medical knowledge to make lists of required medical supplies, rather than carry out actual nursing at Uclés. Madge did both roles but was constantly drawn back to the nursing role out of desire to support her colleagues and patients at Uclés:

> Really Nat, I am almost falling between two stools. Holst said it's confusing. 'Do you consider your hospital work more important than your promises to this committee?' But I do feel you will understand ... Porta and I do all the treatment ... Porta thinks it very curious but is privately very impressed that I would give up my off-duty time to the hospital.[34]

In several of her letters Madge talks fondly of the Spanish medical staff at Uclés, naming several of them. She learned enough Spanish to converse with medical staff and, later in the war, to write letters in Spanish as it was more likely that they would get past the government censors.[35] Beside her medical and social interactions with the Spanish medical staff, she was particularly involved in two aspects of work: the first was persuading the Spanish doctors to train Spanish nurses properly (this was agreed but not without some opposition!) and secondly, helping some of the Spanish staff to learn English.

In a letter intended as propaganda, Madge makes many comments about her Spanish medical colleagues. She described the director of Uclés, Dr Landa, as, 'a gentle sensitive Spanish gentleman' with 'delicate sensitive hands'. She further mentions a 'vivacious little Doctor Gine', going on to say, 'I have seen him operate for 5 hours at a stretch, days together as well as doing his dressings and seeing to his two wards'. The full name of this doctor was Jose Maria Gine Ferre and he was a major in charge of the clinic in 1939. Probably unknown to Madge, this doctor had Fascist sympathies, which might have been the case with some of the other doctors at Uclés. Dr Gine was the first post-Civil War Francoist mayor of Uclés; if he had had Republican sympathies, at the very least he would have been imprisoned in Uclés Monastery, which became a prison after the Nationalists took it over in April 1939.[36] Madge mentions Señor Porta, who was a medical and X-ray doctor. Other doctors she names include Garcia, Sanjurjo, Fernandez and Aranda, who were junior doctors. Madge mentions that she helped Dr Aranda in the operating theatre. She describes the Spanish nurses as 'charming girls who previously had no knowledge of nursing and who are going to our school at the hospital to learn to read and write, all eager to learn'. She names the nurses as Mercedes (who became a good friend), Carmen, Juanita and Gloria. Another known local nurse who served alongside Madge was Teresa Martinez Garcia from the nearby village of Huelves. After the Civil War she, like many of the local nurses, fled Uclés to avoid persecution by the victorious enemy.[37] In another letter Madge writes of the Spanish doctors at Uclés:

> Oh, how I wish you could know some of these doctors. They work on and on with little or no material and very seldom grumble or complain at the lack of it.[38]

One of Madge's major roles in Spain was to train young Spanish women to become fully trained nurses. During her final period of leave in November 1938 it was expected that this would be Madge's main focus when she returned to Spain. While on leave, Madge discussed her prospective role with Leah Manning of the SMAC.[39] Dr Porta, the chief surgeon at Uclés, with whom Madge frequently worked and who she admired greatly, was not altogether supportive of her on this issue. He and other doctors at Uclés believed all nurses needed to know was how to make beds and wash patients. Undeterred, Madge won over the director and set up a school for trainee nurses at Uclés. In her own words:

> I have promised the Director that I will start the girls' lectures on practical nursing, he is going to teach them in anatomy and physiology, and I am going to bully Porta into giving a course on (only elementary) medicine. The director is very pleased, and I do feel that this is a step in the right direction ...[40]

In the same letter Madge mentions that she is teaching English to Dr Porta and he has sent off to Madrid for some English grammar books. In a later letter Madge comments that Dr Porta has been reading English newspapers and *Punch* magazine, which were sent to him, and is receiving an hour's tuition from Madge each day. She now has an eye doctor and a pharmacist also learning English. Madge paints a humorous picture where Spanish doctors are walking around repeating English phrases like 'no thank you', 'thank you very much', 'I have', 'you have', 'he has', 'she has', etc. Madge comments:

> ... there is something about the Spanish temperament, they express their pleasure and their sorrows, their likes and their dislikes simply and unaffectedly.[41]

Madge obviously had great affection and loyalty for her medical colleagues, with whom she voluntarily stayed to the bitter end of the war. By the time of her last birthday in Spain, a Spanish nurse called Mercedes had become her closest companion at Uclés and a Dr Torricilla was teaching her Spanish. Madge, in a very moving letter, describes her last birthday on Spanish soil:

> I was thirty-five the other day and Mercedes, Dr Porta and Dr Torricilla came and had a cup of tea with me, and

some Norwegian bread which Holst had sent down. Porta produced some grains of tobacco which he rolled into a cigarette, and we completed the tea-party, with one cigarette between us. Anyway, I wouldn't have swapped it for the finest birthday party in England. These are my friends, as well as my colleagues, Mercedes being my constant companion. Every evening after we have finished duty she comes round to my digs, and with Dr Torricilla who lives there as well, we sit round the table, our light a pot of olive oil, with some cotton for a wick, and we luxuriously drink tea after which I have a Spanish lesson from Dr. Torricilla, or else a reiterating of the day's wrongs and miseries, and so to bed. I feel that one day we shall all waken up to be told the war is over, such is life at Uclés. I must finish now. My regards to all.[42]

Madge very rarely mentions any fellow British medical staff in her letters. She also only uses first names of individuals with little added details, so it is difficult to decide who she is really talking about. When she returned to Britain in June 1939, she was met at Victoria Station by fellow nursing volunteers from Spain: Louise Jones, Ena Vassie and Patience Darton.[43] Patience Darton was born in Orpington in London in 1911. She was privately educated in St Albans and on leaving school first became a primary school teacher, later a waitress and finally trained as a nurse. Working in the poor East End of London she became politicised and joined the Labour Party. She volunteered to go to Spain in February 1937, at first working in Valencia helping the British commander in Spain, Tom Wintringham, recover from typhoid. She then served at many hospitals in Aragón, Madrid, Teruel, and Valls, finally leaving Spain in late 1938. During the Second World War she taught apprentice nurses for the LCC. After the war she went to China and became an interpreter and later worked for Foreign Language Press. On her return to Britain she became an active member of the IBA and died in 1996 in Madrid during a Spanish Civil War veterans' reunion. It is possible that she served with Madge at the Aragónese hospital of Poleñino during the summer of 1937. Like Louise and Madge, Patience was a strong advocate of training the Spanish nursing assistants.[44]

Ena Vassie (also known as Una, though her name was actually Agnes) was born in London in 1906 and had been a qualified nurse for thirteen years before she went to Spain. She served at Benicàssim, Castellón and Mataró and served with famous British volunteer doctors and surgeons Alexander Tudor-Hart and H. S. Bury. On leaving Spain she worked for the SMAC and lived in a flat with Nan Green and Patience Darton. I do not believe that Madge had met Ena in Spain and think she turned up to greet Madge along with her London flatmates.[45]

In one of her last letters home Madge affirms that she wants the legacy of Louise Jones' efforts at Uclés to be remembered:

> However, you know I am happy at Uclés, and I like to feel that Louise's good work will be terminated here with the same conscientiousness, and that the name of *Misión Sanitaria Británica* will evoke pleasant memories in the minds of all the people here.[46]

In her letters Madge mentions two drivers, Johnny and Pat. Johnny returned with her from Britain in August 1938 and left in October 1938, along with Pat. I have not been able to discover any more information about these men. Madge also mentions several names of other British nurses at Uclés; these include Pat, Beryl, Marion and Elisabeth. These four could be Patience Prior, Beryl Smithson (who also served on the Aragón front and was one of the five who tried to present a letter to Mrs Chamberlain), Marion Campbell and Elisabeth Burr. The first three returned to Britain in September 1938. Madge is quite scathing about the nurse called Elisabeth, who was recalled in October 1938:

> Elisabeth has also been recalled; she has been up to her old tricks of mischief making. She was recalled once before but the Director wrote to the committee asking for her to be given another chance, she was better for a while, so you can see things are anything but lively … causing a lot of trouble so willingly has decided that she had better go home with the boys …[47]

Apart from lacking life's essentials, such as adequate food and proper hygiene, a medical volunteer's life serving in Spain was also harrowing and dangerous. Twelve British medical personnel died there and many more were wounded.[48]

## Head Nurse at Uclés: Madge in Spain 1937–1939

Madge was escorting two wounded nurses to the docks and was herself wounded in June 1938 by a bomb splinter in Valencia, which broke her arm and led her being sent home for a month's sick leave, during which she spent most of the time raising money for Medical Aid to Spain. She describes a bombing raid in detail in an article for the SMAC bulletin. Madge writes that five or six planes supplied by Germany or Italy (likely Italy) flew from Majorca to bomb Valencia. The noise was horrendous with the drone of the planes' engines, fire from the anti-aircraft guns, screaming from women and children and followed by the explosions of the bombs. Each bomb dropped seemed as if it was heading directly for you, and on the ground was total chaos. The earth lifted and houses shook with the concussion of the bomb explosions. A bomb had dropped at the back of the house where Madge was staying. After the air raid was over Madge went to investigate with others. Behind the house in which she was residing, she found a badly damaged smaller house and five mutilated bodies; a family group, all dead. Ambulances and rescue services were screaming around the city as they were expecting another air raid soon; rescue services and ordinary people were digging people out from under the rubble and taking the injured to hospital. Madge claims she had seen children in previous air raids with missing limbs where the wound is cauterised by the white-hot bombs and had personally helped one such child. Other fatalities, Madge says, were killed by the concussive effect of a bomb explosion with blood oozing from their ears and mouth. She described during a previous air raid seeing a mother carrying a mutilated baby wandering around dazed in a total state of shock. Madge ended her appeal for medical aid with a firm commitment to her personal support for the Spanish Republican people:

> I am going back in a day or two, proud to give my services to people who after two years of this awful slaughter can still say *No Pasaran*, to the foreign invaders ...[49]

During the Christmas of 1938 Madge helped to bring fifty refugees from Barcelona to Valencia by sea, as Republican territory was now divided in half by the Nationalist forces. As the boat came into the harbour, an enemy air raid was taking place. Madge described the terror and confusion of the air raid. The ship was approaching Valencia harbour and was almost docking when the air sirens went off. The refugees began to scream and run in all directions. Madge and those in charge of the refugees ordered everyone to lie flat, the ship shook with the concussion from the exploding bombs, but everyone survived the air raid. The ship was not hit but ran aground in the harbour and after the raid Madge and the refugees were rescued by an improvised gangway which they used to 'scramble ashore'.[50]

In January 1939, Madge fell ill for a time, but was back on duty again after a short period of convalescence until the war ended.[51]

A key part of Madge's role in Spain and in Britain was to plead for medical supplies and food. When in Spain, she listed the supplies that were needed, and, when in Britain, helped to raise money required. In an article for a local newspaper, the *Grantham Journal*, Madge states she is a Spanish Medical Aid nurse in a hospital near to Madrid where her job is to raise funds for medical supplies and medical instruments. She had been in Britain for two weeks and will be leaving for Spain again on July 24. In the same newspaper article, she talks about the chronic lack of food in Republican Spain.[52]

In a letter of October 1938 Madge again lists the lack of food and, an essential in wartime, nicotine:

> To make matters still more cheerful we haven't had any cigs for weeks. Really it is hard to keep cheerful without a smoke, and we have neither milk or sugar, we have plenty of tea, but it is pretty ghastly without sugar or milk.[53]

Late in the war Madge continues to request food and medical supplies. In her letter, she uses what would be recognised as racist language today but in the 1930s 'worked like a nigger' meant to work very hard. She pleads that the wounded are dying because of lack of nourishment:

> Do please try to send nourishing food for the very sick, and what you can in the way of surgical instruments from the list that you have. I am getting rations from the hospital. These consist of a small loaf of bread, a handful of rice, beans or lentils and half a litre of wine, which of course I don't drink, and so pass on. One boy died yesterday morning, and I have worked like a nigger with him, but the lack of nourishment

defeated me. I feel very depressed because I know that he and many like him ought not to have died. He had typhoid and I could only get a small ration of milk a day – we have no eggs at the hospital, nothing. Also, we have about 24 towels in the whole hospital. You probably wonder where the things go to, but you cannot take the shirt, pants and vests off them when they are discharged and send them away without, if you have them. However, this lot came with practically nothing, and will have to be discharged practically nude, as we haven't got clothes to give them.[54]

In two *Daily Worker* articles Madge makes sure she describes the lack of both medical and food supplies. In the first article she talks about the difficulties of training young Spanish women to be nurses and then comments: 'But if staffing was difficult, food and medical supplies were a thousand times greater.'

In the second article she comments:

It is heart breaking to watch men die because you cannot get nourishment to keep their strength up. We have only a small quantity of anaesthetic left and so many operations are performed without anything ...[55]

When she returned from her second leave in August 1938 aboard a British ship, the *Stanleigh*, Madge says that the passengers all booked into a hotel in Valencia for two days. However, they never ate in the restaurant of the Hotel Metropol, 'because there was hardly anything to eat'.[56]

In the same letter Madge makes an appeal for crutches for the wounded as well as the usual appeal for cigarettes:

Now another thing do you think if you put out an appeal in the paper you could get any crutches. We have got men legs in plaster and no crutches for them ... they will be a godsend, there is no more wood in Spain and no one comes out to make them. It does not matter how crude they are ... were to contribute 10 Woodbine a week.

Madge ends the letter with a list of what she calls 'points to remember':

> Finishing the theatre (an urgent necessity)
> Crutches (very urgent)
> Cigarettes for the wounded (not a necessity but such a comfort for the brave lads)
> Pyjamas (if possible)
> Sewing cotton white
> Buttons, tape, needles and Singer Sewing Machine needle (These latter, some of the girls might like to collect).[57]

Probably the most heartrending appeal by Madge came after a failed government offensive in Estremadura late in the war (see earlier in the chapter for full details). She ends this letter almost distraught but still requesting aid:

> I could go on and on quoting one heart breaking story after another. In addition to the usual things we need SHEETS, SHIRTS, TOWELS, PILLOW-CASES, PANTS, VESTS, SOCKS. Will you all try and think of some of the misery and suffering that is going on here.[58]

As Madge states in her letters, her role in Spain, beside that of nurse, was that of fund-raiser for the SMAC. She did this in a variety of ways. Madge appealed direct to the SMAC national committee for aid, she wrote letters pleading for aid and articles for SMAC publications and the press. When she was on leave in Britain, she spoke at fundraising events, and found photographs and stories that would be good propaganda pieces in Britain. She reported any problems with the medical supplies sent to Spain, priced up equipment and even set up a charity shop in Britain, finding things in Spain to sell in it. She requested, advised and helped to procure anything, from condensed milk and toilet rolls to incinerators and ambulances.

The SMAC met regularly in London to discuss requests from Spain. In the minutes of a committee meeting from September 1938, they agree to Madge's request to send to Uclés food, toilet rolls, sanitary towels, soap, towels and condensed milk. In the minutes of a meeting in February 1939, the Committee agree, again in response to requests from Madge, to send to Uclés £120 worth of food, particularly milk, and £30 worth of medical supplies. We know that the toilet paper arrived at Uclés as one of Madge's letters describes how the office clerks used the Izal toilet rolls for typing paper![59]

One of Madge's efforts to raise money for medical aid and to support Basque refugee children was to set up a shop in Britain and find things in Spain to sell in that shop. In a letter to the *Grantham Journal*, Madge asks for funds so that the Basque refugee children are not sent back to Spain. She also encourages people to befriend them and suggests that, since many Basque boys enjoy football, maybe a match against local youngsters could be organised. Later in the same article she thanks all those people who have made donations for Spanish Aid:

> … doctors and nurses get a lot of the limelight, but without the people at home to organise, and the generosity of you all, we should not be able to carry on.[60]

The shop was opened in Shaftesbury Avenue in London in November 1938 and included several hundred pounds' worth of pottery and dolls from Spain. It took Madge three months to gather together the stock to sell in the shop. The shop was opened by the Spanish ambassador's wife. In the article there is a picture of Madge in full nursing uniform – all white dress and large hat – this would clearly emphasis the humanitarian aspects of the fundraising (see pictures of Madge at Uclés).[61] The idea for the Christmas bazaar seems to be Madge's, and as early as August in one of her letters she suggests to Dr Malimson that Manchester should also do this:

> In about a month I am going down to Valencia with Mr Holst to purchase a load of Spanish pottery for an Xmas bazaar in London. This idea might come in useful to you, and if you let me know anytime we can always arrange to send some up to Manchester. It is both attractive and very cheap and would be a novelty.[62]

Madge wrote articles for the SMAC and to several newspapers, always with the end goal of raising awareness of the conditions in Spain, but most importantly to collect funds for Spanish medical aid. In every article Madge wrote or contributed to, she always made a plea for aid or made sure people knew where to donate. Below are some typical lines from articles that Madge wrote or contributed to:

> … thanking you sincerely, and I hope when I get back to Spain you will continue your good work.[63]

and

> Señora de Azcarate, wife of the Spanish Ambassador, opened the shop which will be selling goods from Spain and other countries until Christmas Eve.[64]

and

> 'Having been home on a month's sick leave my arm having been broken with shrapnel in one of the air-raids on Valencia'. Writes Nurse Madge Addy, 'I have devoted the whole of my time to trying to raise funds for Medical Aid for Spain'.[65]

In the *Daily Worker*, until the bitter end Madge requested more medical aid be sent out to Republican Spain. As late as March 1939 food, clothes and medical supplies were sent out (they arrived too late) after a letter from Madge that stated medical supplies were needed urgently.[66]

Throughout her time in Spain Madge constantly pleaded for aid and listed what was needed, and sought out potential propaganda material and wrote propaganda pieces to 'tug at people's heart strings'; all aimed at maximising money raised for medical aid, food ships and supporting the Basque refugee children. When in Britain on leave she toured around the country talking at fundraising events and meeting with wealthy and influential groups and individuals who maybe could be persuaded to donate money for medical aid, and so on.

Three stories from Madge's letters show that medical aid could come from some of the most unexpected sources. In the first story she relates how Lord Faringdon, a Labour peer, had visited Spain in his Rolls-Royce and was so appalled by how the wounded were transported that he donated his car to the SMAC, who converted it into an ambulance.

## Head Nurse at Uclés: Madge in Spain 1937–1939

Madge takes up the story describing what eventually happened to Lord Faringdon's Rolls-Royce:

> This ambulance has done duty on all the fronts in Spain and is now back in England full of bullet holes and a complete wreck. It is starting a propaganda tour of the seaside towns … This tour finishes end of August and George (Jeger) says Manchester can have it in September. It is the most wonderful bit of propaganda you ever saw.[67]

It is possible that, when on leave, Madge spoke in Stalybridge, near Manchester, with this bullet-riddled ambulance as a prop. But, although this would be a nice symmetry, it is most likely that the speaker in Stalybridge was local nursing volunteer Lillian Urmston. Nurse Urmston's account of her fundraising activities while on leave from Spain mirror exactly the sort of activities Madge would have done in Britain when on leave. In Lillian's own words:

> They sent an ambulance up with me to Stalybridge and in all the surrounding towns I spoke to the Quakers, Church of England, Congregational, Methodist, Communist, Labour, Co-operative Women, Town's Women's Guild … I deliberately said 'Leave the ambulance as it is, with the blood stains inside …'[68]

Lillian Urmston was born in Stalybridge in 1915. On leaving school she worked in an office before training as a nurse. At the time she volunteered to serve in Spain, she was a Staff Nurse in a Lake District hospital, and also a volunteer nurse in the Territorial Army. She served in Spain at hospitals on the Aragón, Teruel and at Flix. Lillian was part of the mass exodus from Catalonia in early 1939, and was, for a time, interned in a concentration camp. On her return to Britain she helped to raise money for Spanish refugees. In the Second World War she became an army nurse and was seriously wounded at Anzio in Italy. After the war she became a journalist and later moved with her husband to the Far East where she helped prostitutes in Singapore to form a trade union. She died in 1990.[69]

## *The Nurse Who Became a Spy*

When Madge was returning from her second period of leave, with a broken arm due to a wound from a bomb splinter, she became frustrated by the difficulty of finding safe transport arrangements back to Spain. In the end she took the gamble of returning, along with a driver and a truck, on board a merchant ship named the *Stanleigh*. This plan held an element of danger in it; the Nationalists were blockading Republican ports. If they were to intercept the *Stanleigh*, the Nationalists would either board it and confiscate any medical supplies, or, at the very worst, they would fire at the ship and sink it. It seems that Madge made a big impression on the crew during her time on board the *Stanleigh*:

> Oh, I nearly signed on the *Stanleigh* they were so wonderfully good to us. I am loaded with presents from them lovely things …

The crew spent two days in Valencia with Madge and her then partner, Wilhelm Holst, and one night they partied until 4am:

> The night before we left for here Wilhelm (Holst) gave a party in his lovely apartment and I was a hostess. Oh boy! What a party, there were eight men and one other lady and we broke up at 4am.

The Captain of the *Stanleigh* seemed particularly taken with Madge; she comments:

> … the Captain came and ate with me. He is an absolute darling and I am afraid he has fallen good and hard.

Perhaps Madge, knowing that the ship contained supplies that would be useful to her in Spain, was not above flirting with the ship's captain to get what she wanted! She further comments:

> Apart from personal presents, I think they gave me half the ship's stores and the Captain was toying with the idea of doing one more journey, as he was so lucky this time.[70]

Once again, we have a picture of Madge as a very independent, assertive and persuasive woman, who gets what she wants for her hospital by any means possible. In this case though, we can see that Madge held a lot of platonic affection towards the captain and his crew.

In one of her letters there is a suggestion that Madge is encouraging Dr Malimson and his North Manchester SMAC to write to any organisation and individual who may give funds to medical aid for Spain, regardless of the personal views and politics of the person or organisation. So, she was definitely suggesting that the Committee try speculative approaches to groups and individuals with very different political views, maybe even anti-Spanish Republican. Madge illustrates an unlikely success:

> By the way, I had a letter forwarded on from home, from the Whitefield Golf Club enclosing a cheque for a guinea. Do please tell your friend that as he was so sure I should not get anything out of them for Spain.[71]

As well as appealing for basics like food and toilet rolls, Madge was also involved in the procurement of major medical aid. In this case, it was trucks converted into ambulances and an incinerator for the hospital. When she returned on the *Stanleigh*, she brought back with her a two-ton Bedford truck and an incinerator for destroying medical rubbish.[72] Madge was also calculating the cost of ambulances and recommending that they be bought in France as they were cheaper:

> ... France can send ambulances to Spain for £210 complete and duty free. The cheapest ambulance we can get in England costs £345 and another £25 duty etc. So, you can quite see that if ... they are dealt with at a central organisation a great deal of money can be saved.[73]

In another letter she talks about a SMAC meeting in London, which she attended while on leave. At that meeting she explained that smaller and second-hand vehicles had broken down in Spain and had caused the hospital serious difficulties. This led to the agreement to send the two-tonne Bedford truck back with Madge to Uclés. As Madge relates to Dr Malimson in Manchester:

> However, I immediately saw the necessity for the larger tyres, as our truck had given up the ghost.[74]

## The Nurse Who Became a Spy

In Spain and in Britain, Madge seems to have carried out almost every aspect of medical support that it was possible to provide, with the exception of performing surgery! But, incredibly, she found time to fall in love and have a relationship in Spain and planned to marry after the Civil War.

Madge was a married woman when she went to serve in Spain, but the marriage was very strained. It is possible that this state of affairs provided one of her motivations for volunteering. In Spain Madge worked in intense and very difficult environments where friendship and comradeship with other colleagues was essential to the ability to carry on regardless. Madge was very fond of the doctors and nurses at Uclés, but one man became her lover. His name was Wilhelm Holst.

In her letters Madge usually restricted herself to talking about others, describing the conditions at Uclés, doctors and nurses, patients and pleading for medical aid. However, in one particular letter she pours out her plans and emotions and describes her relationship with Holst, in response to a request from Dr Malimson that she talk a bit more about herself when she next writes to him:

> … you asked me to talk about myself. There are so few people I can really have a heart to heart talk with. I have written to (forgot you don't know his name) my husband to ask him if he will divorce me. I know he won't let me divorce him, so I have told him if he will not do so, I will give him grounds. I think you will believe me when I tell you that the idea is abhorrent to me, but apparently there is no other way and when our affairs are quite settled I am going to marry Wilhelm Holst …
>
> Having made up our minds and having a definite effect in mind we are both glad that we have work which interests us and brings us into contact occasionally. Wilhelm is hoping that we should be able to marry in a year. I hope so but knowing my husband and the long-windedness of the law in England I have my doubts. Wilhelm has two sons who are at present in a preparatory school for the University of Paris where we should live. I told my sister about him when I was home, but she didn't take kindly to the idea …[75]

## Head Nurse at Uclés: Madge in Spain 1937–1939

The husband to whom Madge refers is Arthur Lightfoot, whom she married in 1930. Her sister is Florence, who witnessed Madge and Arthur's wedding. We know she visited the family when on leave and she received cigarettes from home, which she distributed to the patients.[76] Wilhelm Holst and Madge married after the Civil War was over, but there is some dispute as to whether the marriage really took place.

Wilhelm Holst was born in 1895 in Drammen, near Oslo in Norway. He was one of six children born into a middle-class family. His father was a shipmaster. Wilhelm went to university to study science but left after two years and became a policeman near Oslo. In 1921 he married a woman called Anna Hval, the daughter of a wealthy farmer. Wilhelm left his job as a policeman and worked for a shipping company, which led to his moving to Hamburg, Germany, in 1922. Anna stayed in Norway at first, but by 1924 she had moved to Hamburg where the couple had two sons. Wilhelm moved to Paris in 1927 to set up a business and lived alone for three years while his family returned to Norway. In 1931, his family joined him for the next five years and a daughter was born. Wilhelm moved to London in March 1936 and the family returned to Norway. Wilhelm tried to set up a shipping company in London but struggled to make a living.[77]

Why Wilhelm volunteered to take part in the Spanish Civil War is unclear. In his letters home to his wife he makes no mention of politics. In a Special Operations Executive report of 1941 Kristian Gleditchs, the husband of Nini Gleditchs, Wilhelm's Norwegian co-worker in Spain, stated that he believed Wilhelm volunteered to serve in Spain from a combination of idealism and a spirit of adventure. Holst was a member of the Norwegian Labour Party, so he had left-wing views, but was not actively involved in politics.[78]

It seems Wilhelm contacted various 'Aid Spain' groups, and was appointed to deliver ambulances and medical supplies. In February 1937 he organised the delivery of three ambulances to Spain for the Quakers (his father was a Quaker). On his arrival, Wilhelm joined the International Brigades and became a stretcher-bearer, but after a short period he was promoted to major in the medical services and was put in charge of evacuating wounded Scandinavian International Brigade volunteers to appropriate hospitals. In August 1937 Wilhelm fell ill with dysentery and was hospitalised for three weeks.

After his recovery, Wilhelm was based in Valencia with fellow Norwegian volunteer Nini Gleditchs. Both Nini and her husband had important roles in the Second World War as part of the staff of the Norwegian government-in-exile. By the autumn of 1937, Wilhelm was the Norwegian representative of the CSI. In 1938 he was also in charge of the hospital at Alcoy, to the south of Valencia in Alicante, having previously been a commissioner for some American hospitals in Spain. An article in a Norwegian newspaper (*Arbeiderbladet*, 28 July 1938) states that Holst was the Head of the CSI in Spain which coordinated medical aid to the Republic. The article praises his personal qualities and highlights both his courage and administrative skills. A large quantity of ambulances from Scandinavia were handed over to the Spanish medical services by Holst.[79]

By 1938 Wilhelm was the main contact for the CSI in Spain as well as a contact for the SMAC and the Quakers. He was a man of significant importance and authority. During the Civil War he continued to write to his wife and family, and even invited his wife to join him. It is hard to judge whether Wilhelm and his wife were drifting apart or whether there was still a bond between them. Wilhelm stayed in Spain till the end of the Civil War and continued dispensing relief in Valencia to the local population, and to children's homes set up by the Quakers and Republican prisoners during the early months of Franco's regime. He was briefly imprisoned, and then released thanks to the efforts of the Swedish consul in Spain. He left the country in July 1939. Wilhelm Holst was obviously a very brave man: if Franco's police had discovered his service in the International Brigades, he would very likely have been executed.[80]

In her letters Madge runs a gamut of different emotions, from being thoroughly depressed by the distress all around to high emotions of solidarity with her fellow doctors and nurses, and her love for Holst. Rarely does she talk about the danger of being killed or injured while serving in Spain. As we know, when Madge's plan to return to Uclés in July 1938 was frustrated by transport problems, she decided to go by sea on the *Stanleigh*. This was a much more dangerous option since Franco's navy was patrolling the Republican coast and regularly sank merchant vessels:

> It is a terrific risk to take but it is better than hanging around for weeks, as it is, it will probably be a fortnight before we get away and you know my view, that if your name is written on the bullet, nothing can save you.[81]

In another letter written on the same day, Madge seems equally unconcerned about what to do if she were to be killed:

> I am afraid to go with John and the stuff on a merchant ship but they thought it would be too expensive to bring my body back, I assured them that my earthly remains would be of no interest, whether they were in Spain, China! Or England, I have no desire for a Christian burial ...[82]

As the Civil War slowly reached its conclusion, Madge was cut off in Uclés. Conditions continued to worsen: soap was virtually non-existent, they had no cigarettes, they had a single syringe for the hospital, there was a shortage of linen and there was very little electricity, often none.[83] In the last month of the Civil War, Casado launched his coup in Madrid against Negrin's Republican government in an attempt to broker a peace deal with Franco. Madge describes the effect on Uclés Hospital:

> After many anxious days, we are all breathing freely. Yesterday we evacuated the whole hospital, (except Juan, my patient), and to-day we are filling up with the wounded from Madrid. It has been a nerve-wracking time, and after two or three days fighting in Madrid with only garbled accounts from this person and that, (I told you previously all wireless had been confiscated) the Colonel in Tarancón gave orders for a wireless to be set up in the schoolroom for wounded and personnel to hear the hourly news bulletins from Madrid. This at once eased the tense atmosphere in the hospital, and the doctors, lieutenants and I gathered in the director's office to hear the news, and at 8 pm. they all went to the schoolroom for the Spanish news, whilst I and Dr Landa listened to the English news (7 pm. in England). Even though the English news was disturbing, there was something very comforting in listening in peace and quietness to the calm, cultured, refined voice of the English announcer. So different from the excitability of the Spanish temperament. At the start of the trouble in Madrid, they sent for our *camions* (lorries) to transport soldiers from the Levant. Every available motor vehicle was commandeered.

Our food has been brought up from Tarancón on a succession of mules and carts. Virtually we have been prisoners in Uclés, and at any moment if there was any trouble in the village or near, the director was going to order all personnel inside the hospital, as this place is strong enough to withstand a siege. However, everything remained quiet in the village, and now the trouble is practically cleared up, and they are sending the troops back to the Levant, and when this is accomplished will return the *camions*. Amongst all this came my own problem. I forgot to mention all telephone communications were suspended, but Holst with his influence managed to get a message through to the hospital to say he had received a telegram from England to say I was to return. This made me very depressed, because of all times I felt this was the worst moment to leave. My heart just ached at the thought of walking out on them all, and Dr Landa kept saying 'the situation is improving Madge, perhaps you needn't go after all'. Then came another message from Holst to say I was to be packed up and ready to go the following morning, (two days ago). I still couldn't get in communication with him nor could Dr Landa. The *Comandancia Militar* at Tarancón refused permission even though Dr Landa went personally to ask. So I very reluctantly packed my things, gave heaps of stuff away, and then with all his influence Holst couldn't get permission to come to Uclés. The Madrid - Valencia Road was militarised and only army transport for Tarancón and Madrid was allowed. He again sent word to say it would be two or three days before he could get a *hoja de ruta* (travel permit) but he would be able to have a telephone communication with me this morning. This morning I was at last able to speak personally with him, and he then told me the contents of your telegram as follows: - 'Advise Madge leave Uclés. Material en route for Uclés.' I was delighted with both portions of the telegram. Naturally he has been very anxious about me and would like me down in Valencia. But I consider my obligation is first to the Spanish Medical Aid and Uclés, and the trouble having subsided, I feel it quite safe to stay on here.[84]

## Head Nurse at Uclés: Madge in Spain 1937–1939

Madge had been encouraged to leave Spain by the SMAC before the end of the Civil War, but was determined to serve to the end. The minutes of a SMAC meeting in London refer to a message sent to them by Holst from Madge on the current situation:

> Madge don't want to leave Uclés now hospital need her more than ever. Am still waiting for news about goods please cable. The Foreign Office had been informed of her whereabouts and asked to make such arrangements for her safety as may be deemed necessary.[85]

By the end of March, the war was over, and Nationalist forces overran the Republican southern zone and took over the running of Uclés Hospital. When the Nationalists arrived, an upper-class Spanish woman asked Madge what she was thinking of in nursing for the 'Reds'.[86] At first Madge was confined to the village of Uclés and was not allowed to leave for three weeks. She was eventually allowed to leave Uclés and travel to Valencia where she contacted the British consulate, and, through them, tried to get exit papers to leave Spain. She stayed in Valencia for three months before being forced to travel to San Sebastian to obtain the documents she needed to leave the country. Madge describes the conditions in post-Civil War Spain. She states that conditions were worse than during the war, with many people starving. She states she 'loathed' the time she spent in Spain after the end of the Civil War where the defeated Republicans were punished (imprisoned or worse) and people lived in abject poverty.[87]

In an article in the *Manchester Guardian*, Madge describes what happened when the Nationalists occupied Uclés; individuals who had been involved in the executions of right-wingers early in the Civil War were themselves executed after a trial, but many innocent men were also killed without a trial. Madge recalls she was in a hairdresser's shop when a woman was dragged in and forced to have her hair cut very short as a punishment because, when she passed a café playing the Fascist national anthem, she did not stop and give the Fascist salute. Madge commented on how difficult it was for Republican soldiers to get work; many who were working were also removed from their employment. Women were forced to dress very conservatively with covered arms, and could only bathe in a 'Victorian-style' bathing costume. Male children were taught military drill from the age of 4. Madge described the new ruling Nationalist regime as having a 'beastly spirit'; she wrote that they missed an opportunity for reconciliation with the end of the Civil War. Most people were thankful the war was over; but the victors had no interest in reconciliation.[88]

Eventually, pressure from the SMAC on the British authorities got Madge her exit visa and she left Spain via San Sebastian and Hendaye.[89] On 30 June she arrived back in Britain and was met at Victoria Station in London by fellow Spanish Civil War nursing veterans Louise Jones, Ena Vassie and Patience Darton. Her meeting with her fellow nurses, as reported in the press, show a very different Madge than the one who first volunteered to serve in Spain:

> As a continental boat train arrived in Victoria station, London, to-day, a young dark-haired woman, wearing a smartly-cut suit, with a red hat and blouse, stepped out. She passed through the barriers, and three young women rushed forward and embraced her.[90]

Madge stayed in London during the summer of 1939 and met other veterans from Spain. She also briefly became a member of the SMAC national committee. Madge had written a report about Spain and it was agreed that parts of the report should be sent to the prime minister and foreign secretary. She was further asked to write a report on post-Civil War Spain, which would be supported by a deputation from the SMAC if necessary and circulated to MPs.[91] At the next meeting of the SMAC national committee in August it was noted that Madge's second report had been passed to the parliamentary committee on Spain, who were arranging for it to be circulated to MPs and sent to the prime minister and foreign secretary. Madge also used her time back in Britain to write up her experiences of being a nurse at Uclés. In two years, Madge had moved a long way from being a married woman running a chiropody business in a Manchester suburb to becoming a national expert on Spain! However, it appears from the SMAC minutes that Madge was no longer a committee member and may even have left the country.[92]

Where was Madge? In 1947 her North Manchester SMAC contact, Dr Malimson, wrote to the IBA in London, asking if they knew anything about Madge's whereabouts. Nan Green wrote back to him to say they

## Head Nurse at Uclés: Madge in Spain 1937–1939

had heard nothing about Madge since 1939, when she last saw her in London.[93] In fact, Madge had left Britain for France to start another, even more dramatic, chapter in her life. She had joined her lover Wilhelm Holst in Paris where she was helping him to organise relief for those Spanish Republicans who had fled to France after Catalonia had fallen to Franco's forces in early 1939. It is hard to believe after her experiences in the Spanish Civil War that the resulting years during the Second World War would be even more remarkable!

## Chapter 6

# Europe 1933–1940: Spanish Republican Exiles, Events Leading to War and the Second World War to the Fall of France

In the period 1936–1939 the major focus of many people in Britain was the Spanish Civil War; however, momentous events were taking place outside Spain that would ultimately lead to the outbreak of the Second World War. While Madge Addy was in Spain between January and June 1939, firstly as a nurse and secondly as a foreign alien, hundreds of thousands of Spanish Republicans had fled across the French frontier in the early months of 1939, as Nationalist forces completed the conquest of Catalonia and arrived at the border with France in late February 1939. British and international aid agencies continued to supply aid both to the southern Republican zone, which fell to the Nationalists in late March 1939, as well as to Spanish Republican refugees in France. Once all of Spain was in Franco's hands, aid was concentrated on those Republicans abroad, particularly those in concentration camps in southern France. For those Spanish Republicans who decided to stay in France rather than face prison and possibly death in Franco's Spain, life was hard, and soon they would be caught up in another war against Nazi Germany. The conventional war between France and Germany was short and brutal and ended with a swift victory for the Germans in 1940, leading to a German-occupied part of the country and a southern part governed by a puppet pro-German and pro-Franco government known as the Vichy regime. From the summer of 1939 Madge was to become involved in aiding Spanish Republican refugees, and, after the fall of France, in clandestine activities opposing the occupying authorities.

## Europe 1933–1940

With the conquest of Catalonia certain and the Republic only capable of delaying the inevitable with rear-guard forces, thousands upon thousands – many on foot – began the trek to the French frontier and ultimately to safety in France. The *retirada* from Catalonia was described by a French reporter who stated that for two days a constant flow of exhausted workers, peasants, women, children, bureaucrats and soldiers trudged towards the French border in 'one vast tide'.[1]

The fleeing populace were bombed and machine-gunned by enemy aircraft; short of food and drenched by rain they advanced slowly to the French border and what they saw as safety. When the roads became too clogged for the refugees to move, thousands of them decided to enter France by climbing over the mountains. In France, tension mounted as the sheer scale of the disaster began to dawn on the French. A huge mass of civilians had already reached the frontier; shortly the defeated Republican army would be there also. On the night of 27–28 January, the border was opened to women and children only. It was decided on 30 January that those able-bodied men who had crossed into France already were to be interned in a camp at Argelès-sur-Mer. The next day wounded men were allowed into France. Newspaper journalist Herbert L. Matthews described the situation in Spain just a few miles from the French frontier: 'not one spare inch of ground near the roads was not occupied by the thousands of "swarming" Spanish refugees. Thousands more waited in lines to receive food from relief agencies.'[2]

In February all but the able-bodied men were to be let in and accommodated in makeshift shelters, which had not yet been built. Extra French troops were sent to the area to keep the refugees under control and to ensure that they did not leave the camps. The first camp on a beach was Argelès-sur-Mer, followed by Saint-Cyprien and Le Barcarès. The camp at Argelès-sur-Mer was staked out and surrounded with barbed wire, initially with no other facilities than the open beach. By early February around 250,000 Spanish refugees had entered France; about a fifth had been dispersed but most were still near the border, living in appalling conditions in the camps. How many died in the camps is not known; official figures say approximately 5,000, but it was probably much higher. On 14 February, the last of the Republican soldiers crossed into France. During January and February 1939 perhaps as many as 500,000 Spanish refugees entered France in chaotic circumstances and with no proper infrastructure in place to support them.[3]

During this period and in the months after, the likes of the Quakers, SMAC, NJCSR and ex-medical volunteers tried their best to help alleviate the suffering. The NJCSR chartered two ships to rescue Republicans and aid workers when the southern zone fell to the Nationalists. One of the ships took 400 Republicans to North Africa and safety, and the other ship rescued aid workers still in Spain. To gain time to get them on board, the Union Jack flag was placed on the dock gates and it was claimed that the docks were British-owned property! In the south of France, the SMAC set up an office in Perpignan which included ex-medical volunteers Nan Green and Una Vassie. Food, milk, blankets, medical supplies and equipment were sent to the camp hospitals. The Quakers organised food canteens at the camps in conjunction with the SMAC, and by April had supplied food and clothing to over 70,000 refugees. The NJCSR's aim was to get as many refugees out of the camps as possible and get them settled elsewhere. By the autumn of 1939, 326 adult Republican refugees were living in Britain. At first, they were supported by fundraising but most, in time, found employment or served in the British armed forces. Like the Basque children, they also took part in fundraising concerts. In addition, Spanish Republican sailors trapped in British ports were given asylum and the seamen's trade union helped them find work on other ships. The biggest single initiative by the British aid agencies was the transport of 8,000 Spanish Republican refugees from France to Mexico. In spring 1939, the NJCSR chartered the ship SS *Sinaia* to take the refugees to Mexico. Looking after the babies on board was the former hospital administrator in Spain, Nan Green. The ship left France on 24 May 1939 and arrived in Vera Cruz in Mexico on 13 June. Former Spanish Civil War nurse Frida Stewart worked with the refugee organisation in Paris until the outbreak of the Second World War in September 1939. She returned to Paris in January 1940 and was later interned and imprisoned. Spanish Republicans helped her to escape to Britain where she worked for the Free French (who aimed to liberate France from German occupation).[4]

The initial reaction and policy of the French authorities to this mass exodus of refugees, which would continue for a couple more months, was to make things as unpleasant as possible in order to encourage the refugees to return home. Conditions in the camps were deliberately harsh and inhumane, and discipline was brutal. Large numbers of military personnel were used to guard the camps and patrol the surrounding areas to make sure no one escaped. All the camps lacked adequate food, housing, sanitation, water supply and medical facilities. Historian Hugh Thomas believes the French government hoped that if they treated the Spanish Republicans poorly enough and openly neglected their needs, then most of them would decide to return to Spain and 'throw themselves on General Franco's mercy'.[5]

Approximately 70,000 refugees were incarcerated at Argelès-sur-Mer, around 85,000 at Saint-Cyprien, and around 55,000 at Le Barcarès, which had barracks for barely a third of that total. A further 75,000 refugees were living in the mountains without shelter. Lillian Urmston, a British nurse who had served in Spain, found herself in the Argelès-sur-Mer camp after retreating across the border and described the conditions in the camp in the first days after crossing the border into France. The camp was situated in open sand dunes surrounded by barbed wire. The wounded were left untreated for several days and nurses like Urmston were not allowed to help the sick. There was only one water supply for thousands of the internees, who received no food until the fifth day. Spanish soldiers who escaped from the camp to find food were badly beaten by the guards; Urmston claims that the guards even bayonetted some of them. She ends her description with a hypothetical question from a Spanish soldier:

> My Spanish friend turned to me and said: 'Would we be treated like this in England?' And I wonder, would they?[6]

British aid worker Francesca Wilson, who had served with the Quakers in Spain, gives a similar description of the camp at Argelès-sur-Mer:

> It is impossible to imagine what eighty thousand men herded together behind barbed wire look like if one hasn't seen it ... a sight so wounding to human dignity. Men pinned into cages like wild animals; exposed to the stare of the passer-by like cattle in the market place.[7]

Thanks to complaints by left-wing French politicians, numbers in the overcrowded camps were reduced, new camps were set up and the building of barracks to house the refugees was accelerated. But progress was slow, as were improvements in the medical and sanitation facilities.

Over half of the camp's inmates suffered from some sort of disease or condition including dysentery, pneumonia, tuberculosis, leprosy, conjunctivitis and scalp ringworm and everyone suffered from lice. Many wounded soldiers suffered amputations as French surgeons did not know the new techniques that had been developed during the Civil War. Although hospital barracks were installed, most patients slept on the floor on straw pallets. The death in February 1939 of the world-famous Spanish poet Antonio Machado from exhaustion and illness was widely published in the world press.[8] A report by a French doctor who visited the camps complained that health and sanitation needs were still not being met and described the situation as 'repugnant'. Anybody defined as a troublemaker – generally Communists, Anarchists or International Brigaders – were placed in prison camps at places like Le Vernet and Collioure where conditions were even harsher.[9]

At first the French government's policy was to make living conditions for the Spanish Republicans as unpleasant as possible in the hope they would voluntarily return to Spain. Franco's harsh policies towards returners, which included imprisonment and sometimes death, led to fewer Spanish refugees returning home than the French government expected. It is difficult to estimate the number of refugees who returned to Spain during 1939, but possibly around a fifth of those who entered France returned. In addition, the French government was keen for other countries to receive some of the Republican exiles. Mexico took in over 12,000 Spanish refugees, other Central and South American countries took in some exiles, and Britain and America received much smaller numbers. The Soviet Union took in around 4,000 Spanish Communists. It is estimated that 30,000 Spanish Republicans settled outside France.[10]

From around April 1939 conditions for the Spanish refugees began to improve and repatriation was no longer seen as essential. Instead, the French government looked to utilise the skills of the exiles for the benefit of the French economy. More camps were built and overcrowding in the old camps was greatly reduced. Spanish Republicans were contracted out to local farmers as farm labour. In the camps, the barracks huts, sanitation and medical facilities were all improved and the building of any new facilities was greatly accelerated. With conditions in France improving for the Republican exiles, they could have hoped for a period of continuing improvements in their living conditions. But the dark clouds of another war were getting ever closer and when the Second

## Europe 1933–1940

World War broke out, the lives of the Spanish Republican refugees would be thrown into turmoil once again.[11]

From September 1939 to June 1940 many former Spanish Republican soldiers joined the French Foreign Legion and the regular French army, and saw action in France, Belgium and Norway. As many as 6,000 would die fighting in the French army during this period. Those captured by the Germans as PoWs were sent to the Mauthausen concentration camp, where as many as 10,000 may have perished. Others would be forcibly enrolled in labour units, working on the farms and in the defence industries, leaving only the old, young, sick and so-called 'undesirables' in the camps and punishment centres. With the defeat of France by Germany in June 1940 and the formation of the puppet regime of Vichy, many Spanish Republicans took up arms in their own formations in southern France to fight as guerrilla fighters, or joined the Free French forces abroad.[12]

The new Vichy regime was on friendly terms with Franco's Spain, which, although pro-German for most of the Second World War, skilfully remained neutral. The Vichy regime sent almost 1,000 Spanish political exiles back to Spain to face either death or very long prison sentences. The most famous individual sent back to be executed was the former leader of the Catalan government, Luis Companys.[13] Surprisingly though, the Vichy regime decided to keep the Republican exiles rather than send them back to Spain, and used them as slave labour. The Republicans were put to work in industry and on the farms, some were sent to Germany to work and thousands were enrolled in the Todt Organisation, building coastal defences for the Germans on the Atlantic coast. Not surprisingly, some Republicans began to resist the Vichy authorities and their German masters. One of the first ways they opposed the occupying authorities was by becoming involved in the 'escape lines', which helped Allied and British military personnel, particularly pilots, to reach Spain, often acting as guides over the Pyrenees.

By 1942 there were many Spanish Resistance groups in existence who liaised with other Spanish and French guerrilla units. The Spanish Resistance groups, alone or working with French groups, liberated almost fifty cities in France. Thousands of Spanish refugees also served in the Free French forces, the Foreign Legion and in General Leclerc's 1st and 2nd armoured divisions.[14] Spanish troops were the first troops to enter Paris during its liberation in August 1944. Some Republican exiles serving with the Free French fought all the way into Germany and entered Hitler's mountain retreat, Berchtesgaden. The number of Spanish Republicans who fought in the Resistance and Free French forces is unknown; however, possibly as many as 60,000 Republicans served in the Resistance. British former foreign secretary, Anthony Eden, claimed that three out of every five Resistance fighters were Spaniards. In all, the cost in the lives of Spanish Republicans who resisted Fascism a second time was possibly as high as 25,000.[15] During the war only one serious attempt was made by Spanish Republicans to attempt to oust Franco. In December 1944, 2,000 Spanish Resistance fighters armed by the Allies invaded the Aran valley in Spain and occupied sixteen villages for ten days. However, they were forced to retire to France after Franco assembled overwhelming forces against them; there was no 'People's Uprising' to support them and so the Allies ordered them to return to France.[16]

After the end of the Second World War, the Spanish Republicans expected the Allies to remove Franco and allow democracy to return to Spain. While many countries denounced the Franco regime during 1945 – in particular France, which had benefitted most from Spanish Republican assistance – nothing was done militarily to overthrow Franco. Spanish Republican guerrillas continued to resist the regime, but no popular uprising occurred from a populace worn down by starvation and oppression. Difficulties also arose from divisions over who exactly was the legitimate Republican government-in-exile, as the ex-prime minister Negrin was omitted from the exiled *Cortes* because of his Communist connections during the Civil War. The Spanish Republicans now put their trust in the United Nations to overthrow the Franco regime. In 1945–1946 the UN banned Franco's Spain from membership of any part of the UN and recommended all countries withdraw their ambassadors. But from 1947 Spain was seen by America as a strategic country (a place to have military air bases and port facilities) in the fight against Communism, and by 1955 Spain was given full membership of the UN. This effectively kept Franco in power until his death in 1975. Armed guerrilla resistance to the regime lasted into the 1960s; the last guerrillero was executed in 1974. It is likely that as many as 15,000 guerrillas resisted the Franco regime in post-Civil War Spain.[17] Louis Stein comments:

> Franco remained in power primarily because the United States and Great Britain feared the possibility of a red Spain more than they feared the actuality of a Fascist one.[18]

*Europe 1933–1940*

While the Spanish Civil War was running its course, and during Madge's time in Spain, momentous events were taking place in Europe and further afield which were leading step-by-step towards a global catastrophe. Madge returned to Britain from Spain in June 1939; within a few months the Second World War would break out. Madge, who by this time was helping refugees in Paris, would become part of this war after Germany conquered France, joining the opposition to that occupying power. The Spanish Civil War is seen as one of the events that led to the Second World War, as Britain and France openly ignored the flagrant breaking of the Non-Intervention Agreement by Germany, Italy and the Soviet Union, who openly supplied arms to both sides. Was the Spanish Civil War just one of a few diplomatic and military conflicts that ultimately led to the Second World War?

The Great War had ended with the defeat of Germany; the terms of its surrender being dictated by the Treaty of Versailles in 1919. This treaty was designed both to punish Germany financially for its four-year occupation of Belgium and parts of northern France, and to limit its armed forces to keep Germany weak so that there would never again be another world war. Problems with the implementation of the treaty quickly became apparent: the Americans decided to withdraw from involvement in European politics, Italy felt that it was harshly treated (and would soon have a Fascist regime led by Mussolini), the treaty enforcement relied on Britain and France working closely together but this was often not the case. France wished to contain Germany and keep her weak, while Britain was happy to accept Germany's breaking of minor aspects of the Treaty of Versailles in order to remain on friendly terms. In eastern Europe a mass of new small independent states had come into being after Versailles, replacing the former Habsburg Empire and parts of the old Russian Empire. Farther east was the new pariah state of the Soviet Union, which was very much an unknown quantity. The treaty also relied on Germany's acceptance of the treaty, and many of its politicians never did. In the Far East the growth of Japanese power threatened both British and French interests there. The desire to overturn the Versailles Treaty and the economic depression which hit Europe, and particularly Germany, played a significant role in the rise of the Nazis in Germany and the eventual rise to power of Adolf Hitler.[19]

In the early 1930s several events occurred that weakened the Treaty of Versailles, saw the ineffectiveness of the League of Nations – the international organisation set up in 1920 to prevent war – and a further increase in countries ruled by right-wing dictators. In Germany, Hitler came to power legally in January 1933; by the summer all opposition parties had been banned and its leaders and cadres imprisoned. In the neighbouring country of Austria, a right-wing dictator called Dollfuss was also coming to power, and in February his forces crushed the Socialist militia in Vienna in a mini civil war. But the Austrian right wing was divided and in July 1934 Dollfuss was assassinated by Austrian Nazis who were demanding Austria be united with Germany.[20] Under the Versailles agreement a small former part of Germany called Saarland was to be supervised by the League of Nations for fifteen years. In the plebiscite of January 1935, the people of Saarland voted overwhelmingly to return to German rule.[21]

The first major failure of the League of Nations – the precursor of the UN – to support a league member was Japan's invasion of Manchuria in 1931. Italy's invasion of Abyssinia was to be its second major failure. Abyssinia was the only independent state in Africa; in 1896 it had inflicted a serious military defeat on Italy at Adowa when the Italians invaded. The Italian dictator Mussolini was desperate to create an Italian Empire in Africa and avenge the defeat of 1896. In October 1935 the Italians invaded Abyssinia from the Italian colony of Eritrea. The League of Nations' response was to impose sanctions on Italy, but, critically, they did not include oil. Attempts by Britain and France to find a diplomatic solution proved a disaster as the plan was leaked to the press and led to uproar when it was proposed that Mussolini would get most of his demands, leaving only a smaller independent Abyssinia. This led to the new British foreign secretary, Eden, calling for stronger economic sanctions against Italy. France's reluctance to introduce sanctions and Britain's lack of desire to close the Suez Canal meant that the League of Nations' actions were ineffectual. Italy was able to crush Abyssinia using large motorised columns of troops, as well as bombs and poison gas dropped from the air. Abyssinia was fully under Italian control by May 1936.[22]

Abyssinia and Manchuria were seen as faraway places, but the next crisis was to be in the heart of Europe. Under the Treaty of Versailles, the former German territory of the Rhineland, which bordered France, was to contain no German military forces or fortresses. This had been re-affirmed at the Treaty of Locarno in 1925. Using the excuse of a treaty between France and the Soviet Union in 1935, Hitler ordered 10,000 German

*Above left*: (1) Madge Addy's father, Frederick William Addy.

*Above right*: (2) Madge's mother, Mary, with younger brother, Edward.

*Right*: (3) Madge as a child with younger brother, Edward.

(4) Madge, 1923; trainee nurse at Hope Hospital (right side) in concert party outfit.

(5) Madge with fellow trainee nurses and Miss Hayes, centre. Madge is fourth on the right, top row. Again in concert party clothes.

(6) 34 Manchester Road (on the right), Madge's home 1932–1937. Two of her brothers lived at what is now the dry cleaners (photo taken 2020).

(7) Madge's pet dog 'Lion'.

(8) Picture House Cinema, which was directly opposite 34 Manchester Road.

(9) Chorlton-cum-Hardy Public Library, across the road from 34 Manchester Road.

*Above*: (10) Uclés Monastery (photo taken 2019).

*Right*: (11) Entrance to Uclés, ornate door described by Madge in her letters (photo taken 2019).

(12) Madge giving the clenched fist anti-Fascist salute alongside British-supplied ambulance.

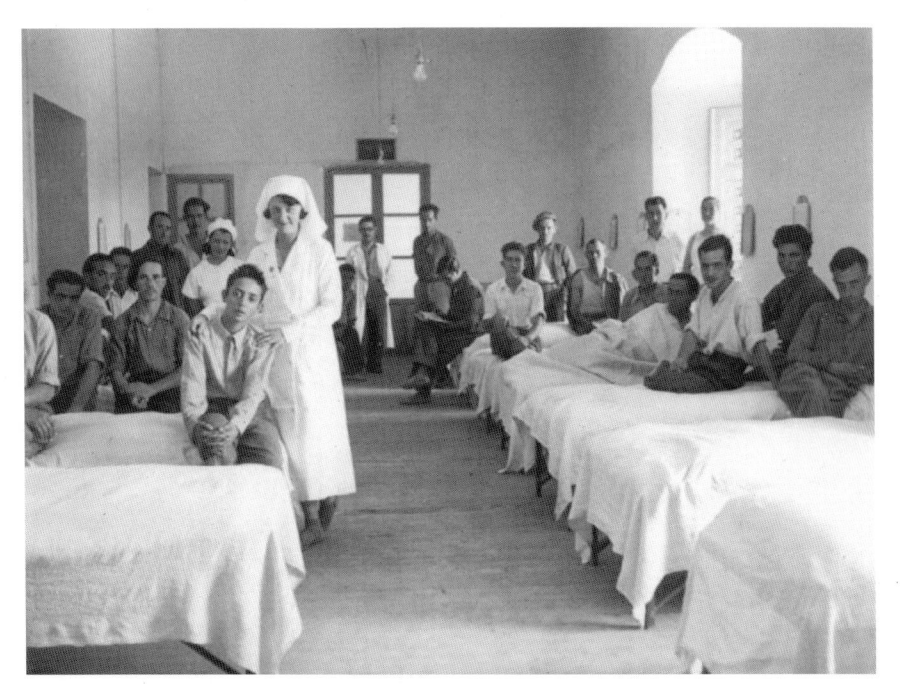

(13) Madge posing with injured Republican soldiers.

(14) Madge outside the operating theatre with Spanish doctor.

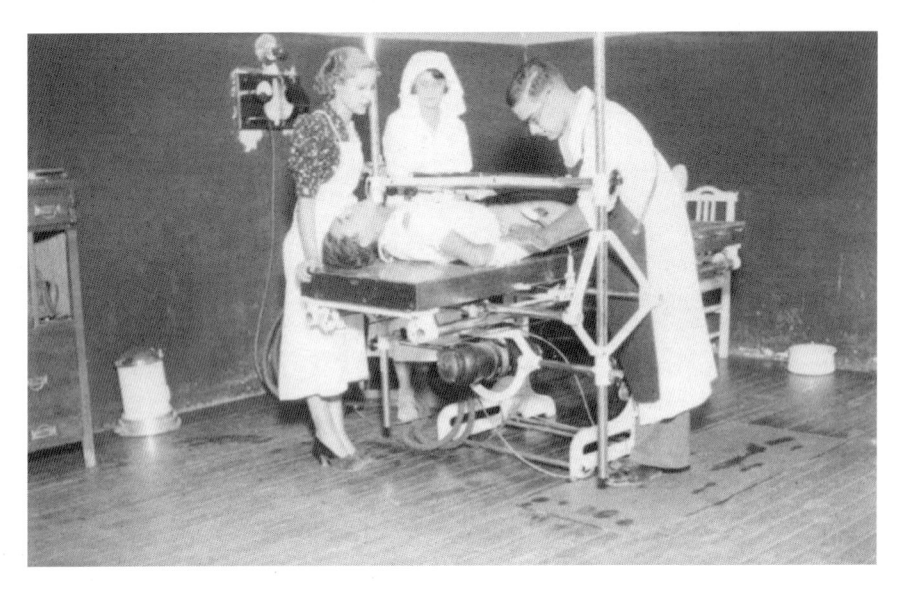

(15) Madge, centre, working in the X-ray department.

(16) Group picture of medical staff at Uclés; Madge is the woman on the left; last on the right on the front row is Wilhelm Holst.

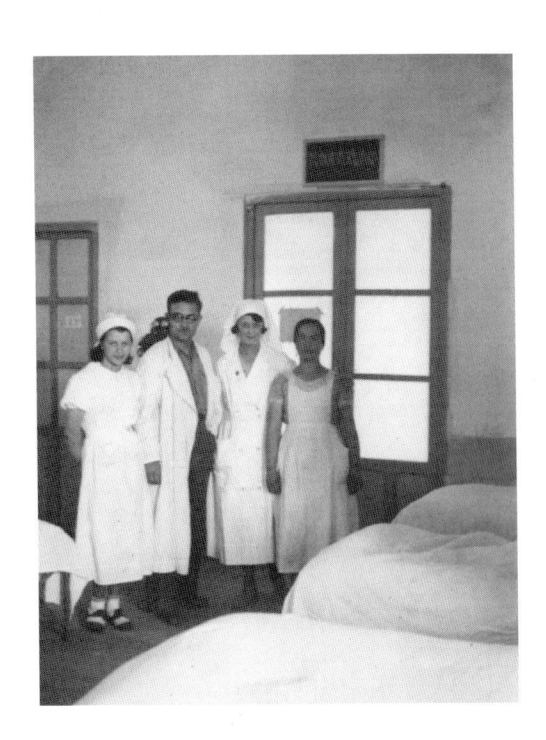

(17) Madge, third right, with medical colleagues in the 'Manchester Ward'.

(18) Teresa Martinez Garcia, a Spanish nurse at Uclés.

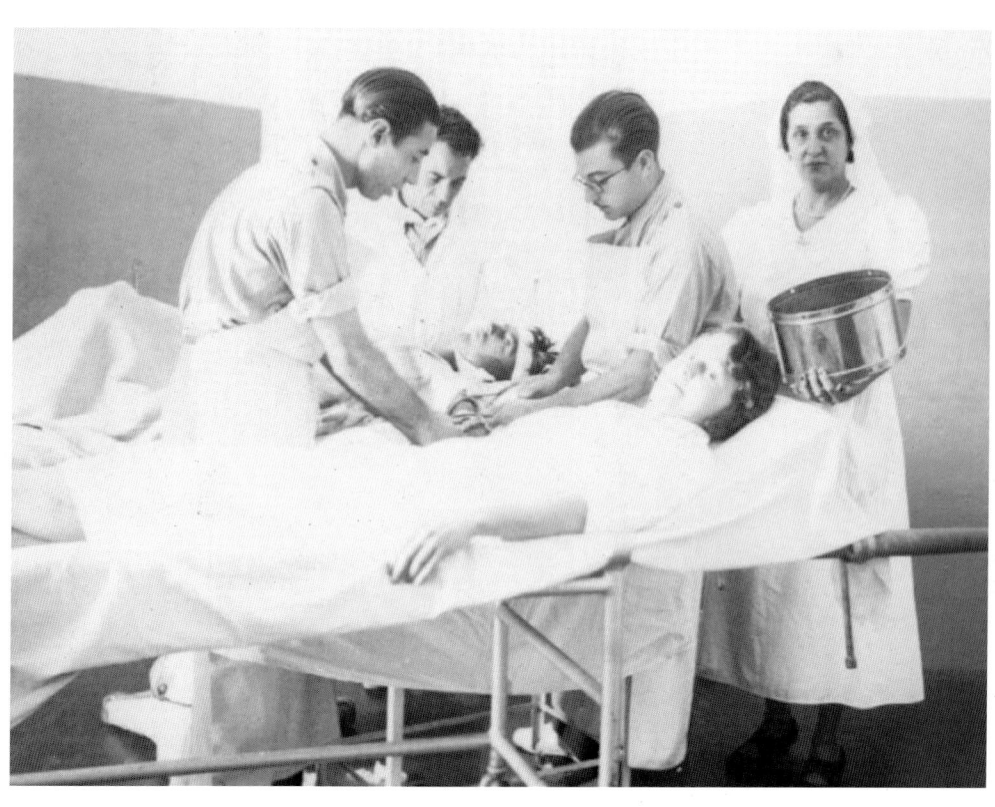

(19) Madge giving blood as part of a blood transfusion to a wounded patient.

(20) Wilhelm Holst in the uniform of a Republican Army Major.

(21) Wilhelm's two sons, Per and Einar Andreas, in 1931. Later murdered by the Germans during the invasion of Norway in 1940.

(22) Madge and Wilhelm in Marseille around 1940.

(23) 'Mrs Oats', photo of Madge in Wilhelm Holst's SOE file.

(24) Thorkild Hansen, photo from his SOE file.

(25) Photo taken of the front of Madge and Wilhelm's house in Marseille, 48 Rue Boudouresque (photo taken in 2020).

(26) Rear of 48 Rue Boudouresque, showing the small harbour (photo taken 2020).

(27) Back of the house in Marseille, Madge with little boy. Wilhelm is standing on the steps.

(28) Group picture taken during the war. Madge is seated far left, front row. Wilhelm is standing on the far left.

(29) Group picture taken during the war. Madge is standing far right and Wilhelm second left.

*Left*: (30) Top row, Thorkild Hansen's medals: Danish medal for serving in the Second World War, British King's Medal for Courage in the Cause of Freedom, French Legion of Honour, French *Croix de Guerre* and French Resistance medal. Second row, Madge's medals: OBE and French *Croix de Guerre* with bronze oakleaf.

*Below*: (31) City of Manchester commemorative plaque in honour of Madge, located at 34 Manchester Road, Chorlton-cum-Hardy (photo taken 2019).

soldiers to occupy the Rhineland in March 1936. Britain had already shown it was willing to allow Germany to re-take the Rhineland in return for some agreements on limiting German re-armament. France was hostile to this invasion but unwilling to do anything without Britain. German actions were condemned by the League of Nations, but no punishment was invoked. Many Conservative politicians in Britain believed Germany was merely taking back what was its own. Hitler had gambled on Britain and France doing nothing and he was proved correct.[23]

Some of the key terms of the Versailles Treaty included strict limits on the size of the German armed forces. From Hitler's accession to power he worked constantly to undermine the limits placed on the size of Germany's armed forces and he was determined to restore the military might of Germany by both diplomatic and illegal means.

On coming to power in Germany, Hitler's major goal was to restore German power by building up its military strength. The Treaty of Versailles had set limits on the size of German armed forces to keep them weak and to prevent a future war. The fleet was limited to 24 warships, the army to 100,000 soldiers and they were forbidden to have an air force. By 1936 the German military was planning to have a peacetime army of 700,000 and a wartime army of 3,000,000, more than in 1914. Hitler believed that the development of an air force was critical to preventing any attack on Germany. Britain had some sympathy with Germany's desire to re-arm, because Britain had reduced its military spending after the Treaty of Versailles (as all nations were expected to do), but France had increased hers. By 1935 Germany had introduced military conscription to increase its army to 500,000 men and the Nazis boasted they had set up an air force under their own ministry. Britain's response to Germany's flagrant breaking of the Versailles Treaty regarding re-armament was one of appeasement and of trying to limit Germany's ambition, whereas France tried to halt any infringement of the treaty, if it could, by any means except war. Hitler, it seemed, preferred direct action rather than diplomatic means to reach his goals, and with Britain and France unwilling to oppose his re-armament, except by harsh words, he could continue to increase the size of his armed forces without any serious threat. Hitler had less interest in his navy and was happy to sign a treaty with Britain in 1935 to keep the German fleet around a third the size of the British Navy and his submarine fleet just under half that of Britain's.[24]

From 1934 onwards, the Nazi economy was geared towards re-armament, with imports linked to military expansion given priority over domestic products. The pace of German re-armament caused economic problems for the country including food shortages, but Hitler personally intervened to continue to prevent any slowing down of the re-armament process. But even into 1938–1939, shortages in manpower and raw materials meant the growth of the German military forces did not happen at the speed at which Hitler wished. By the middle of 1939 the German army stood at 730,000 men and it could mobilise 3,700,000 men in time of war. By the time of the outbreak of the Second World War its air force stood at approximately 4,000 planes. Between 1933 and 1939 Germany had transformed itself from being one of the weakest military powers in Europe to being the strongest. Although its armed forces had many defects because the rapid creation of many of its planes, tanks and military equipment meant they were inferior in quality to those of their neighbours, numerically the German armed forces were superior. Why was Hitler gearing up the German economy for war and rapidly expanding his armed forces? Was it to help him prepare for a world war of revenge or to support him diplomatically in a series of small wars with his neighbours?[25]

While Spain ripped itself apart in its Civil War, major world events were taking place that also helped lead to the start of the Second World War. In the Far East in 1932, Japan had conquered Manchuria from China and declared it an independent state. In 1937, Japan invaded China itself and by 1938 held most of the country, which it then exploited economically as Japan sought raw materials to help it to become the leading power in the Far East at the expense of Britain, France and America. Japan's aggressive policy in the Far East meant Britain always had one eye on this area and was concerned as to how to protect her empire. This meant Britain was more likely to give in to German demands in Europe because it did not want to become involved in any war on the continent when it might need to protect its far eastern empire from the Japanese.[26]

The Treaty of Versailles had been designed to keep Germany weak; part of this policy was to reduce the size of Germany and give pieces of her territory to the new countries in eastern Europe. Germany's neighbour Austria was formerly part of the Habsburg Empire, but the Austrians were seen by Hitler as Germanic people who should be part of

*Europe 1933–1940*

a new greater Germany. After the death of Dollfuss in 1934, the power of the Austrian Nazis was increasing, and they were becoming ever more disruptive. The new Austrian chancellor included two Nazis in his cabinet, but was still losing control of the political situation and so he agreed to meet with Hitler. At the meeting Hitler demanded that a Nazi be made minister of the interior; on returning home the Austrian leader did as Hitler requested. He then unwisely announced there would be a plebiscite to ask the people to support an independent and Germany-free Austria. Hitler demanded the plebiscite be cancelled, and when the Austrian government received no help from the major powers, Hitler's army invaded Austria on 12 March 1938. Hitler announced to cheering crowds the union of the two countries or *Anschluss*. He was greeted in Vienna by around 250,000 people.[27]

Hitler's success in Austria had aroused the passions of Germans living in the Sudetenland area of Czechoslovakia. The leaders of the Sudeten Germans wished to be re-united with Germany. In May 1938 the Czech government refused what would mean the breakup of their country, but were willing to give the Sudeten Germans some increased rights to self-government within Czechoslovakia. Czechoslovakia had an alliance with the Soviet Union who were also allied with France, so potentially the Czechs had powerful friends. At this juncture, fearing a possible world war, the British prime minister, Neville Chamberlain, requested a meeting with Hitler. In their first meeting an agreement was reached that any area in Czechoslovakia with a German majority would peacefully be restored to Germany. A week later, in Chamberlain's second meeting, Hitler demanded the military occupation of the Sudetenland, plebiscites in other areas of Czechoslovakia, and also demanded that the territorial claims of Hungary, Poland and Germany should be honoured. The Czech response was to mobilise their army. A third meeting between Chamberlain and Hitler took place at Munich on 29 September 1938, which also included Mussolini and the French prime minister. It was agreed that Germany would occupy part of Czechoslovakia on 1 October and an international boundary commission would draw up a new border on the 10th. Hitler signed this agreement, which led to Chamberlain's historic announcement on his return to Britain while waving the agreement declaring, 'Peace for our time'. In early 1939 Hitler encouraged Czechoslovakia's neighbours to make territorial claims and supported the Slovaks in declaring independence.

On 15 March 1939 German troops occupied what was left of the Czech state. Finally, Britain and France acted; in March 1939 both promised military assistance to Poland if it were invaded.[28]

One major European power was not represented at Munich and that was the Soviet Union. France and the Soviets had made a pact in 1935 but little had happened since then. Stalin, the leader of the Soviet Union, interpreted the Munich Agreement as France and Britain encouraging Hitler in his desires in eastern Europe and towards an inevitable clash with the Soviet Union. Nevertheless, both Britain and France attempted to make the Soviets part of a grand pact against Germany. Not trusting Britain and France, Stalin demanded precise commitments from France and Britain regarding military assistance, and an agreement that he could enter the territory of other eastern European states to prevent any attacks on those states. Not surprisingly, Britain and France would not commit to this, so Stalin stunned Europe in August 1939 by making a non-aggression pact with Nazi Germany. In the pact it was agreed that Poland would be partitioned between the two powers, the Soviets would be given a free hand in the Baltic states and Finland, and neither side would support any powers at war with the other country. Hitler was gambling that France and Britain would be so shocked by the non-aggression pact that they would no longer oppose his planned invasion of Poland. To Hitler's surprise, France and Britain made it known they would stand by their treaty obligations to Poland. Hitler, still gambling that they would do nothing, ordered his military forces to invade Poland on 1 September 1939. Two days later, both Britain and France declared war on Germany and the Second World War had formally begun.[29]

In the inter-war years, France was a country divided by class and politics, and was led by a myriad of different weak governments – forty-two in all – from 1920–1940. By the 1930s, as in Spain there were growing clashes between the extreme right on one side and the Communists and the left wing of the Socialists on the other side. This came to a head on 6 February 1934 when the head of the Paris police (the *Sureté*), a known right-winger, was removed from office by the new French government. This led to an attempted right-wing coup in Paris involving small parties that included monarchists, conservatives, Fascists and anti-Semites. But by far the largest right-wing force in France was the *Croix de Feu*, an ex-servicemen's organisation led by a retired lieutenant-colonel called de la Roque. There were running street battles for six hours. Fourteen right-wing supporters were killed and over 200 hospitalised in the defeat of the coup. Three days later the Communists organised a demonstration that ended in bloodshed and riots, but this also was crushed. The events of February 1934 seem to have strongly affected the French left-wing parties into uniting to prevent the rise of Fascism in France. In June 1934 the French Communist Party proposed an alliance with the Socialist Party to oppose Fascism, and in July 1934 the two parties reached agreement. In July 1935 the Radical Party of France (right-wing Liberals) joined the agreement, and there was a huge Bastille Day parade in Paris in the same month with supporters of all three parties involved. By January 1936 the alliance known as the Popular Front published its political programme. In the election of April 1936, a united Left were successful in winning the General Election.[30]

The leader of the Popular Front was the Socialist Léon Blum. The party came to power when the economy was distressed, and the supporters of the Popular Front were expecting far-reaching social reforms. The new government was immediately faced by a mass of strike actions and sit-in strikes where workers occupied the factories. So, the first job of the government was to restore industrial peace. An agreement was reached with the strikers whereby in some cases wages were increased by twelve per cent. Other social policies introduced by the Popular Front government were the forty-hour week and holidays with pay. But the French economy struggled to cope with these reforms; in October 1936 the franc had to be devalued and by March 1937 a halt had to be put on any more social reforms. Troubles in Europe and the Civil War in neighbouring Spain were adversely affecting domestic affairs in France. Less than two years after taking office, with the economic situation in France worsening, Blum resigned. The Popular Front was replaced by a succession of weak Radical Party governments. Throughout the interwar period France had been dogged by economic backwardness and at times chronic class conflict, but events outside France and eventually war were to bring down the Third French Republic. By 1937, French foreign policy was in disarray and the French people were divided, except that the majority wanted to avoid war.[31]

In the 1920s, the French government had reduced the period that men had to serve in the army as part of national conscription, and had begun to construct an extensive system of forts called the 'Maginot Line' from the Swiss frontier to the Belgian frontier. By 1936 the French army was led by Great War hero Marshal Pétain; his experiences of the horrific losses suffered by France in that war meant that his military strategies were mainly based on defence. However, the policy of non-intervention in Spain resulted in a second Fascist dictatorship bordering France. When Hitler occupied Austria in March 1938, Léon Blum, who was briefly back in power, called for a unity government because of the crisis. This was rejected and a government of unity led by the Radical Party took office instead. Throughout 1938–1939 the French government, led by Daladier, followed the foreign policy initiatives of Neville Chamberlain. In France itself there were both strong pacifist and pro-Nazi elements which influenced government decision-making. The dismemberment of Czechoslovakia effectively saw the end of the Versailles Treaty, which France had fought so hard to maintain throughout the 1920s and 1930s. In December 1938 things looked a little more hopeful when Germany signed a pact of friendship with France. Internally there were still domestic economic problems and the government looked to reduce their spending by reducing its number of employees, increasing taxes and lengthening the working week. As the Civil War came to an end in Spain, the French government recognised the Franco government and sent Marshal Pétain to Madrid as ambassador. France sided with Britain in the failed negotiations with the Soviet Union, and in promising aid to Poland if it was invaded. On 3 September 1939, a few hours after Britain had declared war on Germany for invading Poland, France followed suit. When war was declared, the 'Maginot Line' was garrisoned and conscripts were called up. Rationing was slow to get off the ground as it was opposed by peasant farmers who were government supporters. In the first winter of the war the French army did virtually nothing, as it was hoped that a defensive posture would ensure that any German attack would be fruitless against French defences while Germany, blockaded by the Anglo-French navies, would be starved of resources. In March 1940, Daladier was replaced as prime minister by Paul Reynaud. Reynaud made an agreement with the British government that neither country would make a separate peace treaty with Germany. In May 1940 the end of the so-called 'phoney war' was shattered by the German invasion of Holland.[32]

When Hitler ordered his armed forces to invade Poland in 1939, the likelihood of Britain and France being able to help Poland in any effective way was remote. The actual physical distance between the three allies meant it would be very difficult to intervene in any meaningful way to help Poland, and there was little political will to do so. The Poles' only real hope of success against the German armed forces was if the Germans were forced to divide their forces to defend themselves against an attack by Britain and France as well. France promised to attack Germany's border defences – the 'Siegfried Line' – within two weeks of mobilisation, and Britain promised air attacks on German cities. Neither of these promises were kept, or were even intended to be. The French sent a small force into Saarland and then halted. On 17 September 1939 – the day the Poles were expecting a major French offensive in the west – they were taken totally off-guard as Soviet Union forces invaded Poland from the east. Britain and France condemned the Soviet action but were at pains to explain that the treaty with Poland only covered military action against Germany, not the Soviet Union. France neither used her army to attack Germany while the bulk of her forces were in Poland, nor used her air force to bomb Germany while the bulk of her air force was away in Poland. The British RAF also did nothing. In the words of the historian Max Hastings: 'The Poles should have anticipated the passivity of their allies, but its cynicism was breath-taking.'[33]

On 28 September the Polish capital, Warsaw, surrendered to the Germans. The campaign continued with mopping-up operations by the German armed forces, the last recorded military action of the campaign taking place on 5 October. Germany took over the bulk of Poland, including Warsaw, with the Soviet Union taking the rest, as agreed by their secret pact.[34]

After the rapid fall of Poland, what would happen next was unknown, although decisive action by France or Britain was not something that was to be expected. The Allies waited apprehensively for what Hitler would do next. During the winter of 1939 Britain and France continued to build up their military armaments, which as yet did not match those of Germany. After the invasion of Poland there were months of inaction which became known as the 'phoney war'; this inaction led to a considerable drop in morale in both the Allies' civilian populations and their armed forces. As spring 1940 began, the British began to stir and planned to mine Norwegian waters to stop Germany accessing mine ores from Sweden that were essential for her munitions industry. But as usual, Hitler was one step ahead of Britain and France; in April 1940, when the British Navy laying mines off the coast of Norway discovered there was a lot of activity amongst the German fleet, they misread the situation and believed the German fleet was going to attack British merchant ships. So, the British Navy left Norwegian waters to protect home merchant vessels. While the British fleet was absent, the German Navy and air force embarked on a full invasion of Norway on 9 April 1940.[35]

The Allies had missed a golden opportunity to inflict a serious defeat on the Germans at sea. Poor intelligence had allowed the Allies, with far greater naval forces, to miss the German fleet which, together with its air force, had landed German forces on neutral Norway. A combination of audacity by Hitler and Allied arrogance that the Germans would never be able to invade Norway led to the end of the 'phoney war' and the first major armed clashes between Germany and the Allies. The Allied forces sent to Norway were of poor quality; the best British troops were in France. Those sent to Norway were amateurs of the Territorial Army. The British force was poorly armed, had few vehicles and not even proper maps. The British promised the neutral Norwegians large-scale support if they resisted the invasion, which Britain could not provide. The only real plan was to occupy the port of Narvik and hold it against the Germans, since this was the port used to ship iron ore from Sweden to Germany. By late April, with the campaign going nowhere, the British government informed the French they planned to evacuate their forces from Norway, much to the anger of the French. Britain also decided that the Norwegians were not to be informed of the British decision – a truly shameful act. The fighting around Narvik continued until late May, with the Allies capturing the port on 27 May 1940. Part of the French Foreign Legion that captured Narvik included Spanish Republican exiles. The Allies quickly realised they could not hold Narvik and they evacuated their forces by sea; this led to the Norwegian King and government sailing to Britain on a Royal Navy vessel on 7 June 1940. The loss of Norway led to the resignation of the British prime minister, Neville Chamberlain, who was replaced by Winston Churchill on 11 May 1940. On the same day as Chamberlain resigned, 10 May 1940, German forces began their attack on Holland and Belgium, which would lead to the invasion of France.[36]

The French commander Maurice Gamelin responded to the news by sending the French army and its British Allied force into Belgium. As the Germans were easily overcoming the weak Dutch army, a second, much stronger force was advancing through the Ardennes forest to attack the weak central part of the French armed forces through an area the Allies deemed impassable. The French military saw the 'Maginot Line' defences not only as border defences, but as something that would enable the French army to fight outside France. The German plan was that one force would conquer Holland and northern Belgium, and another was to make a feigned attack against the 'Maginot Line'. The decisive blow would be the force coming through the Ardennes forest, which contained most of the German tanks who were to crush the outnumbered French forces, cross the River Meuse and then swing north-west to the Channel ports and cut off the French and British forces in Belgium. Although over 400 Allied aircraft were used to try to destroy the bridges the Germans built to cross the River Meuse, the Germans were able to cross with relatively light losses. Once across the Meuse, the French command ordered a series of uncoordinated attacks on the Germans. These all failed, and, to the horror of the French, they realised the true destination of the German tanks. French counterattacks continued against the advancing Germans but never in enough numbers to be decisive. The reaction of the French civilian population was total panic; so many people left their homes that it impeded the French army's ability to move and deploy. As many as 8 million French civilians abandoned their homes in the next few months and fled from the Germans. It was the largest ever mass migration in western European history. After crossing the Meuse, the German army was constantly on the move, whereas the Allied forces seemed in slow motion in comparison. On the same day that German tanks reached the Channel coast, French prime minister Reynaud sacked Gamelin as the French Commander-in-Chief, replacing him with 73-year-old Maxime Weygand. On 28 May 1940 the Belgian king surrendered to the Germans while British forces had retreated to the port of Dunkirk to evacuate its forces by sea.[37]

The Dunkirk evacuation was announced to the British public on 29 May 1940. By a combination of the bravery of the Royal Navy, hundreds of small civilian boats and the RAF, more of the British forces were rescued and returned home than was ever thought possible. In all, 338,000 men were evacuated from Dunkirk, of which 229,000 were British. In France the war continued into June; the French forces fought better than in May, but they had lost too much already to be able to defeat the Germans. By 6 June the French frontline based on the Somme was breached, and four days later the French government left Paris, along with thousands of the city's inhabitants. On 14 June 1940 the German army entered Paris; two days later the French prime minister Reynaud broadcast to the nation that the French government were seeking armistice terms from the Germans and French forces should stop fighting. As many as 1.5 million French soldiers were captured and became prisoners. France had been defeated, not by superior forces but by a more dynamic opponent led by much more skilful commanders, who took opportunities when they arose. Morale was also a key element; the German armed forces fought with the conviction that they would win, while the French and British forces showed little and sometimes no conviction in their actions. French troops seem to have had little faith in their national leaders and generals and this undoubtedly affected their ability to resist the German forces. After their defeat, few French went into exile to continue the fight against the Germans, as had been the case with the Poles. On 22 June 1940 the French surrender was signed in the same railway carriage in which the Germans had been forced to sign their surrender at the end of the Great War.[38]

By the summer of 1939, Madge was in Paris with Wilhelm Holst and his two sons, helping Spanish Republican refugees. During the events that ultimately led to war and the early part of the Second World War, Madge remained in Paris. When it became too dangerous to live in Paris, she and Wilhelm relocated to the south of France, having earlier sent Wilhelm's sons home to Norway for greater safety. With the defeat of France, Madge, along with Wilhelm, would become part of the cloak-and-dagger world of underground Resistance to the German occupation, and she would continue to dedicate her life to opposing Fascism wherever she happened to be. She had come to Spain to oppose Fascism as an experienced nurse to help the Republican war effort, she had come to France to help Spanish Republican anti-Fascist exiles and now she was about to embark upon espionage activities against another Fascist enemy. Before we cover the story of Madge and Wilhelm from the summer of 1939 to the end of the Second World War, and also introduce into the story a Danish man called Thorkild Hansen who became Madge's third husband, we need to explore the underground world of British agents in enemy-occupied territory and the Resistance to the German occupation of France.

## Chapter 7

# France 1940–1944: Vichy, the Resistance and British Support

The prime minister of France resigned on 16 June 1940, and the following day the head of the new French government, the Great War hero Marshal Pétain, asked the Germans for an armistice. In Vichy, one month later the Third French Republic ended and Pétain took on almost dictatorial powers as head of the Vichy regime in southern France. The armistice was signed on 22 June and three days later France was effectively occupied and ruled by Germany. At first, the armistice terms seemed generous. The French Vichy government had jurisdiction in the southern unoccupied zone and in the German-occupied northern zone. The Vichy regime still controlled the French navy and colonial forces, although the national army was greatly reduced in size. Even the old German areas of Alsace and Lorraine were not claimed by Hitler. Pétain called it 'peace with honour' and many of the French people believed Pétain had saved them from a harsher peace.[1] Many French people looked simply to survive the occupation. As Kedward states:

> In general, the French turned further away from the war and concentrated single-mindedly on day-to-day survival and the search for some return to a semblance of acceptable normality.[2]

The two zones were separated by a military frontier. In the German zone French flags disappeared from public buildings and there was an evening curfew. French cars and lorries disappeared from the roads and German signs appeared throughout the zone. Unemployment rose, raw materials for industry were in short supply, food was strictly rationed and any French vehicles on the roads had to use gazogene burners instead of petrol. The 1.5 million French PoWs were kept by the Germans as a free labour force. Hitler annexed Alsace and Lorraine in August 1940, contrary to the armistice terms, and drove out any elements who were hostile to the Germanisation from those areas. To control the German zone there was an army of occupation, the French police and many willing French collaborators, and also the German counter-espionage agencies. These agencies included the military-controlled Abwehr and the Nazi Party-controlled Gestapo. In June 1944 the Abwehr was taken over by the Gestapo.[3]

In the early days of the regime, Pétain, the leader of Vichy France, was very popular and seen as the saviour of France. Although he held strong right-wing views, at this time he was seen as the leader who ruled with common sense and realism. The cult of 'The Marshal' saw thousands regularly greeting his appearance and millions having his image in their house. Blaming the weak governments of the 1930s for failing France, Pétain looked to introduce his own revolution. With the help of a former Socialist and right-wing Independent called Pierre Laval, Vichy France attempted to set up a new society that would avoid the weaknesses of the past. In October 1940 Pétain and Laval met with Hitler as heads of state, but Hitler lost interest once it became obvious Pétain was not offering him anything extra. Laval's policy towards Germany was to offer them more than the armistice terms in return for France having a stronger position in a German-occupied Europe. Laval was sacked in December 1940, but returned to power again in April 1942. During the course of 1941 Pétain came around to Laval's point of view.[4]

Pétain's Vichy regime passed a series of decrees and laws that idealised the family and peasant life; young people were to be mobilised to carry out work for the good of society and left-wing organisations were to be repressed. The slogan of the so-called 'National Revolution' was 'Labour, Family and Fatherland'. At first there was little opposition to the imposition of reactionary conservative policies. These policies helped to unify Vichy France and to reduce the impact of the military defeat. During 1942–1943 the peasantry received small subsidies and tax concessions from the Vichy government, were made immune from being conscripted for labour in Germany, and were happy with the regime. But as the regime forced the peasants to supply food for the towns and cities, and increased the conscription of peasants for forced labour in Germany, the relationship went from being strained to a total breakdown.[5]

Women were put on a pedestal by the Vichy regime; their number one duty was to have large families and stay at home. A typical Vichy view on womanhood is stated by Gustave Combes:

> The mother's place is in the home, not in the factory. The mother's task is to protect the home ... to give birth to strong and healthy children. The day she undertakes this mission – which will return her halo – France will regain her health and strength.[6]

Since the husbands of hundreds of thousands of women were PoWs or forced labourers in Germany, this ideal was impossible for many women in Vichy France even if they had wished to emulate this ideal. Women without children were paid a small subsidy to stay at home and not work. Employers were actively encouraged to sack women workers, even those whose husbands were PoWs. In schools, teachers were told to pass more boys than girls in their examinations. As early as the winter of 1941–1942 the subsidies for women to stay at home were inadequate compensation for not working. By 1943–1944 Laval was looking to force women into work to replace all the men lost working in Germany. Many women in both zones had been involved in the mass exodus fleeing from the German armies, and it fell mainly on them to set up home again. The burden of providing and caring for the family became harder as shortages of goods increased as the war progressed.[7]

Pétain had no political organisation to back him, unlike Hitler with the Nazi Party, or Franco and the *Falange* in Spain. In the Vichy zone, two attempts were made to set up a sort of Pétainist party; army veterans' associations were amalgamated into the *Légion des Anciens Combattants* and young men who would in the past be eligible for military service were sent to work camps for six to eight months. The radio and press were heavily censored and only the message of the Vichy regime reached its citizens. Legislation was passed against so-called 'dark forces' such as freemasons, Communists, trade unions and immigrant Jews. You could be dismissed from public office for belonging to a masonic lodge. Communism was illegal and any act of opposition was seen as the work of Communists. In August 1940, all trade unions were banned. Within two weeks of the setting up of the Vichy regime, immigrant Jews with French citizenship were stripped of their rights; a common slogan of

Vichy was 'France for the French'. The Vichy regime led by Pétain began as the saviour of France, with its collaboration with Hitler being widely accepted. However, as the true nature of the German occupation unfolded, the regime's popularity declined and resistance increased dramatically.[8]

The Vichy government viewed collaboration with Germany as a key part of their policy to transform French society. Collaboration was seen as the necessary policy to once again return France to being one of the major powers in Europe. The armistice and making peace with Germany were portrayed as the best choice for France. This being the case, anyone who opposed the peace and the collaboration with Germany was seen as anti-French, whether this was another country like Britain or those French who refused to make peace with Germany. Pétain saw collaboration as an economic choice, but many right-wing French supporters of Pétain were sympathetic to the ideals of Nazi Germany. Laval saw that Vichy must collaborate with the Germans, but try to negotiate the best it could for the benefit of France, or try to manage as well as possible any demands from Germany that were detrimental to France. During Laval's period out of office, he was replaced by Admiral Darlan. During 1941 the admiral almost committed France to fighting alongside Germany. He agreed to let them use Syrian airfields to attack British forces in Iran, and when the British attacked Vichy forces in Syria he almost agreed to co-belligerent status for Vichy forces. This would have meant that they were effectively fighting alongside German forces. Pétain rejected this. From the minute the armistice was signed, British forces and Free French forces attacked the old French colonial empire, taking control of many of the smaller countries. The British fleet sunk the main French fleet at Mers-el-Kébir off North Africa, which led to significant anti-British feeling for a time. Any defeats inflicted on British or Free French forces were greeted enthusiastically in the Vichy press, where the Free French were portrayed as traitors. The only French force to fight with the German army was a small volunteer force including many French Fascists which fought on the eastern front against the Communist Soviet Union.[9]

The German invasion of the Soviet Union in 1941 was supported ideologically by Vichy; however, it meant extra demands on France and living conditions began to worsen significantly. The German invasion of Russia led the Communist Party in France to begin armed resistance against both German occupation forces and the Vichy regime.

*France 1940–1944: Vichy, the Resistance and British Support*

Communist assassinations of German officials led to the execution of hostages by the Germans. On behalf of the Germans, Vichy officials chose hostages, arrested resisters, recruited labour for Germany and rounded up Jews for deportation. Some officials in the Vichy regime saw this as 'shielding' the French people from the excesses of the German occupiers, and also from openly Fascist French supporters of Nazism. Yet known French Fascists like Philippe Henriot, the Vichy propaganda minister, and Joseph Darnand, the head of police, held important positions in the Vichy regime. Darnand set up the *Milice*, Vichy's own armed police force, who were effectively involved in a civil war with the Resistance forces in 1944. Perhaps as many as 150,000 French were openly Fascist or pro-Nazi to the extent of wearing Nazi uniform and eating and dining with German officers, being a *Milice* member, a Vichy official, a volunteer fighting in Russia or a civilian supporter. Many more collaborators would have had no ideological hue, but for many French people, collaboration meant the desire to survive by any means possible. If this meant getting a German soldier boyfriend or a Vichy official who could get them extra food or stop them being deported to Germany to work, then so be it. Others may have been settling old scores by denouncing a neighbour or passing on information about the Resistance to the authorities for preferential treatment. But for the majority of the French population, the only seeming alternative to collaboration in the first years of the Vichy regime was *attentisme*, which basically meant waiting to see what happens.[10]

In the first two years of the German occupation and Vichy regime there were very few acts of resistance against the authorities. In November 1940 students in Paris were prevented from trying to lay wreaths to commemorate the Great War dead, and there was a major strike by miners in May 1941 in north-east France. Even in 1940, there were executions for resisting. Jacques Bonsergent was part of a group that clashed with German soldiers and one was struck. Although not the assailant, Bonsergent took the blame and was executed. Israel Karp, a Jew of Polish origin, waved a stick at a parade of German soldiers and was later executed. A young Communist called Pierre Roche cut a telephone cable, which led to his execution. In the same year five other men were executed for minor acts of sabotage. But the vast majority of the French people, although unhappy with the situation, were not willing to oppose it. The 50-year-old French General Charles de Gaulle broadcast from London on 18 June 1940 on the BBC, encouraging those French people who wished to resist the occupation to join him in London. At this stage, the broadcast had little effect and he was seen as a voice 'crying in the wilderness'. Similarly, the first French 'resisters' often were alone and had no knowledge of any other 'resisters'. The first signs of resistance were pamphlets and news sheets encouraging the population to resist the authorities, usually at this stage by acts of sabotage. These acts could include something as easy and crude as turning road signs so that German troops went in the wrong direction. This progressed to the hiding of armaments and, eventually, to armed resistance. As the Resistance groups grew in size and began to communicate with each other, aid from abroad was provided by the Free French and by the Special Operations Executive (SOE).[11]

Many people who became resisters in the Vichy zone belonged to persecuted groups such as trade unionists, Communists, masons, Jews and women. Towns and cities became the first places for resistance, since in the early years of the Vichy regime the peasants were given preferential treatment by the government so that they would oppose and denounce any Resistance activities in the countryside. In a city or town, it was also much easier to find access to, and to hide, a printer to print clandestine information. It was also easier in towns and cities to escape the authorities, using a combination of local knowledge and by running away into labyrinthine small side streets, particularly in places like Montpellier, Toulouse and Marseille, which still had very narrow medieval streets. In January 1941, a paper called *Resistance* appeared in Paris, but only a month later those involved began to be arrested. The first actual pamphlet suggesting any sort of resistance appeared as early as July 1940. Some people resisted quietly by listening secretly to the BBC News; if discovered you could be fined and even deported. Other resisters who did not oppose the authorities but refused to follow its orders included individuals who refused to report for labour in Germany and hid from the police. Other individuals would help by providing 'safe houses' for Resistance fighters, and there were doctors who were willing to treat wounded Resistance members, and individuals who could forge documents so that the Resistance could travel more easily and hide their identity. Smugglers sprang up who would smuggle groups or individuals into and out of occupied France and into neighbouring neutral countries like Switzerland and Spain.[12]

*France 1940–1944: Vichy, the Resistance and British Support*

The Germans classed any resistance as acts of terrorism, so the normal rules of war did not apply. Vichy authorities classed resisters as political opponents and portrayed them as dominated by foreign powers. The early Resistance bands were poorly armed and lacked unity. Only one political party – the Communists – had any sort of structure and leadership and control of Resistance groups. In 1942 the Free French decided they needed to link up with the Resistance and help to supply them with arms and to become more unified and organised. Jean Moulin was sent to France and worked to unite the various Resistance groups. By the time of his betrayal and death in July 1943, he had had some success; he also persuaded them to accept the leadership of De Gaulle. In return, De Gaulle sent a message to the Resistance groups to show that he was committed to restoring a democratic French government. The Free French and the British provided money to arm the Resistance, but in return the Resistance groups had to agree to be led by Gaullist or British agents. The Communists ignored this and began to assassinate German officers, which led to the shooting of masses of hostages by the Germans. The Communists' refusal to accept British or Free French leadership led them to be starved of money and weapons. Nevertheless, efforts to unify the disparate Resistance groups with the Free French forces outside France led to the formation of the *Forces françaises de l'intérieur* in February 1944, which was to cause the Germans many problems during the D-Day landings in June of that year.[13]

In June 1942, the Vichy first minister, Laval, agreed a scheme with the Germans whereby some of the French PoWs would be returned to France and in return more French workers would be sent to Germany. By February 1943, this labour in Germany had become compulsory and the numbers requested by the Germans increased with each request. More and more Frenchmen ordered to work in Germany failed to turn up, and either went into hiding or joined the Resistance. Laval had urged his prefects (regional administrators) to comply fully with German requests. This was also the case in rounding up naturalised Jews: over 15,000 men, women and children were put into rail trucks and handed over to the German SS. Immigrant Jews had earlier been put into concentration camps in inhumane conditions before being sent to the East to be murdered. The Vichy regime also made no attempt to intervene in the rounding up of Jews in the occupied zone, where technically they had some jurisdiction. The idea that the Vichy government was providing some sort of 'shield-like' protection to workers and Jews from the occupying Germans was no more than an illusion. On 11 November 1942, after the Allied invasion of North Africa, the Germans occupied the Vichy zone. They ordered the disbandment of the French army in France and the French fleet in Toulon was scuttled. What tiny bit of independence Vichy had had now disappeared. The reactions of lower level Vichy officials to the new situation varied; some became openly Fascist and increased efforts to hunt down the Resistance and those in hiding from forced labour. However, more officials, possibly sensing that the Germans were losing the war, either turned a blind eye to Resistance activities and labour avoiders, or openly assisted them.[14]

Founded in January 1943, the *Milice* were seen as the paramilitary vanguard of *Pétainisme*. At first, any attempts to arm them and use them to fight Resistance groups were opposed by most Vichy prefects. But, armed instead by the Germans, they began to hunt down Resistance groups and by January 1944 were operating in the former German zone as well working alongside German troops. The war against the Resistance groups in 1943, and particularly in 1944, took on the qualities of a civil war. By 1943 De Gaulle was the acknowledged leader of both the Free French and the Resistance in France, which was moving towards full-on armed resistance to the German occupying forces. The transformation of the Resistance to German occupation was caused by the compulsory orders for more French labour in Germany. This led to more and more people fleeing to the countryside to avoid this compulsory order. Those individuals who refused to work in Germany were often protected by Resistance groups, while others joined the armed struggle. These countryside Resistance groups became known as the *Maquis*, after the Corsican name for scrubland.[15]

Women played a major role in the Resistance movement and were some of the first to oppose the Germans or Vichy government. As early as 1940, women were protesting for the release of husbands who were PoWs. This progressed to protesting about shortages, in particular, food. Women were involved in all aspects of Resistance activities, although few were leaders and only a minority took part in actual fighting and sabotage activities. Women resisters tended to be young, because young women had more freedom to move away from home than married and older women. Girls as young as 13 and 14 ran messages and helped to supply the *Maquis*. When on clandestine missions, women had the added complication of finding accommodation; many single women would be refused a room because it was seen as morally suspect for a woman to travel alone. In addition, if German soldiers or local police were showing an interest in them, were they suspicious of what the woman was doing or was it just a physical attraction? Women ran 'safe houses', deciphered codes, acted as typists at clandestine meetings, distributed leaflets and pamphlets, and printed pamphlets and newspapers. Many were imprisoned, sent to concentration camps, tortured and executed.[16]

There were many brave women who served in the Resistance, but brief biographies of three will give examples of their heroic efforts in opposing the Germans and Vichy regimes. Lucienne Guezennec joined the 'Combat' Resistance group and helped to print its newspaper. She injured an arm badly in the printing press but returned to work quickly because she was needed. When the secret printing facilities were raided, she was the sole survivor. As she was wounded, she was taken to hospital, where she was rescued by the Resistance. France Pejot and her sister joined the Communist Resistance while continuing to manage the family store in Lyon. Secret documents were hidden at the family apartment. She avoided arrest several times and prevented male comrades from being arrested by her coolness, quick thinking and acting skills. But her luck ran out after her third arrest when she was deported to the concentration camp of Ravensbrück. Evelyne Sullerot was 17 years old in 1940 and had to look after her two younger siblings. She also assisted her father in his psychiatric clinic in Compiègne as well as taking part in Resistance activities. She hid Jews and fugitives at her father's house and later assisted a *Maquis* unit in the Orléans region.[17]

The countryside peasantry, who had at first favoured the Vichy regime, had found its crops seized by the German army and many found themselves economically ruined. By 1944 they were not immune from being conscripted as forced labour in Germany. So, in the countryside, farmers and peasants now sympathised and helped the *Maquis* and some even joined them. Most *Maquis* units were poorly armed and were rarely supplied by either the British or Gaullist agents. Those *Maquis* forces that became known to British or Gaullist agents and were willing to accept their leadership received arms and radio equipment. The *Maquis* worked best in small groups in sabotage operations like blowing up railway lines. Attempts to fight the Germans in large numbers in a pitched battle led to two disastrous actions in 1944, where over 1,200 *Maquisards*

*The Nurse Who Became a Spy*

were killed. In spring 1944, the Germans took over from local Vichy officials to hunt down the Resistance and labour dodgers. By this stage, the Resistance had infiltrated the French police, local civil service and other public services.[18]

The only French forces on whom the Germans could rely were the *Milice* and French Fascists. Before the Allied D-Day landings in France in June 1944, the Resistance received the coded messages from the BBC broadcasts and began to try to create havoc behind the German frontlines. Railway lines were dug up or blown up, trees were felled to block roads, electric cables were cut and German forces moving across the country were continually ambushed. Allied Commander-in-Chief Eisenhower stated that the Resistance forces had helped to divert many German forces from deploying in the frontlines against Allied forces. In some cases, the German forces who were constantly ambushed and slowed down reacted with atrocities, the worst being at Oradour-sur-Glane, where an SS unit murdered 600 men, women and children. With the liberation of France by Allied forces, including units of Free French, the Vichy government was moved to Germany. There were some atrocities by the Resistance forces as they took over villages, towns and cities with collaborators and *Milice* being executed or publicly humiliated before the Free French took over. De Gaulle was seen as the saviour and leader of France and, on 26 August 1944, he walked the length of the Champs-Élysées to show that Paris was liberated and was the capital of the country once again. Resistance groups accepted De Gaulle's authority and any fear that Communist and *Maquis* groups would set up an alternative left-wing state were proved to be false. After the war, the leaders of Vichy France were put on trial and sentenced to death, with only Pétain sentenced to life imprisonment instead because of his great age.[19]

British support for the French Resistance and the *Maquis* was channelled through various security, intelligence and espionage bodies, and irregular armed personnel. At the start of the Second World War, Britain had two main intelligence security organisations: MI5 and MI6. During the war, a bewildering array of organisations were established for various purposes, but mostly to support the French Resistance. Two significant new bodies set up during the war were MI9 and the SOE. The SOE and MI9 became both famous and notorious because of their operatives' bravery and heroic acts, and their willingness to undertake actions at huge personal risk, which often resulted in death.

## France 1940–1944: Vichy, the Resistance and British Support

SOE and MI9 were also known for their 'cloak-and-dagger' activities, the improvisation and amateurism of many of their operations and the use of a vast array of innovative gadgets. The world of James Bond and his gadget man 'Q' is not a world away from some SOE/MI9 agents and the boffins who designed devices to support them in the field! During the course of the war the number of agents grew, as did the headquarters and support staff in Britain and the buildings they occupied. Organisations divided and sub-divided into a baffling number of sections, each with an acronym reflecting a specific area of responsibility. The proliferation of the security, intelligence, espionage and irregular warfare services often led to overlapping of activities and disagreements over areas of activity, particularly between the established pre-war organisations and the newer ones. There were also often dilemmas in the field as to which Resistance and *Maquis* groups to support; Free French only or other groups like the Communists, or even foreign groups like the Spanish Republicans.[20]

The two pre-war intelligence and security agencies were MI5 and MI6. The home intelligence service, MI5, was founded in 1909 and was one half of the Secret Service Bureau. During the Great War it played a major role in capturing many German spies in Britain. Post-war and into the 1920s, the service was reduced to save money and only started to grow again in the 1930s to counter internal Communist and Fascist subversive activities. During the Second World War it played a key role in combatting enemy espionage, intercepting German communications and replying with false information. MI6 was the foreign arm of the British intelligence and security services and the other half of the Secret Service Bureau. During the Great War it worked with Army Intelligence and had a network of spies in occupied Belgium who were able to pass on information such as German troop movements. In 1920 it became known as the Secret Intelligence Service, although during the Second World War it was known as MI6. In the inter-war years, it set up a code and cipher facility at Bletchley Park. During the Second World War the organisation grew rapidly and had agents gathering intelligence throughout occupied Europe. At Bletchley Park, MI6 played a key role in winning the war with its work of cracking the German military codes. These very professional organisations had a key role in intelligence and information, but it was not their role to take the fight to the enemy or to help rescue British and Allied military personnel trapped in enemy territory.[21]

MI9 was founded in December 1939 and was headed by Norman Crockatt, who had served with distinction in the Great War. Its key role was to help the escape of British PoWs and help those British, Commonwealth and Allied military personnel trapped in enemy territory to return to Britain. It also gathered information from returning military personnel and from agents on the ground, as well as from captured enemy PoWs. MI9a dealt with captured enemy personnel and MI9b dealt with intelligence, evasion and escapes. The training of MI9 agents, the individuals who became agents, the use of women as agents and the use of amazing gadgets very much mirrored what the SOE was doing.[22]

In July 1940 the new British prime minister, Winston Churchill, handed over to Labour politician Hugh Dalton the management of the newly created SOE, with the instruction to 'set Europe ablaze'. The aim of the SOE was to support local resisters to oppose the occupying forces by sending in supplies and agents to equip, train and plan sabotage activities with them. Although Churchill was in favour of setting up the SOE, the established intelligence agencies saw the ethos of the SOE and its agents as 'amateur, dangerous and bogus' and a threat to their own agents. At first, the SOE was a small secret organisation based at 64 Baker Street in London. During the course of the war the organisation grew enormously and acquired many buildings both in Britain and abroad. It had its own training schools, airfields, code and deciphering facilities, research and development centres where many strange devices were developed to aid agents with communication and sabotage. They acquired so many buildings SOE was jokingly referred to as 'Stately 'Omes of England'. The French section of the SOE was called F section. During the course of the war F section sent over 400 agents to France, of whom around fifty were women.[23]

From its foundation in 1940 until its dissolution in 1946, the SOE was involved in clandestine operations throughout Europe, in North Africa and Abyssinia, and in Asia. Its operatives had both spectacular successes and disasters and were quite ruthless in supporting guerrilla or partisan factions that they believed were best able to oppose the enemy. Famous SOE-inspired actions included the blowing up of the railway viaduct of Gorgopotamos in Greece, which linked Thessaloniki and Athens and its port. In Czechoslovakia, Czechs trained by the SOE assassinated Reinhard Heydrich, who was the leading Nazi official in Czechoslovakia. A major action in Norway was the destruction of the German heavy

## France 1940–1944: Vichy, the Resistance and British Support

water facility which put back potential German development of nuclear weapons. In France, the Pessac power station was destroyed. Before D-Day in 1944 the SOE dropped 'Jedburgh' teams of three men – two officers and a wireless operator – to link and lead Resistance and *Maquis* forces in causing mayhem behind the German frontlines, and delaying reinforcements reaching the front. They accomplished this successfully. On the reverse side, the SOE was criticised for always wanting to act for action's sake. Indiscretions by SOE agents and badly planned actions led, on occasion, to the deaths of Resistance fighters and, more often, civilian helpers. For a time in Holland, German intelligence was able to capture many SOE agents, civilian helpers and Resistance fighters because security checks and coded warnings were ignored. Generally, the SOE tended to support non-Communist guerrillas; however, in Yugoslavia, where the Communists proved to be the most effective opposition to German occupation, the SOE had no qualms about supporting them with arms and agents.[24]

The SOE had no recruiting policy as such; sometimes individuals were simply invited to join. These tended to be people with previous experience or training in irregular warfare, or who had been members of the intelligence services, but every person who served in SOE was a volunteer. Most SOE operatives came from the business and professional world rather than the upper classes. The quality of the agents varied from first-class to poor, and included a number of oddballs. The volunteers needed to be British subjects by birth (although this was not strictly enforced) and a key attribute for service in France was the ability to speak near-native French; if you could not pass yourself off as a local then discovery and capture were very likely. Many agents in France were, like Madge, people already residing in France.[25]

All SOE agents sent out from Britain to France received some sort of training. Until 1943 this began with a few weeks of physical and military training; later this was replaced by a psychological assessment of new volunteers. After preliminary training or assessment, volunteers undertook a more intensive training programme of several weeks' duration, concentrating on irregular warfare. This training included hand-to-hand combat, map-reading, Morse code, use of pistols and sub-machine guns, how to creep up and kill someone with a knife, and sabotage techniques, including the use of explosives. Trainees were taught how to blend in with the locals and not draw attention to themselves. Training was given on coding and ciphering, and the importance of security. Throughout training the volunteers were expected to speak French most of the time. Those who spoke English in their sleep or while drunk, or merely forgot, were removed from the process. Some agents received specialist training as wireless operators, others were given parachute training and some were taught forgery and burglary techniques by criminals! After several months, the volunteers were coming to the end of their training. At this stage they were instructed about the German counter-espionage services and local police forces. They were also dragged out of bed in the middle of the night and interrogated for hours; at least one agent said this part of the training saved them in the field. A captured agent was expected to say nothing for forty-eight hours. This was deemed enough time for all their contacts to be able to relocate and cover their tracks; after that the agent was free to say anything. Once an agent had passed the course and was ready to be sent to France, they were given the appropriate clothing, an alias, false papers and a backstory, which they had to know off by heart.[26]

British based SOE agents travelled to France in three ways. One way was by sea, which was done in a variety of ways: submarine, fast torpedo boats, local fishing vessels and sailing boats. The second was by air; the agent could either parachute down to the destination or rendezvous point, or smaller planes could land at a designated improvised runway and drop the operative off in France. The final way to enter France was on foot from neutral Spain, often crossing the Pyrenees. The SOE were dependent on support from the Royal Navy and RAF, on whose list of priorities the SOE was quite often very low. In time, the SOE were to have their own small force of planes, which they used not only to take agents to France but also to extract agents and important individuals. The planes were also used to supply agents in the field and Resistance groups.[27]

Before he or she arrived in in France, the SOE agent would have been told the area of the country in which they would operate. This area of operations was known as a Circuit or Network and could cover a large area, sometimes hundreds of miles. Each Circuit or Network had a code name, called after a profession or job, so that if wireless communication were intercepted it would be difficult for the enemy to understand. All members of the Circuit or Network had code names and false identities and all communications were in code. A typical SOE group in France would include at least three agents. Firstly, a leader who planned the activities of the group, arranged for arms drops, made links with Resistance groups, planned and carried out acts of sabotage, and looked for potential civilian recruits. Secondly, a courier who travelled around the area of operations, usually on a bicycle, passing on messages and instructions and often explosives. This role was a good one for a female agent as it was common to see women travelling around the cities and countryside looking for food and supplies. The third member was the wireless operator who sent coded messages to London, using Morse code, to request arms, a pick-up by plane etc. This was a perilous occupation; the wireless sets were bulky and difficult to disguise when on the move, and the aerials were huge and could easily be spotted. If a wireless operator either spent too long sending a message or stayed in one location for too long, they were likely to be discovered by enemy intelligence.[28]

Any SOE agent captured by the counter-espionage forces of the Germans could expect little mercy. Captured agents faced torture to force them to reveal the details of their Circuit or Network, and then either execution or a slow death from starvation and overwork in a concentration camp. A few agents survived the concentration camps and were liberated by the advancing Allied troops in 1945. For some agents, their cover story was so good and the agent so convincing that they were released. Others were helped by some rather dumb policing: one wireless operator, caught red-handed while travelling, claimed the wireless was a Dictaphone, which was believed. Also, Vichy or French police would occasionally deliberately look the other way and pretend they had seen nothing. But all SOE volunteers were aware of what would happen to them if they were captured by the enemy.[29]

One aspect of the SOE activity that has caught the popular imagination is the mass of quirky weapons and gadgets. To look at them in detail would be outside the scope of this story, but we will look at three to give a flavour of SOE ingenuity. Wireless sets were always difficult to disguise because they were big and heavy. To try to help wireless operatives in the field, the SOE boffins devised ways of hiding the wireless in bundles of faggots (sticks), or hiding it in a portable gramophone or even in a vacuum cleaner carrying-case. Agents were advised that they could overcome the problem of hiding the very large aerial by hiding it among tree branches and tendrils, and wrapping rope around it from clothes lines and sash window cords.[30] SOE agents used camouflage to hide weapons and explosives. Plaster fruit was used for transporting ammunition and plastic explosives. Plaster logs containing hidden weapons were left in wooded areas covered with moss. Plaster coal was used to contain plastic explosive: once in position a fuse was added, coal dust was used to hide it and then it was ignited.[31] A final ingenious invention was a tube of face cream that, if spread thinly on any window, made it frosted, so that an agent could not be seen from the outside.[32]

The SOE employed women in large numbers, mostly in Britain. They worked as cipher operators, base wireless personnel, clerks, drivers and telephone operators, or in the various training schools. A small number of women were used in the field and by the SOE in France. Most female agents were either couriers or wireless operators; very few were involved in sabotage and armed actions. One SOE operative, Pearl Withington, commanded 2,000 *Maquisards*. After the war she was awarded the MBE, a civil award, which she sent back, commenting that she had done nothing civil![33] Many women volunteers were members of First Aid Nursing Yeomanry, the name for the Women's Transport Service before they joined the SOE. Many of the women who were sent to France were given Women's Auxiliary Air Force officer commissions. Most of the volunteers tended to be middle-class or came from professional families, but this was not true of all of them. The key factor was the ability to speak French and to be able to blend in with the native population. Of the forty female SOE agents (Foot lists fifty-two female agents) who were sent to France, fourteen were killed.[34]

Several of the women who served in the SOE have rightly become well-known and their heroic efforts celebrated in print. These include the likes of Odette Sansom, Noor-un-Nissa Inayat Khan and Violette Szabo, to name only three. The stories of three of the lesser-known and first SOE operatives in France will give a picture of what these brave women did as SOE agents in France.

Virginia Hall was born in America in 1906. She attended some of the best schools in America and in Europe, and was a talented linguist. In 1933 she lost the lower part of one leg in a shooting accident. She was sent to France in August 1941 as an SOE agent and a journalist for the *New York Post*. She made her base in Lyon where, from a bar, she organised supplies to the Resistance, assisted new agents, helped escaping and evading Allied soldiers, recruited locals who were willing to resist the occupation, and increased the number of 'safe houses' to hide wanted people. When the Germans occupied the Vichy territory in

*France 1940–1944: Vichy, the Resistance and British Support*

November 1942 she fled to Spain. On her return to Britain she was sent to Spain to gather information for the escape lines. She became bored with the lack of action and was once again assigned to work in France, this time as a member of the American Office of Strategic Services – the American equivalent of the SOE. In Spain she had been trained as a wireless operator, and after returning from there she landed again in France in March 1944. Initially she served in central France then moved to the south where she linked up with a 'Jedburgh' team and the local *Maquis*.[35]

Yvonne Rudellat was born near Paris in 1897, moving to London in her teens. In May 1942 she volunteered to join the SOE. Her first trainer called her 'little old lady'. She landed secretly in France in July 1942 and took a train on her own to Lyon, where she met Virginia Hall, and then left for Paris, finally arriving in Tours. Here she became a courier and cycled all around the area distributing messages, explosives and looking for suitable places where planes could land or parachutists could be dropped. She also delivered messages while travelling on the train to Paris and Bordeaux. In a three-month spell in 1943 she was involved in receiving twenty parachute drops and also in sabotage activities. In June 1943 her luck ran out when she was trying to escape by car after the arrest of two Canadian agents. She was shot in the head and was treated by the local hospital but was moved to Fresnes prison when still very weak. Here she was interrogated by the Gestapo; she exaggerated her confusion. Rudellat was then sent to the concentration camp at Ravensbrück in August 1944, and in March 1945 was transferred to the Belsen death camp. She was still alive when the Allies arrived, but was too weak to tell them who she was and died in April 1945.[36]

Blanche Charlet was born in Belgium in 1898 and fled to Britain when her country was invaded. She was one of the first four women volunteers of the SOE, her excellent French being a major factor in her recruitment. She was landed by sea into southern France in September 1942, but, finding no contacts, she travelled to Lyon where she met Virginia Hall. Here she was assigned to a new network. In October 1942 she was arrested along with the wireless operator. After interrogation they were sent to the prison at Castres from where she managed to escape with another female escape lines agent after help from a Yugoslav cleaner at the prison. They were taken in for two months by Benedictine monks, who even put them in touch with an escape line.

Twice they unsuccessfully attempted to cross into Spain. Blanche ended up returning to Paris in January 1944 and then went back to Lyon, where she did some courier work until the SOE arranged her return to Britain via Brittany in April 1944.[37]

Critics of the SOE saw them as a band of amateurs who achieved little and often caused severe reprisals by German occupying forces. SOE agents did receive some training in how to survive in occupied territory and how to carry out sabotage and espionage activities; however, this training was often inadequate for the conditions they faced. Most agents knew the dangers they would encounter and were willing to take the associated risks. In France the majority of the population at first had little interest in supporting the SOE in opposing the occupying authorities, whether German or Vichy. When Germany was in the ascendant between 1941 and 1943, being betrayed was a constant danger for an SOE agent. Only in 1944, when it looked like the Axis forces were losing the war, did the majority of the French population support the overthrow of the German occupation (although this was mostly a passive opposition). In all, around 400–500 SOE agents were sent to France, and of these 126 were killed.[38] Max Hastings makes this comment on the role of the SOE in Europe in the Second World War:

> Yet SOE's operations were important then, and seem justified now, by their moral impact and contribution to fomenting insecurity, tension and sometimes murderous hysteria among German occupying forces.[39]

## Chapter 8

# Resisting Fascism Again: Madge, Wilhelm and Thorkild: France 1940–1944

In the waiting room at Marseille airport a variety of people are waiting for the next German DLH flight to Lisbon. There are French, German and Portuguese businessmen, German officers, some with their wives, others with their girlfriends. There is also a shadowy figure who does not talk but silently watches the other passengers. A lone, well-dressed woman waits with this group for the flight. On the outside she – Madge – is confident and sociable, speaking French fluently and German well. Inwardly she is very aware of the secret messages sewn into her fur coat; secret messages for the British secret services, which, if discovered, would lead to her imprisonment, torture and almost certain death. Madge is travelling on a Norwegian passport; although Norway is now a conquered country and part of the German empire, the Nazis see Norwegians as ethnically Aryan like them, and so they despise them less than they despise other races. The travel documents are fake and so are Madge's reasons for going to Lisbon. Once on the plane, Madge continues to play her role of a rich Norwegian woman travelling to Lisbon for health reasons, or whatever cover story she has been given. On landing in Portugal, Madge follows the instructions given to her and meets up with her contacts. The lining of her coat is unpicked, and the messages passed on to the British secret services.

This was just one of the activities in which Madge Addy/Holst became involved during the German occupation of France and the rule of the Vichy regime.

Piecing together Madge's role in intelligence and Resistance work was a difficult process and, in some cases, assumptions had to be made.

Madge left no letters from this period, did not keep a diary, was never interviewed about her activities, and features in no newspaper article; almost the perfect spy. But there is enough information to piece together her story. She is mentioned very briefly in several books written about the SOE in France, MI9 and the Garrow-O'Leary escape line. Her second husband, Wilhelm Holst, has two SOE files which contain information about Madge. In the *Service Historique de la Défense* archive there is a brief but enlightening file on Madge's wartime activities. Madge appears in the recommendations files for an OBE, which lists briefly her wartime accomplishments. After her death in 1970, her OBE was sold, along with some personal papers whose contents were briefly described by the auction house. Unfortunately, the personal papers are no longer accessible.

Madge Addy was not your typical special agent. She was not recruited by an intelligence agency in London, neither did she volunteer in Britain to serve abroad. She was not trained in Britain by the SOE or any other intelligence agency. She was not directly involved in sabotage or armed activities. In Britain, MI6, the established intelligence agency, tended to look down on the young upstarts of the SOE and MI9 as amateurs who might get in the way of their information-gathering. The head of MI6 espionage abroad, Sir Claude Dansey,[1] demanded little contact between each organisation's agents. In the field this was regularly ignored, and members of the different organisations often worked together.[2]

Madge began her Resistance activities in 1940 by helping Ian Garrow to find suitable people to help British soldiers and officers to escape from Marseille. One of this group of people was Thorkild Hansen, who later became her third husband. Another was Nancy Fiocca, better known as Nancy Wake, who became the most decorated woman SOE operative in the war. In the initial stages of planning the escape line to Spain there was no input from British Intelligence. At first, possibly unbeknown to Madge, her husband Wilhelm Holst had become an SOE agent. Madge was to support her husband's and Ian Garrow's activities by acting as a courier to and from Lisbon. She was taught how to use to use secret inks to write messages. In Marseille she housed agents at their house, dealt with secret correspondence and answered the phone. Madge worked for two SOE networks led by Holst: Billet and Alexandre, becoming his second-in-command with the rank of lieutenant. When Holst was ill and hospitalised, Madge led the network. Her role changed during the course of the occupation of France from brave amateur to full time paid P2 agent. Her aliases or code names included Mrs Oats, which was probably the name on her Norwegian passport, and *Billette*. She acted as a courier and messenger for a variety of British intelligence agencies, carrying messages and receiving replies, and regularly returning with large sums of money to support the running of the escape lines and SOE networks. She was involved with the MI9 escape lines, helping to get Allied armed forces personnel (mainly airmen) into Spain. Madge helped to set up probably the most famous escape line: the Garrow-O'Leary line. While working on the Garrow-O'Leary escape line she worked with the legendary Albert Guernisse, whose alias was Pat O'Leary. She also helped to setup the Pierre-Jacques line, which was an SOE escape line to get agents in trouble out of France. Here she worked with her future third husband, Thorkild Hansen, whom she knew from 1940 in the early days of helping Ian Garrow. The joint head of the Pierre-Jacques line, along with Hansen, was a flamboyant character known as Pierre Lalande, whose real name was Guido Zembsch-Schreve. For four years, Madge opposed the Vichy regime and the German occupation, commenting, 'I believe in taking the war into the enemy's camp.'[3]

In August 1939 Madge left Britain to join her lover Wilhelm Holst in Paris, where he was living with his two sons. Since leaving Spain, Holst had continued with his humanitarian work, which included working for the CSI, the Norwegian aid committee and the Quakers. Working from an office in Paris, he was organising relief for Spanish Republican refugees. Madge would almost certainly have been involved with Holst and others in providing aid to the refugees. Her affection for the Spanish Republicans was strongly evoked in her letters written from Spain. When war broke out in September 1939, Holst and Madge were working for two organisations providing aid to Spanish Republican refugees: the Quakers and a Swedish relief organisation.[4] During the so-called 'phoney war' period, from September 1939 to March 1940, little changed in Madge's and Wilhelm's day-to-day lives; however, two major decisions were made in their personal lives, one with tragic consequences. Now both divorced from their first partners, Madge and Wilhelm married. Secondly, and fatefully, Wilhelm decided to send his sons back to his ex-wife and daughter in Norway for safety because a major clash between Germany and France was expected at any moment. In April 1940, Germany invaded Norway and Holst's two sons, aged only 15 and 17, joined the Norwegian Army. Tragically, they were both killed in battles around Honefoss in April 1940.[5] In a letter to his friend Nini written a year later, Holst writes about his sense of loss; he was finding it difficult to overcome his feelings of grief and felt that their deaths were a cruel blow and so unnecessary, but he goes onto comment that many Norwegians are suffering like him.[6] The following month the German armed forces invaded the Low Countries and by May 1940 they had invaded France. With the war going disastrously for the Allies and the Germans' capture of Paris seeming a certainty, Madge and Wilhelm made the decision to move south and take up residence in Marseille.[7]

As the victorious German army swept all before them, a mass of French refugees headed south away from them. Among these fleeing millions were Madge and Wilhelm, but also many Allied and British service personnel who were keen to avoid becoming PoWs. In 1940 Marseille was a major port city situated on the southern Mediterranean coast of France. Refugees and weary soldiers arriving in the city were fed by Red Cross volunteers and a Vichy government canteen. Marseille had suffered little in the war with Germany and, except for the influx of refugees, seemed little changed. There were no longer British ships in the harbour and the consulate had left, and German-Italian armistice staff had taken up residence in the main hotel. Besides Marseille's fame as a port city, it was infamous for the Le Vieux Port district around the dock area; an area of labyrinthine streets controlled by gangsters who also ran the black market, particularly in food.[8]

The new Vichy regime looked to round up all Allied military personnel who had fled into their zone. Captured British military personnel in Marseille were imprisoned in an old Foreign Legion fort called St Jean. For those new inmates who could read French, the Foreign Legion motto over the gate reading 'You have asked for death. I will give it to you' was not a very welcome greeting. Officers were released on parole if they reported for roll call once a week; they were issued with ration cards and allowed to come and go as they pleased. Many sold their ration cards and lived in modest hotels. The American consulate was happy to help any British citizen in trouble. However, in the very early days of the defeat of France, two Scotsmen were willing to organise the shelter, feeding and escape from Marseille of British and Allied personnel, with support from an ever-growing number of locals and people of all nationalities. These two Scotsman were Ian Garrow and Donald Caskie.[9]

Donald Caskie was a minister of the Church of Scotland and had a church in Paris when the Germans invaded France. He was born in Scotland in 1902 and studied at Edinburgh University; first gaining an Arts degree, then studying for the church. His first post as a minister was in Edinburgh. He was to take up a further two ministerial posts in Scotland before moving to Paris. He was well-travelled and had visited Libya, Egypt, the Holy Land, America and Canada. As a minister in Paris, Caskie was known for his sermons denouncing Fascism and the dictators, so, with the German army advancing on Paris, he fled south and ended up in Marseille. On his arrival, Caskie reported encountering a city in turmoil, with many wounded, starving and desperate British soldiers wandering the streets. Caskie went to the American consulate, where he met the British consul, who asked him if he could help these soldiers. Caskie went to the local French police to ask for help in finding accommodation for distressed British civilians; however, it was made clear that he would be closed down if they found he was sheltering British soldiers. He was given the empty British Seaman's Mission at 46 Rue de Forbin; a large building close to the notorious Le Vieux Port harbour district known for its lawlessness. A sign over the door of the refuge said, 'Open to British civilians and seamen only'.[10]

Once the refuge had been made habitable, Caskie began to take in soldiers. Secret spaces were created in the fabric of the building, so that when the police searched it, they found nothing. Through contacts he had made with criminal elements, the American consulate and brave local individuals, Caskie was able to overcome problems like dressing the soldiers in civilian clothes and getting rid of the uniforms, feeding large bodies of men, getting identity cards, forged documents and being able to find other 'safe houses' for the soldiers to hide in, once the refuge was full. Locals provided cash for the upkeep of the men in Caskie's care. According to Caskie, twenty to twenty-five men a week escaped to their freedom, most across the border into Spain. The final total probably numbered in the hundreds. The refuge, and the soldiers and airman it housed, became part of an organised escape line called the Pat O'Leary line, which, at its height, involved hundreds of helpers. Eventually disaster struck when a British traitor named names, implicating Caskie, and he was given one week to leave Marseille. He also had to settle a suitable distance away from the city in lieu of two years' imprisonment.[11]

Caskie settled in Grenoble, where he worked at the university as a teacher of English while continuing to preach to local British residents and interned British military personnel. He claims that he helped British PoWs to escape from *La Turbie* prison by smuggling in items such as scissors and knives. His luck ran out in 1943 and he was imprisoned in poor conditions in various prisons in France and Italy until the liberation of Paris in August 1944, when he was residing in the city's notorious Fresnes prison. After the war he was an awarded an OBE and in 1957 the Queen laid the founding stone of a new Scottish church in Paris. He returned to Scotland and died there in 1983.[12]

Madge was in Marseille during the period that Caskie was running the 'Seamen's Refuge'. There is no definite evidence to link the two, or that their paths even crossed, but this does not make this unlikely. Madge was one of the earliest resisters; as we shall see, she had strong links with Ian Garrow. In Marseille in the early days of the French defeat there was a small group of people who knew each other and were determined to do what they could to resist the occupying forces, be they Vichy or German. Caskie was one of these individuals and so was Madge, so with such a small group of liked-minded individuals in the early days, it is probable their paths crossed. In the cold winter of 1940–1941 Caskie talks about the support he received from local *résistants*: '… but for the stealthy friends who brought us aid. They included natives of Marseille, some of them of British ancestry …'[13]

There would only be a limited number of individuals of British ancestry helping Caskie; just maybe Madge was one of them? A strange coincidence, but perhaps not; in the same letter to Sir Robert Knox, both Donald Caskie and Mrs Holst are recommended for an OBE for their services in France. In his autobiography Caskie makes no mention of Madge, so maybe they never worked together or at best only briefly.[14]

Before the intelligence services had organised anything related to helping soldiers, and in particular airmen, to escape from occupied France, with no training and at first little support, Ian Garrow, a British officer on parole in Marseille, decided to organise the escape of British servicemen out of France and into Spain. In this endeavour Madge was to be one of his earliest helpers, and she supported Garrow bravely during his time in France. Garrow had been an officer in the 51st Highland Division, which had been forced to surrender in May 1940 to the Germans in Normandy, in northern France. With a group of soldiers, Garrow escaped from the

Germans and was able to make it to the south of France, unaided by any organisation. The group was arrested by French police and interned in Marseille. As an officer, Garrow was allowed parole and so, because of this freedom, he decided to organise the escape of armed services personnel out of France. Garrow spoke French well, although with a distinctive Scottish accent, so even dressed in civilian clothes he could not pass as a Frenchman. He was also very tall and walked with a strange gait. Yet this person became the head of the first properly organised escape line. He contacted Donald Caskie and had a small band of devoted civilian helpers in Marseille. Garrow began to organise 'safe houses' where the soldiers and airmen could be hidden. Identity cards and false documents were obtained for the men, money was raised to support the cost of clothing and feeding them, and for procuring guides to get the men into Spain. By January 1941, he had made links with the British consulate in Barcelona and British embassy in Madrid to help to get British military personnel out of Spain and back to Britain.[15]

So far, Garrow's efforts and the aid provided by his helpers had been done alone, with no support from Britain, until, in its very early days, the British intelligence organisation MI9 contacted Garrow. This contact with MI9 provided support such as money, couriers and the setup of more regular communication channels, including coded messages in BBC broadcasts. In the summer of 1941 Garrow met up with a remarkable man whom he knew as Pat O'Leary, and together they began to run the escape line which took their names. Eventually Garrow's luck was to run out, and he was betrayed by a traitor in the organisation. Garrow was imprisoned at Fort Saint-Nicolas in Marseille, where his health was badly affected by the lack of food he was given. He was sentenced to ten years' imprisonment and was moved to Meauzac prison in the Dordogne area of southern France, many miles from Marseille. His health continued to decline, so, with a group of helpers, O'Leary planned to rescue Garrow by dressing him up as a guard and walking out of the prison when the guards changed shift. Remarkably, this worked. Garrow was then taken to the Spanish border and was back in Britain by February 1943. In Britain he worked for MI9 and was promoted to major. Later he was promoted to lieutenant-colonel and was an interpreter in Berlin from 1945–1947. He left the army in 1947 and died in Scotland in 1976.[16]

So, what was Madge's connection with Ian Garrow? Once Garrow had made the decision to help British military personnel to escape to

Spain one of his earliest supporters was Madge. It was Madge who contacted Garrow to help him in his endeavour. To help him to reduce his contact with the local police authorities, Madge allowed Garrow to live with her and Holst in their house in Marseille at 48 Rue Boudouresque, both to shelter Garrow and offer him accommodation. Until Garrow was able to arrange financial support for the escape line through the intelligence services, Madge provided him with money to support his activities; this was probably done through her husband Wilhelm, who was a successful businessman. Madge put Garrow in touch with a group of people who were to become major helpers and were fundamental in making the Garrow-O'Leary escape line such a success. These helpers included Dr George Rodocanachi and his wife, George Zafiri, Mario Prassinos, Thorkild Hansen, Nancy Fiocca, and Louis Nouveau and his wife.[17] Madge's citation for an OBE states that she was a major figure in the original setting up of the Garrow-O'Leary line and helped it to become an established escape organisation in the south of France.[18]

When Garrow was imprisoned, Madge maintained contact with him and sent him food. When he was in the prison in Marseille, it is likely that Madge visited him. This was very brave – even foolhardy – as it may have made her a suspect person to the authorities. Once he was transferred to the prison in the Dordogne region it was more likely Madge's communication and food would have been sent to helpers in that region to pass onto to Garrow, or it could have been sent directly to the prison, or maybe Madge did actually travel to the prison and saw him in person. As we shall see later, Madge was quite prepared to travel large distances alone. She may also have had a role in planning the escape of Garrow from Meauzac prison. What that role was is unknown. Maybe she did visit him in person at Meauzac prison; if that was the case she could have passed on information about his physical state, what the guards were wearing, the work patterns of the guards, and maybe she was used to try to influence a sympathetic guard to support them in smuggling Garrow out of the prison or providing them with confidential information. Madge was not involved in the springing of Garrow from Meauzac prison, but it is likely that information provided by her played a role in his rescue.[19]

In the early days of the Garrow-O'Leary escape line, Madge put Ian Garrow in touch with some remarkable local people. George Rodocanachi was born in 1876 in Britain of Greek parents; he attended school in Marseille, going on to train as a doctor in Paris. He qualified as a doctor in 1903, serving as a doctor in the Great War. He married his wife, Fanny, in 1884. Dr Rodocanachi was to play a major role in the Garrow-O'Leary escape line in several ways. Firstly, his flat on the Rue Roux de Brignoles was very large; this enabled Garrow, and later O'Leary, to hide many British and Allied personnel there. Dr Rodocanachi spoke excellent English and was also a member of the Medical Repatriation Board; if any Allied military man was declared unfit to be able to take up arms again, he would be released to Britain. The good doctor used various methods of faking serious ailments in a way that was convincing enough for a perfectly fit airman or soldier to be sent back to Britain. Any injured soldiers, airmen, agents or helpers were secretly taken to him for treatment. As well as allowing his flat to be used as a 'safe house', Dr Rodocanachi allowed radio transmissions to London to be made from his flat, with the serious danger of being located by the local enemy secret services. Eventually he was arrested and, being an old man with heart disease, he died in Buchenwald concentration camp in February 1944. His wife Fanny loyally supported him in his endeavours; she came to Britain after the war and died in 1959.[20]

Two other helpers of Greek extraction who were introduced to Ian Garrow were George Zafiri and Mario Prassinos. George Zafiri was a nephew of Dr Rodocanachi. His father ran a macaroni factory and George gave large quantities of this foodstuff to help feed the military personnel hiding in his uncle's flat. On occasions, George travelled throughout France on behalf of the escape line, warning other helpers to be more discreet and helping injured agents to get medical treatment. In April 1943, with the enemy having infiltrated the escape line, Zafiri escaped to Spain where he was imprisoned in various prisons and the concentration camp of Miranda de Ebro, until the British were able to gain his release in August 1943. In Britain he joined De Gaulle and the Free French. After the war he returned to Marseille and became a businessman.[21] Mario Prassinos was a very dapper and suavely dressed individual, who was often used to greet soldiers and airman entering Marseille by train. When O'Leary was absent, Prassinos was put in charge of the organisation. He was one of the people who smuggled food to Garrow when Garrow was imprisoned in Marseille. He also helped O'Leary to evacuate a large group of airmen by sea. After this he was warned by O'Leary that the authorities were on to him, so he was helped to escape to Spain and then on to Britain. There he trained as a SOE operative and returned to France where he was captured by the Germans. He was either executed or died of disease in Germany in a concentration camp, and was later awarded a posthumous OBE.[22]

Louis Nouveau and his wife Renée were a well-to-do middle-class and middle-aged couple. He was a successful merchant banker, stockbroker and businessman who spoke excellent English and dressed in English-style clothes. He invited some British officers to tea, and this was where he met Ian Garrow. After this they agreed they would hide British military personnel in their flat. In a volume of Voltaire (the house was full of books) Louis Nouveau kept a record of all the military people who lodged in his flat. He reckoned 156 airmen and soldiers – all British, except eleven Frenchmen – were hidden in his flat. Louis collected his 'parcels', as Allied soldiers and airman were known, from a particular bar. Airey Neave – a future MP, an escaped PoW from Germany and later a major figure in MI9 – stayed for a time in the Nouveaus' flat. He had to wear fluffy slippers so the military personnel hiding in the flat would not be heard by neighbours. Neave hated wearing the slippers as it made him feel weak and unable to escape if needed. Louis also took part in evacuating many airmen by sea. By June 1942 the Gestapo were closely watching the Nouveaus, so it was decided that Louis would go to Paris to take charge of operations there and Renée was to go to Toulouse. In Paris, Louis Nouveau was betrayed by a traitor at the main station and ended up in Buchenwald concentration camp where, incredibly, he survived. He was awarded the George Cross for his escape line activities. On Louis' arrest, Renée was sent to Britain for safety. After the war she returned to France and was awarded the MBE.[23]

Another of Ian Garrow's escape network helpers was a remarkable New Zealand-born woman who, in 1940, was known as Nancy Fiocca. When she was 2, Nancy's family moved to Australia, where she spent her childhood and adolescence. Nancy had a desire to travel and lived in Canada, New York and London before becoming a journalist in Paris. In 1934 she was sent on an assignment to Marseille to cover the visit of the King of Yugoslavia, who was assassinated there. Her next assignment saw her in Vienna, where she witnessed local Nazis attacking Jewish residents, and her final assignment was a visit to Berlin to see the Nazis in power. It was not until 1936 that Nancy returned to the south of France, where her love for the high life saw her partying on the French Riviera. Here the flirtatious and very attractive Nancy caught the eye of a middle-aged local businessman from one of the richest families in the region, who was called Henri Fiocca. The two became engaged to be married, although it was agreed that Nancy would continue with her journalism job in Paris. When war broke out Nancy was in Britain at a health resort, but left to volunteer to serve in the British armed forces. She was offered work in a canteen. With that she returned disdainfully to France.[24]

Nancy married Henri Fiocca in November 1939, with a reception at Marseille town hall. Henri was called up into the French army and Nancy converted a truck from his factory into an ambulance and took herself to near the French-Belgian border as a volunteer nurse. With the defeat of France, Nancy and Henri eventually made their way back to Marseille. While Henri returned to his business, he was happy to let Nancy become involved in supporting the British and Allied PoWs in Marseille by providing food, cigarettes and a radio for them to listen to the BBC. Through 1940 and 1941 she was a part of the Garrow-O'Leary escape line, acting as a courier and using Henri's factory as a place for the servicemen to hide on their way to the border. When Garrow was arrested, Nancy was involved in the plan to rescue him and provided the money to finance the operation supplied by her husband. In 1943 Nancy was working as courier for the O'Leary line and the French Resistance. The German intelligence services were on to her but could not catch her; they nicknamed her the 'White Mouse' because she was so difficult to find. With the Gestapo closing in on Nancy, it was decided to get her out of France. After various narrow escapes, including being imprisoned by the French police for several days, she was eventually able to cross over the Pyrenees into Spain, where she was again arrested and rescued by British officials. She arrived in London via Gibraltar in June 1943. Henri had become fully involved in the work of the escape line, but he was eventually caught, tortured by the Gestapo and executed in October 1943.[25]

Back in Britain, Nancy volunteered for the SOE. She was trained as an SOE operator, where she was criticised for her light-heartedness and lack of seriousness, although her trainers praised her determination. She was eventually accepted for service abroad and landed by plane back into France in April 1944. Her exploits in France led her to be accepted by the *Maquis* Resistance groups and eventually Nancy was the effective leader of thousands of *Maquis* fighters. As one *Maquis* leader said about Nancy: 'She is the most feminine woman I know until the fighting starts. Then she is like five men.'[26]

After the war she married an RAF officer and returned to Australia to live. Because of her exploits, she was one of the most decorated individuals of the Second World War, being awarded medals from New Zealand, Australia, America, France (two) and the George Cross from Britain for her almost unbelievable wartime achievements.[27]

Another Briton linked with the early efforts of Ian Garrow was Elizabeth Haden-Guest. She had some previous espionage experience and had worked for Red Aid and helped German political prisoners to escape. Like Madge, she also had a connection with Spain; in this case her brother-in-law, David Haden-Guest, had been killed fighting in the International Brigades. Also, her father-in-law was an MP. In 1940 she escaped with her young son from a prison in the German zone in France, but by the time she arrived in Marseille, the rigours of getting to the port city had caused the boy to become ill. She went to Dr Rodocanachi, who treated the boy on that occasion and on several other occasions afterwards. She had already contacted Garrow and asked the doctor to join them in helping British servicemen to escape into Spain, and as we have seen, he agreed. Haden-Guest became a courier for Garrow, delivering messages, money and servicemen to the appropriate place. She hid servicemen in local brothels, where sometimes she left her son if she was working for Garrow. In 1941 Haden-Guest was betrayed and arrested whereby she was interrogated, beaten and imprisoned for several months. After her release she was sent to Lisbon with her son and arrived in Britain in 1942. Her desire to return to France to continue her espionage activities was rejected on the grounds that she was 'burnt out'.[28]

From the summer of 1940, a small group of individuals in Marseille led by Ian Garrow had set up and grown an organisation – with no outside help from British Intelligence – to help British and Allied servicemen escape across the border into Spain. This organisation had been set up by amateurs as their contribution to help Britain win the war, and to oppose both the German occupation of France and the Vichy regime. In the words of Donald Darling (who became MI9's contact with the Garrow organisation):

> To be honest, the Marseille group did contain some unexpected people, beside the English wife of a Norwegian. There were three Greeks, a Dane, and a French Australian.

Garrow was a Scot ... Louis Nouveau and his wife Renee ... Dr Rodocanachi, they formed a highly active, if amateur team.[29]

It seems these amateurs overcame their lack of experience by personal loyalty to each other and 'thinking on their feet'. This was a small network of people compared to much later larger organisations. It was the first network to organise the escape of British and Allied military personnel trapped in France. They were all aware of the dire consequences of being discovered by the occupying authorities. Although untrained, they were able to keep the network going for a significant period of time: '... composed of a particularly united team, all reasonable intelligent and enthusiastic people ...'[30]

Jimmy Langley, who became a major figure in MI9, talks about the Marseille group in the early days: 'Marseille itself had a number of devoted helpers who would hide evaders awaiting departure to Spain ...'[31]

This small group of individuals, some of the first to resist the German occupation, formed the backbone of what became known as the Garrow-O'Leary escape line: 'In time, he [Garrow] organised a group of people who served as some of the line's staunchest and most dependable workers throughout its existence.'[32]

Involved along with Madge and these remarkable individuals was her then-husband Wilhelm Holst who, perhaps unbeknownst to Madge, was also working for the SOE, and a Dane called Thorkild Hansen, who would later become her third husband and who also worked for the SOE. What Ian Garrow and his bunch of very brave amateurs needed was help from Britain and a contact person. The newly formed MI9 was to provide that support, with their contact person being Donald Darling, who knew Madge's husband Wilhelm, having met him in 1938 in Paris when both were involved in organising medical aid for Republican Spain.[33]

MI9 was very much the junior member of the intelligence services and was under-resourced in both funds and personnel throughout the war. In addition, it struggled to get its message across of the importance of returning Allied servicemen back to Britain to continue the war against the Germans. Pilots, in particular, were very expensive to train and also highly skilled, so it was an asset to the war effort to get these men back to Britain; in terms of morale, it was important to show that if you were shot down in enemy territory there was an organisation in place that could get you back home. In May and June 1940 there were many British soldiers from the British Expeditionary Force who had evaded capture and a significant number of RAF pilots who had been shot down in now enemy territory. Most of these evaders headed for Vichy France. With large numbers of British and Allied servicemen heading for southern France, MI6 offered to set up an escape line from Marseille to Spain for MI9. Dansey, the head of MI6, chose Donald Darling, one of his own agents, to go to Spain to set up links with France. His instructions were to set up an escape line running from Marseille to Barcelona and then to Lisbon or Gibraltar. Darling spoke both French and Spanish well, having lived in both countries, and knew the Pyrenees well. He arrived in Lisbon in July 1940. The British ambassador in Madrid, Sir Samuel Hoare,[34] did not want him in Spain, as he believed Britain should do nothing to antagonise General Franco which might lead him to join the Axis powers, so Darling based himself in Lisbon. His cover was that of British vice-consul in charge of refugees and he was given the codename 'Sunday'.[35]

Later, Darling was to receive support from two famous escapers, Airey Neave and Jimmy Langley. Langley had been an officer in the Coldstream Guards and had been badly wounded as part of the rear guard at Dunkirk. He was too ill to be put on a boat and be evacuated, so he was left behind and became a PoW. His arm had to be amputated, but even though it was not fully healed he escaped from a hospital in Lille and made his way south to Marseille, where the MRB declared him unfit for further military action and he was sent back to Britain. On his return to Britain he was recruited by British Intelligence and joined MI9, where his code name was P15. Another famous escaper was Airey Neave; he was an officer in the ill-fated defence of Calais and was wounded and taken to Germany as a PoW. Having made one failed attempt to escape, he was sent to Colditz Castle. This was the notorious German PoW camp which housed men who had made regular attempts to escape. In January 1942 Neave became the first escaper from Colditz and returned to Britain via Switzerland, Marseille and Spain and on return to Britain, he joined Langley in working for MI9, where his code name was 'Saturday'.[36]

MI9's key role was to help servicemen, especially pilots, to escape from enemy-occupied territory. There were two types of servicemen in enemy territory. First, escapers who were the smaller group. These were men who had been captured by enemy forces for as long as a few minutes to several years. Captured servicemen were encouraged to try to escape as soon after capture as possible, as this was their best chance of getting away. Once in a PoW camp, MI9 would send a variety of packages, mostly unsuspicious food stuffs and toiletries; however, hidden in some packages were secret aids to escape, such as metal files. A British officer's sworn duty was to try to escape. Conversely, those who were not captured by the enemy forces and were alone or in a small group were known as 'evaders' and in France they mostly headed south, where many were discovered by escape line operatives and moved to secure accommodation before being moved across the border into Spain. MI9's role with evaders was to provide money, offer support, send in agents and set up regular communication with the leaders of the escape lines. It was also to help members of the escape lines to return to Britain if it became too dangerous for them to continue. Another important role of MI9 in Britain was training pilots in ways to evade capture, and designing an escape kit for pilots that would allow them to survive for several days. When the Americans entered the war, MI9 worked alongside its US counterpart, MIS-X, for the rest of the war, without the frictions they had had with MI6.[37]

Darling, now in Lisbon, began to use previous contacts to try to set up an escape organisation in Spain. He was aware of the situation in Marseille and was instructed to make contact with Garrow and supply him with money. Darling persuaded an American working for a Jewish refugee organisation to make contact with Garrow. Darling wanted to employ Spanish Republicans as guides to get British servicemen across the Pyrenees into Spain, but the British ambassador banned the use of Franco's enemies and Darling had to revert to smugglers. This was all part of Hoare's policy of 'keep Spain neutral'. British servicemen arriving in Spain were arrested and often sent to the concentration camp at Miranda de Ebro; they were released to British officials, but this could take several weeks. Neutral Lisbon became a centre of intrigue, with spies from both sides living side by side and radio masts being thrown up all around the city. The British embassy grew to 200 individuals and had to move to a bigger residence. Lisbon also became the place to where British residents who had lived on the south coast of France fled before returning to Britain. Darling continued to use trusted Americans to send messages to Garrow and O'Leary in Marseille. Another useful courier used by Darling in the early days of his links with the Marseille group was a very wealthy Armenian oil tycoon's son called Nubar Gulbenkian, who was able to travel on a neutral passport and had reasons to visit Vichy France as his father lived there. But Darling needed a trusted regular courier from Marseille. That trusted courier was to be Madge. Darling left Lisbon for Gibraltar in January 1942 and remained there until March 1944. He then moved to London, where he was chief of the Evasion Office. He ended up in Paris, where he was put in charge of the Awards Bureau, which recommended medals for individuals involved in the Resistance and escape organisations. He died in 1977.[38]

Wilhelm Holst, Madge's second husband, was one of the very first SOE operatives and was known as Billet. He travelled in both French zones and to Lisbon using his Quaker credentials. In the early days it is possible this was not known to Madge, or at least, this was what Wilhelm told his superiors. Wilhelm's activities will be looked at later in the chapter. Wilhelm was having difficulties getting to Lisbon, so he suggested Madge should do it instead. It also seems that Garrow and O'Leary were looking for someone to be a courier to link up with Darling in Lisbon. Madge may have been chosen not only for her personal qualities, which will be looked at later, but because she knew Darling from her time in Paris. It is just possible that both Wilhelm and Madge had been recruited by the intelligence services just before the Second World War. Donald Darling states:

> She was Mrs Madge Holst, the Yorkshire-born wife of a Norwegian businessman I had known in Paris in 1938 and had a branch of his business in Marseille. Both had joined the organisation.[39]

Madge was actually born in Manchester, although the family had lived in Yorkshire before Madge was born. It seems Madge had met Darling before their first meeting in Lisbon. Does Darling mean they joined the intelligence services before 1939 or had joined during the war? The latter option seems the more likely.[40]

Madge first travelled to Lisbon with Wilhelm in the spring of 1941, where they met with Darling and passed on important information to him; possibly on this trip Madge agreed to be a courier. Subsequently, Madge travelled on her own to Lisbon. Darling describes the time they met up when Madge had arrived in Lisbon on her own. She had arrived in the city without his knowledge and booked into the same hotel as Darling; she rang him, and they agreed to meet in his hotel room. When they met, Darling turned his radio up high so no one could hear them talking. Madge told him she had travelled on a Norwegian passport on a German Lufthansa plane. Madge then took some nail scissors out of her bag and cut open the sleeve of her coat to reveal a large tube of toothpaste; inside was important information from Garrow and O'Leary written on rice paper. Madge told Darling that she would be returning to Marseille in a week's time to take provisions, money (this could be large amounts) and information from Darling back to Garrow and O'Leary. It is also quite likely in Lisbon that she would have passed on SOE information from Wilhelm, either to Darling or an SOE contact there. Darling sent her letters to London and requested a reply; when this was received Madge took it back to Marseille for Garrow and O'Leary. On one visit to Lisbon she was carrying so much stuff inside her fur coat that they had to rip it open in Darling's hotel room and then sew it back together. Once Darling left for Gibraltar, Madge's new contact was a confidential secretary, a Canadian woman who was the wife of a British diplomat.[41]

On one of her trips to Lisbon, Madge was shown how to use magic inks for correspondence. She was given an address in Lisbon to write to in French. She was to write as if to an elderly relative, then write between the lines with magic ink, which she took away in her make-up bag. Wilhelm Holst was sent detailed instructions in the use of magic ink for correspondence by the SOE. It is quite possible that Madge may have used these techniques in her correspondence with Lisbon. Instructions for using the magic ink included the need for the pen to be a ball-point to avoid scratching, and the need for it to be clean and washed, otherwise the secret writing would show up. When writing, use little pressure on the pen, and have a powerful light because the ink is clear; this will allow you to see what you are writing and check if there are any scratches which may betray the secret message. When the writing is complete, let it dry for ten minutes, then rub with a clean piece of paper on both sides. Then expose both sides of the paper to steam from a boiling kettle for around one minute. Next, lay the paper between two sheets of blotting paper and press together under a weight, such as a few books. The piece of paper is ready to receive the visible print, which should be written at right angles to the secret message. This preparation of the paper only needs to be done if chemical testing by the enemy is feared. To make the secret ink, use one tablet of Pyramidon (headache tablets) which should be dissolved in enough water to make a 0.1 per cent solution. If the label on the bottle states each tablet is 0.1 gm, the tablet should be dissolved in 100 cubic centimetres of water, if the tablets were 0.2 gm then 200 cubic centimetres of water and so on. Any writing paper except shiny paper could be used.[42]

Madge's trips to Lisbon were an essential way of maintaining communication with the British intelligence agencies and of receiving aid. Madge knew what would happen to her if she was discovered – almost certainly imprisonment, torture and either execution or a slow death in a concentration camp. It seems that Madge was an effective courier and an important part of the Garrow-O'Leary escape line organisation, as well as having contacts with the SOE. Helen Long describes her: 'Another valuable courier in the early days was Madge Holst …'[43]

Donald Darling comments: 'With communications with Marseille now on a firm basis, through Madge Holst, I felt I could leave matters in the hands of the confidential secretary …'[44]

Jimmy Langley adds: '… the courier service set up by Donald Darling was functioning well and we received regular, if of necessity brief, reports from Ian Garrow.'[45]

Darling also says of Madge that she was 'calm and self-possessed' and 'cool as a cucumber'. This theme is continued in a letter recommending her for an award where her coolness and bravery, and her willingness to take on any requested task, are praised. Madge seems to have been a very effective courier with an ability to stay calm and collected and to play a role while travelling that hid the real purpose for her journey. Madge was a woman who had a quite extraordinary nerve and mental toughness that is hard to understand in the modern world.[46]

The Garrow-O'Leary escape line was better known as the Pat O'Leary line, after the charismatic Belgian who turned it into one of the most effective escape lines during the war. As we have seen earlier, many British servicemen had headed into the south of France after the fall of France to escape being captured and made a PoW. Ian Garrow, a Seaforth Highland officer, became the driving force of the organisation of the escape from France of these British and Allied servicemen, with help from a small band of helpers in Marseille consisting of various nationalities and including Madge. The Germans' file on the escape line was called Acropolis because of the number of Greeks helping the organisation. The original small, very amateur setup had developed with support from Donald Darling in Lisbon and MI9 had helped Garrow and his support organisation to expand his network of operatives and get more servicemen out of France. The original escape line saw both evaders and escapers travel from northern France, often with help at first from French civilians with no link to Garrow, then to Marseille, from there on to the Pyrenees and eventually to Gibraltar. In April 1941 an SOE agent called Pat O'Leary, who was really a Belgian named Albert-Marie Guérisse, was forced ashore off the coast of France after the boat he was using broke down. After being captured, he escaped and arrived in Marseille, where after a short time he met Garrow. Both men got on well and O'Leary agreed to join Garrow in managing the escape line. When Garrow was arrested in October 1941, O'Leary became the leader of the escape line.

As the escape line grew, the routes they used increased and became more varied. Most servicemen came from northern France, from such places as Lille, Rheims, and Paris and its surrounds. Some escapers from Italy and Germany entered Switzerland, where they were interned; to get back home, they had to enter France and avoid capture again, like Airey Neave. As the O'Leary line expanded rapidly, once the escapers and evaders entered southern France they were either contacted by a member of the escape line organisation, or a friendly civilian would put them in touch with the organisation if they knew someone, or send them to a particular bar where organisation members visited to check for servicemen and pilots on the run.

The O'Leary line tended to use the eastern Pyrenees to take the servicemen over into Spain, as they were the easier part of the range to cross. When German intelligence infiltrated the escape line network, they were forced to take the 'parcels' across the central Pyrenees, which were much higher and more difficult to climb. Crossing the Pyrenees was very dangerous; besides being an arduous climb, the mountains were well-guarded and there was a chance of capture or being shot. Organising the journey over the Pyrenees was a key role for both the escape line and British Intelligence. Suitable guides needed to be found and paid, clothing and footwear needed to be able to withstand the cold and ice of the climb. A safe route was essential.

Once in Spain, the evaders' troubles did not suddenly stop; Spain was neutral but Gestapo agents could move freely around the country. Evaders were often imprisoned in local prisons before being moved to the concentration camp at Miranda de Ebro. The camp at Miranda was typical of a concentration camp: very overcrowded, filthy, and the prisoners were fed a starvation diet. Some British servicemen were held for months in the camp before being released by British consular officials. If the British servicemen could prove they were an escaper they were released; if not, they were interned in Spain. Once this became known, all evaders declared that they were escapers! Thousands of servicemen and pilots were to make their way through Spain and back to Britain. Many left for Britain via Gibraltar, where Donald Darling would interrogate them to see if they had any useful intelligence which would be useful for the war effort. Other escape lines like the Belgian 'Comet' also evacuated escapers and evaders into Spain over the Pyrenees. All the main British intelligence agencies – SOE, MI9 and SIS – used the Pyrenees to enable their agents to enter and leave France.

The O'Leary escape line also used sailing boats, which usually landed at the small port of Canet Plage near Perpignan and then sailed on to Gibraltar. These boats were crewed by Polish SOE agents; both the 'parcels' and the intelligence agents were evacuated by these boats, which also inserted agents into southern France. These agents tended to be from all branches of the British intelligence services. Two other, bigger vessels called HMS *Tarana* and HMS *Fidelity* were also used; they pretended to be fishing ships. This had to be abandoned by the end of 1942 with the German occupation of Vichy France.

In December 1941 the organisation was devastated when a major member of the escape line called Harold Cole, a criminal from London, turned traitor. In 1940 he was a sergeant in the Territorial Royal Engineers and absconded with the sergeants' mess funds. In northern France he became a very successful courier based in Lille, taking evaders across the German zone into southern France and to Marseille. It appears that he was embezzling money raised to support the helpers in northern France. When confronted by O'Leary, Cole escaped, but was captured by the Gestapo. Cole changed sides and denounced many helpers and leaders of the O'Leary line in the north of France. This led to many deaths and imprisonments. Many other members of the organisation known to Cole had to be helped out of France to avoid capture by the authorities. Nevertheless, the line continued throughout 1942. By early 1943 the network in the north had recovered but another disaster was to occur in Paris. This time the traitor known as Roger le Neveu or Roger the Legionary, as he had once been a member of the Foreign Legion, was able to betray the likes of Louis Nouveau and the escape line leader O'Leary. This led to the arrest of many members of the organisation in northern France, but also in the south of France in Toulouse and Marseille the escape line was effectively finished. Unbelievably, the line re-grouped, based in Toulouse, although it was greatly reduced in size. It was led by an elderly woman called Françoise Dissart and continued to help evaders until May 1944. The former Pat O'Leary line was reconstituted as the Françoise line.[47]

During the period 1940–1944, Madge met and worked with a group of remarkable and very brave individuals. Two of these people were famous Resistance fighters and were highly decorated for their efforts. The first was Nancy Fiocca (or Nancy Wake), and the other was Pat O'Leary. O'Leary became the leader of the most famous escape line until his capture. Madge was part of the original Marseille group of helpers who had worked with Ian Garrow and continued to work with O'Leary. When O'Leary arrived in Marseille, Madge arranged for him to meet up with Garrow and may well have been a courier passing messages from one man to the other and organising meetings.[48]

Madge became the escape line's courier to and from Lisbon, and was trained in the use of magic inks to pass on secret messages to British Intelligence by post. She also worked with O'Leary and others in planning the release from prison of Ian Garrow. Who was Pat O'Leary?[49]

Pat O'Leary's code names were Joseph and Adolphe, but his real name was Albert-Marie Guérisse and he was a Belgian doctor. When Germany invaded Belgium, he was a doctor in a cavalry regiment. When the King of Belgium surrendered to the Germans on 28 May 1940, he took a ship and landed in Britain. Belgian officers in Britain were sent back to France in June 1940 and O'Leary found himself based in the south of France. Pat was determined to escape and sailed for Gibraltar with a group of Belgians and Czechs. Here, Pat joined a small French trawler called the SS *Rhin* which was taken over by the British and became known as HMS *Fidelity*. This vessel became an armed 'Q ship' (disguised merchant vessel) and was used by the SOE for secret operations. O'Leary joined the SOE and was given the background story of being French-Canadian. Pat became second-in-command of this ship with the rank of lieutenant-commander in the Royal Navy. During a sabotage operation off the south coast of France, the small boat that O'Leary was using to return to HMS *Fidelity* capsized. This led to a half-drowned O'Leary being taken prisoner by French coastguards. As he was wearing Royal Navy uniform, O'Leary was taken to the prison for British PoWs at St Hippolyte near Nîmes. As a British officer PoW like Ian Garrow, Pat was free to do pretty much what he wanted under the parole system, as long as he did not escape. Pat had no intention of honouring his parole and planned to escape at the first opportunity.[50]

Thanks to his freedom under parole, O'Leary was able to contact Garrow and they decided on a plan of escape. O'Leary was able to saw through prison iron bars while his fellow inmates distracted the guards, which enabled him to escape from the prison. During his escape he was hidden in a convent and helped to escape from Nîmes by the Mother Superior. Once he had arrived in in Marseille, O'Leary's first thought was to return to Britain and continue his SOE activities. But Garrow believed that O'Leary would be a great addition to the escape line, and persuaded him to stay put until they received permission for O'Leary to stay in France and work for the escape line organisation. It was agreed through the Admiralty that the BBC would broadcast a secret message if O'Leary could stay. The message was '*Adolphe doit rester*', or in English, 'Adolphe must stay' (Adolphe was O'Leary's code name). To Garrow's delight, one night the message was broadcast by the BBC and repeated for clarity. Garrow now had a joint leader who had a combination of daring and native language skills. Every week, pilots, ex-soldiers and compromised Resistance men and women arrived in Marseille to be moved to safety abroad. In October 1941 Ian Garrow was arrested, and O'Leary became the single leader of the escape organisation.[51]

Pat travelled throughout France expanding the escape line, setting up new 'safe houses' and adding more couriers to the organisation. He himself also moved 'parcels' around the country. This often meant having nerves of steel; in one incident his two RAF pilots who spoke no French had to sit next to two German soldiers in a very busy rail dining carriage. Pat ordered beers for the three of them, but one of the pilots knocked his beer over one of the Germans. Fortunately, the Germans thought it was hilarious. Pat remarked after the incident: 'Never tell me the Germans haven't got a sense of humour.'[52]

One of the organisation's couriers in northern France was Paul or Harold Cole, who at face value seemed a very efficient courier, although a little over-confident. After the first meeting with Cole, O'Leary was suspicious of his loyalty. Shortly after this meeting, O'Leary was arrested but was released by the authorities for lack of evidence and his cover story was suitably solid. But many others had been arrested and O'Leary suspected Cole. O'Leary travelled to northern France and discovered that the money Cole was receiving to pay the helpers and couriers there was not being handed out to them but being kept by Cole. In Marseille, Cole was interrogated by O'Leary and other leaders of the organisation. Pat lost his temper and struck Cole. O'Leary wished to send him back to Britain because he was not reliable. Another leader recommended killing Cole; while they were discussing how to proceed, Cole took the opportunity to escape. O'Leary was to discover that Cole was a traitor and had caused the imprisonment and deaths of many members of the escape line.[53]

O'Leary travelled secretly to Gibraltar to speak with Donald Darling, crossing the border from Spain into Gibraltar in the boot of a car. There he and Darling discussed expanding the line, and it was agreed to make it known that Cole was a traitor. During his stay in Gibraltar, Pat met with Jimmy Langley, who supplied him with a trained radio operator who proved to be totally unsuitable. After the meeting, O'Leary returned by boat to France with his radio operator.[54]

Pat O'Leary was famous for his daring and audacity. He expanded the escape line so it reached the borders of Belgium, Italy and Spain, included over 200 couriers and helpers, and may have helped as many as 600 airmen and servicemen to escape from France. He was also involved in many remarkable escapes. He was able to organise the escape of the socialite, racing car driver and air ace Whitney Straight back to Britain before the occupying authorities realised who they had in their midst. He led the planning and escape of Ian Garrow from Meauzac prison and was present when he was whisked away by car from the area. When O'Leary said goodbye to Garrow as he prepared to cross the Pyrenees into Spain, he shook his hand and commented prophetically: 'Can this go on much longer?'[55]

O'Leary also rescued Nancy Fiocca from a French prison by claiming to be her lover. He planned and carried out six large sea evacuations of servicemen from southern France as well as one evacuation of service personnel by submarine. The successful growth of the organisation did have its problems. In the early days, all the couriers and helpers could be properly vetted for reliability, but as the organisation grew, the vetting became less thorough and, in some cases, impossible. This led to another traitor appearing on the scene called Roger le Neveu; in March 1943, he was to betray Pat to the authorities, and this led to the effective end of the escape line as a major organisation.[56]

After capture, O'Leary was interrogated and tortured at various prisons in France before eventually being sent to concentration camps to rot and starve to death. He managed to survive two of the most notorious concentration camps: Mauthausen, where thousands of Spanish Republicans died, and Dachau, from where he was finally set free in April 1945. At the liberation of the camp he stayed behind as a doctor to assist with a typhus epidemic. In 1946 he was awarded the George Cross for his services during the war and became one of the most decorated Resistance fighters of the Second World War. Shortly after his release from Dachau, he identified the body of the traitor Harry (Paul) Cole in Paris; he had been shot dead by French police. After the war, he re-joined the Belgian army and was medical officer for the 1st Lancers. He became Chief Medical Officer for the Belgian forces who fought in the Korean War in 1951. In 1947 he married an English woman called Sylvia, who had worked with Donald Darling in Paris. In later life, Pat suffered badly with his eyes due to his severe wartime experiences (torture and malnutrition). He died in 1989 in Belgium.[57]

Madge also had links with a significant SOE escape line for agents, known as the Pierre-Jacques line. In a letter from the Dutch General Staff dated March 1945, Madge is thanked for her bravery under the German occupation but, more significantly, for having assisted 'Pierre' in establishing an Allied escape line. How this was done is not made clear; it could have been by putting 'Pierre' in contact with helpers, couriers, full time agents and safe houses. But who was 'Pierre'? Pierre's full code name was 'Pierre Lalande', also known as Guido Zwikker, but the real name of this Dutch agent was Guido Zembsch-Schreve. He was an SOE-trained agent. 'Jacques' was short for the code name of 'Jacques Cornet', whose real name was Claude Planel; he was a British citizen born in Mauritius, who spoke excellent French, and was to become Guido's radio operator. Guido Zembsch-Schreve was yet another remarkable person with whom Madge worked during her Resistance years.[58]

Guido Zembsch-Schreve was born in Berne, Switzerland, in 1916 but his nationality was Dutch. His father was a doctor and he had a brother and sister. By 1943, his father was living in Belgium and had retired as a doctor, his mother was dead, his brother lived in Holland and his sister was married and lived in Austria. Guido went to school in Geneva and Brussels before spending two years at Brussels University. In 1936–1937 he spent one year in London before spending two years in America. He spoke perfect Dutch, English and French, good German, and spoke Spanish moderately well. When the Second World War broke out, he was working in Antwerp in Belgium as a manager in a shipping company. When the Germans invaded, he fled south into France in his American Chevrolet car and finally ended up in Marseille, where, according to Guido, the Dutch consul introduced him to the local Resistance. Perhaps they included Madge, Wilhelm Holst and Thorkild Hansen? Early in 1941, Guido left France for Spain and entered Portugal, from where he sailed to America. In America he decided he needed to do something to fight the Germans and help to free his country.[59]

He decided to move to Canada, where those Dutch who wished to fight for the Allies were recruiting a volunteer Dutch Brigade. He joined this unit in July 1941 and trained near Ontario before arriving in Britain in October 1941. In Britain he was offered the opportunity to become an officer in the Dutch Brigade, which was known as the 'Princess Irene' Brigade, after a member of the Dutch royal family; but he declined the offer. Instead he volunteered to serve in 12 Commando and started his training in March 1942. During his time with 12 Commando, he took part in a raid on the Channel Island of Sark, which was occupied by the Germans. Here, his group captured a German soldier. They brought him to Britain where Guido interrogated him in German. After this raid he transferred to 10 Commando, a multi-national group of volunteers. During the training in North Wales, he got in trouble for climbing up the clock tower of a local church. In early 1943, Guido was invited to London and offered the chance to be an SOE operative, which he accepted with alacrity.[60]

During his SOE training Guido's commando expertise was very evident in his physical fitness, weapon handling and fieldcraft, although he was less good at signalling and communication and sabotage. He was viewed by his trainers as an incredibly confident man in everything that he undertook, and excessively thorough – almost too much so.[61] Further comments by his instructor and commander point to a very capable, although vain, man. His good points were his thoroughness, his previous experiences and great self-confidence. On the negative side, his superiors noted that he was not leader material, he was unpopular with the other men, keen to praise himself and never accepted responsibility when he had made mistakes. Nevertheless, it was decided to drop Guido by parachute into occupied France in July 1943, with the job of taking over the leadership of an existing network and expanding it to incorporate the passing of individuals and special materials out of France.[62]

In his own words Guido describes his mission as the establishment of a network separate from all existing organisations. It was to be a network where SOE agents could be brought into enemy-occupied territory, and was also to be used to extract compromised agents. Its scope was to range from north of Holland to the border with Spain. In addition, specialist equipment was to be sent to Britain via Spain and Switzerland.[63] He was provided with the names of contacts in Marseille; it is highly probable that two were Madge and Thorkild Hansen, and likely also Wilhelm Holst.[64]

Guido was to be parachuted into France with his wireless operator, Claude Planel. The first part of the mission involved Guido visiting Switzerland and Holland, while his radio operator found good places near Paris where he could make transmissions. The second part was to set up as soon as possible escape and infiltration routes for SOE agents based in Denmark, Holland, Belgium and France. Guido was given a contact in Holland and in Marseille, an agent code named 'Berger', who was Thorkild Hansen. In addition, Guido was to locate places where equipment and agents could be dropped by air, or places where light aircraft could land. The two agents parachuted into France at night and landed near a German army driving school. They were helped by a local farmer, and then managed to bluff a lift to Paris from two German NCOs. In Paris, Guido contacted a friend of Thorkild, code named 'Doris'. It was agreed that 'Doris' would set up a network in Paris, while Guido would go to Switzerland and the radio operator would scour Paris for suitable places to transmit. Having visited Switzerland and set up 'safe houses' in Paris, Guido travelled to the Spanish border to organise a new Pyrenean crossing, where he was helped by a Basque priest. After that he visited Hansen in Marseille to tell him what he had organised and then he returned to Paris in September 1943.[65]

The organisation grew to cover 1500km; there was a transmitter in the Paris area for quick communication, as well as couriers who were paid but were not part of the organisation. Madge may have been one of these couriers. A sea escape route to Spain was already in place at

## Resisting Fascism Again

Collioure, near the Spanish border, which used local fisherman and their boats to transfer at-sea agents onto Spanish fishing boats, from where they were landed in Spain. This was already in place and had been set up by Thorkild Hansen. The organisation was organised geographically with regional heads; these included the Paris region, south-east France, south-west France, northern France, and Belgium and Holland.[66]

Guido comments: 'Thanks to the courage and determination of all those brave men and women who had answered my calls for assistance, the Pierre-Jacques network was now up and running.'[67]

These men and women included Madge and Thorkild Hansen, her future husband.

Guido organised his network in the following way: in each town was a reception house, a safe house and a headquarters. The headquarters only had contact with the safe house and the reception house. The links were maintained using a 'cut-out' (a way of passing on messages with minimum contact between agents; often something was placed in a shop window, or could be a message in code left with a loyal third party). On arrival, an agent was taken by a guide or courier to the reception house. The people at the reception house would ring headquarters using a pre-arranged message that an agent had arrived, usually via a cut-out. Headquarters would then send someone to take the agent to the safe house. The reception houses were intended to be used just for an overnight stay; the safe houses were selected so that an agent could stay for a long time if needed. Headquarters then arranged for the agent to be taken to the reception house at the next town, and everything was repeated. This way, a guide, helper or courier had the minimum amount of information about the network and, if captured, would only be able to pass on limited information to the enemy. The Pierre-Jacques network people in Lille in northern France were to collect any fleeing agents from across the border in Belgium. The Lille organisation received details from London about the fleeing agent, including a physical description and a password. The fleeing agent was then passed along the network, always accompanied by a member of the organisation, who then introduced them to the relevant people in each town they passed through.[68]

The SOE ordered Guido to supply various Resistance groups with funds and help agents by supplying them with wireless sets, or, if their cover had been blown, to help them to return to Britain. During Christmas and New Year 1943–1944 Guido stayed in Marseille, where he organised for several agents to be sent home. In March 1944, he was told to help an agent in Paris called 'Julian' to leave France via Spain. However, when Guido went to meet 'Julian' in Paris, he was betrayed and captured by the Gestapo. He was interrogated and tortured but kept to his cover story. He was then sent off to the concentration camp of Buchenwald to starve and rot. From there, later in 1944, he was moved to another concentration camp called Dora, and finally in April 1945 to Ravensbrück. At Ravensbrück, Guido managed to escape with two American pilots, but they were captured by the Soviets. The Soviets allowed them to cross over the River Elbe, where they were taken to the American headquarters and freedom. On his return to Britain, Guido claims he was greeted by General Gubbins, the SOE chief, and Churchill. He then left Britain to return to newly liberated Holland. For his wartime activities he was awarded an OBE.[69]

Madge was an amateur resister from the summer of 1940 when she first helped Ian Garrow. During the war she became second-in-command of the Alexandre *réseau*, or network, led by Wilhelm Holst, and a paid full time P2 agent. It is not clear, although very possible, that Madge was aware of Wilhelm's clandestine work from the beginning and that he misled his superiors as to Madge's knowledge of his activities. In secret discussions about Madge's involvement in Wilhelm's activities there is a description of Madge written in April 1941, the month before she became a member of the Billet network. At first it lists the usual information: date of birth, maiden name, place where she lived most of her life; then it states that she is 1.65m tall, with dark brown hair, grey eyes, slim, weight about 55kg. Donald Darling describes Madge thus: 'Madge was an extraordinarily normal woman slight and delicately built, but calm and self-possessed.'[70]

She is described as a typical English type who speaks good French with a strong English accent. It was agreed that Madge had to know something of the special correspondence with which Wilhelm was dealing, so that she would be able to receive and send it on.[71]

So, Madge became a member of the Billet *réseau*. How much she knew about the organisation in the early days is open to question; it was agreed in secret meetings that she would know only as much as Wilhelm decided to tell her. Although intelligence services were reluctant for Madge to be fully informed, it is likely that Wilhelm told her all about his involvement in the intelligence services. The decision to get Madge involved came about because Wilhelm was often travelling abroad, both as head of the network and with his Quaker work. Besides taking in special correspondence and forwarding it on, Madge was to answer any telephone calls relating to the network. It was also agreed she would house special agents in their Marseille home until Wilhelm's return. Wilhelm's trips away lasted several weeks, on occasions. Any agent wishing to enter their house had to know the password *'de la part de Monsieur Scholl'*, with Scholl pronounced as Skoll. Wilhelm emphasised that it would be helpful if Madge was told of his activities, so that at an early stage Madge would have known what Wilhelm was doing, and what she was letting herself in for. When asked by the intelligence services if Madge would be a willing participant, Wilhelm commented: 'wife should play', which strongly suggests he trusted her completely and believed she would be an asset to his organisation.[72]

Madge and Wilhelm lived at 48 Rue Boudouresque in Marseille. It was a small house close to the sea, with access to a small port at the back of the house. It was also within 50m of a military installation. Whether this was their choice or the intelligence services' decision is difficult to say; if it was the choice of MI9 or similar it could have been chosen so they could keep an eye on the military location nearby. In a letter to a friend, Wilhelm writes that he and Madge are living in a small house by the sea 'quietly and peacefully'; in this case Wilhelm is keeping his friend in the dark as to his and Madge's activities. By 1941 Madge was now a naturalised Norwegian and so she could travel abroad as a Norwegian citizen. As Madge said to Donald Darling about the occupying authorities: 'Anyhow they think I am Norwegian.'[73]

At first, probably because of her courier activities to Lisbon, Madge played a junior role in Wilhelm's SOE Billet and Alexandre networks, handling correspondence, answering the telephone and accommodating and hiding agents. However, during the course of the war Madge's role in the SOE networks and her relationship with Wilhelm were to change.[74]

The Billet network, which may have existed in some form from 1940, became the Alexandre network in April 1941 until it was closed down in September 1944, after the Germans had been driven out of most of France. The Alexandre network was linked with several others, including the Pierre-Jacques circuit. This could explain Madge's early role in helping Zembsch-Schreve to set up his network. At its disbandment, the Alexandre core network consisted of two women and four men, including Madge and Wilhelm. The main role of these SOE networks was information-gathering, recruiting agents, money transactions and working with the French Resistance. Madge had the code name of Billette and Mrs Oats. She was the network's company secretary, or *secrétaire générale de réseau*, and second-in-command of the network with the rank of lieutenant. She became a full time P2 agent paid by the Free French *Forces françaises combattantes*. She also took over the command of the network for a period when Wilhelm was ill.[75] A letter to a Captain Liger written in April 1945, asking permission to allow Madge to travel to Paris, states that she had opposed the occupying forces throughout the war and she was a major reason for the success of Billet and Alexandre networks.[76]

In the document which ended the existence of the Alexandre network, Madge is listed as *célibataire*, which translates as single woman, while Wilhelm is listed as married with one child, although both have the same address in Paris in 1944. By 1945 Wilhelm is living and working in Paris and Madge has a different address in Marseille from their wartime house. Perhaps by 1944 their relationship was strained, or they had separated. There is a picture of Madge and Wilhelm and a young child at their Marseille house (see plates); there is no record of this child being their adopted child or it being their child. It is likely that the child was an orphan that the Quakers were supporting who was visiting Madge and Wilhelm. Madge would later marry Thorkild Hansen, whom she probably knew from the early days via Ian Garrow in Marseille, and through her work with the Pierre-Jacques escape line. It is just possible that Wilhelm and Madge never actually married, or it was faked; there is no evidence of a marriage having taken place, or of Wilhelm divorcing his Norwegian wife. So perhaps, once the Alexandre network was closed down, they went their separate ways, with Madge in time becoming romantically involved with Thorkild Hansen. Why Wilhelm and Madge separated is hard to surmise; they certainly loved each other early in their relationship. Possibly wartime stresses, or regularly being apart from one another had an effect; maybe Wilhelm, having lost two sons, wanted to get his remaining family back together. Or perhaps his links with a known collaborator and possible financial irregularities alienated Madge? Perhaps they had simply grown apart and no longer loved each other.[77]

From 1940, Wilhelm Holst had three roles, which he continued through to 1944 when the Germans were driven out of France. These three roles included businessman, Quaker relief work and his British Intelligence and Resistance activities.

Wilhelm's business activities involved transmission and transport, and ship brokering. As a shipbroker, Wilhelm would have been the middleman between ship-owners and people who wished to charter the ship to transport cargo, or between buyers and sellers of ships. He could also have been involved in providing insurance for shipping.[78]

From 1940 and throughout the war years, Wilhelm worked for Quaker relief. He worked first for the American Friends Service Committee which had offices in Paris and Marseille. He was Director-in-Charge of Quaker relief in Marseille. In this role as a member of the AFSC he was free to travel freely between both the Vichy and German zones of France and he could travel abroad with relative ease. This was ideal cover for his espionage and Resistance activities, as he could travel with ease around France, and he was not strictly security checked. In his work with the Quakers, he was able to provide relief to refugees and displaced children and was able to get some Jews out of France to safety. From the end of 1942, Holst was working for the French Quakers.[79]

Holst's role as a resister and intelligence agent spanned the period 1940–1944. Wilhelm was one of the SOE's earliest agents and was recruited in April 1941. It is very possible that Wilhelm was working for both MI9 and the SOE. He had two code names: Billet and Mr Oats, and led two SOE networks or lines: Billet and Alexandre. He was a full time paid P2 agent with the rank of captain paid by the FFC. The Alexandre network was under the supervision of Lieutenant-Colonel Humphreys of the SOE. Wilhelm communicated with the British military attaché in Switzerland and made trips to Lisbon to pass on messages and receive instructions (Madge later took over this role). He played a major role in delivering financial funds to other SOE groups and networks. He also worked closely with another SOE network called 'Rossi'. He helped to get agents in and out of the two zones in France and made frequent trips to the Pyrenees area, Bordeaux, Paris, Brittany, Lyon and the Côte d'Azur.[80]

Wilhelm Holst was a complicated figure, but the death of his two sons in Norway seems to have turned him into a convinced anti-Fascist and someone who would do all he could to oppose the occupying authorities.

In the first official history of the SOE, Foot describes Holst thus:

> ... behind his ponderous appearance he kept a swift intellect, a painstaking character and a strong dislike of the Nazis. He was able to put together several useful lines for passing messages and parcels round south-west Europe.[81]

His physical attributes are described in an SOE file. Holst was a big man; his height was 1.89m and he weighed 117 kg. He had dark brown hair going grey on the sides, with blue eyes, but needed always to wear glasses. The file comments on his personal attributes, which included words and phrases like extraordinary, good organiser, accomplishes things, cynical, worldly-wise and shrewd. In another letter written by a Major Nagell, Wilhelm is referred to as a 'good Norwegian patriot'.[82]

After the Germans had been expelled from France, Holst wished to secure a post with the Norwegian government in Paris. In 1941 he had shown interest in working for the Norwegian government-in-exile, but did not follow up on this. In 1945 Holst was lobbying to try to get a Norwegian government post looking after Norwegian refugees in France. He was unpopular among the Norwegian community in France because he had worked with, and was friendly with, a known collaborator called Wilhelm Heineman, who had carried out fortification work for the Germans using slave labour. Holst claimed that Heineman had helped him in his Resistance activities several times. Although Holst's link with Heineman was condemned, his loyalty to the Allied cause was never doubted. In correspondence linked to his lobbying for support in getting a job with the Norwegian government, comments are made about Holst's financial transactions and the fact that he made plenty of money during the war and had a large bank account in Lisbon.[83]

After separating from Madge, Wilhelm was back in Paris running his own company and also becoming the representative of the Norwegian Spanish Committee in Paris. He was decorated many times for his wartime exploits, receiving medals from France and Norway. In 1947 he was back with his first wife, Anna, and divided his time between Paris and Oslo. In 1949 he set up a new business in Oslo but died suddenly in November 1949, leaving behind his wife Anna and daughter Lissen. His sudden death was possibly caused by his size and the stresses of his Spanish Civil War and Second World War experiences.[84]

*Resisting Fascism Again*

Thorkild Hansen was a Dane; he became friends with Madge and Wilhelm in Marseille from 1940, and was involved with assisting Ian Garrow's activities. He was a co-leader of the Pierre-Jacques line and it is likely he worked with Madge again on helping to set up the line. Towards the end of the war he and Madge became romantically involved and post-war he became Madge's third husband.

Hansen was born in Copenhagen in January 1900. His father was called Lars Peter and was deceased by the time of the Second World War; his mother was called Johanne. He said his parents were 'simple people', who had thirteen children, of which Thorkild was the twelfth. Most of the family were still living in Denmark. He went to school until he was 17 and spoke Danish, French and English fluently, German well and also had basic Spanish. From 1917–1919 he worked in marine insurance in Copenhagen. In 1920 he moved to Paris, where up to 1926 he worked in two different banks. From 1927–1933 he worked in import and export between France and Denmark and Norway. Then from 1934 up to the outbreak of war he was organising and teaching about life-insurance. At first glance, he was not somebody who would be expected to be a heroic Resistance fighter. He was married in 1924 to Marie and had two children; he and his wife later separated and then divorced, and Marie and the children were living elsewhere in France.[85]

Thorkild joined the French army in August 1939, just before the outbreak of war. He was mobilised into the army in February 1940 and was sent to the Chalons/Marne front in northern France in June 1940. He was captured by the Germans and made a PoW on 18 June. At the PoW camp at Fourchambault the Germans discovered he was distributing anti-German propaganda and condemned him for his activities; this was 23 December 1940. The next day Thorkild escaped and managed to the cross the demarcation line dividing France, arriving in Marseille in January 1941. In Marseille he became part of the AFSC, which is where he would have first met Wilhelm and through him, Madge. Within a short space of time, Wilhelm and Thorkild became friends. He was put in charge of purchases, food distribution and transport until the American Quakers left in November 1942. When he describes the Marseille group helping British service men and pilots to escape to Spain, Donald Darling mentions a Dane; this is almost certainly Thorkild Hansen. From October 1941, Hansen was also the leader of an SOE circuit. His code name or alias was 'Henri Berger'.[86]

In September 1942, he left Marseille for Lisbon and was put in charge of setting up a network for the passage of messages, propaganda and other material from Belgium to Portugal through France. This organisation developed into one of the biggest SOE circuits and Thorkild was joint organiser. This organisation then linked up with the Pierre-Jacques line, where Thorkild became the joint leader, and it helped to extract agents in danger out of France into Spain. The Spanish escape route was organised by Thorkild. Setting up the initial network involved Hansen in much travelling, where he had on his person a great deal of compromising material such as wireless sets, faked papers for agents and subversive propaganda. He, like Wilhelm, was also involved in distributing large sums of money amongst the various networks and circuits. In March 1944, Zembsch-Schreve, co-leader of the Pierre-Jacques line, was betrayed and captured. To prevent mass arrests, Hansen needed to act quickly.[87]

Thorkild did indeed act quickly, getting rid of evidence and warning other agents and helpers. He needed to destroy any compromising material, which, if it fell into the hands of the Gestapo, would have been disastrous for himself and the organisation. Hansen was never in robust health, but nonetheless he crossed the Pyrenees on foot in July 1944 to make a personal report to his intelligence chief in Madrid. He then re-crossed the Pyrenees back into France to continue his Resistance work until Allied forces liberated France.[88] The head of SOE, Major-General Gubbins, recommended Thorkild for the King's Medal for Courage in the Cause of Freedom, based on his exploits during the war. His recommendation mentioned his bravery, quick thinking and the fact that he carried out his duty regardless of the dangers involved.[89] Thorkild was also decorated for his wartime services by the French and the Danes.[90]

With the closure of the Alexandre *réseau* in September 1944, Madge's wartime exploits had come to an end. When she first decided to oppose the occupying forces, she would have known of the dire consequences of being captured. During her involvement in Resistance activities, people she knew had been tortured, imprisoned and killed. Although she never received more than basic training (in the use of magic inks in Lisbon) Madge rose to be second-in-command of an SOE network, and even led it for a time. Madge had links with the SIS, MI9, SOE and the French Resistance. She had links and worked with incredibly brave men and women like Ian Garrow, Albert-Marie Guérisse/Pat O'Leary, Nancy Fiocca/Wake, Guido Zembsch-Schreve and her two remarkable lovers, Wilhelm Holst and Thorkild Hansen, to name only a few. Madge had come a long way from being a thirty-something unhappy housewife with a chiropody practice in a Manchester suburb. After almost eight years of total upheaval fighting against Fascism in Spain, France and Portugal as a nurse, fund-raiser and Resistance woman, and with two failed relationships but a new one developing, would things ever be the same again?

# Epilogue

Saturday, 12 May 2018 in Chorlton-cum-Hardy, Manchester was a beautiful sunny spring day. From early morning people had been gathering outside 34 Manchester Road, Madge's last Manchester address before leaving to serve in Spain. Her old house would have been recognisable to Madge, although the ground floor was now a hairdresser's shop with a wooden ramped decking entrance. Her brothers' house two doors down was more altered and was now a dry cleaner. The variety of people gathering outside her old house included interested locals, trade unionists, Labour Party members, IBMT members, Royal British Legion members and an enthusiastic group of young Spaniards living in Manchester. The crowd grew in size to around a hundred; some carried flags, predominately the Spanish Republican tricolour flag of red, yellow and purple and a red Communist flag also flapped in the wind. Some of the people wore political t-shirts linked to the Spanish Civil War, particularly to the British Battalion of the International Brigades.

Hanging on the wall of 34 Manchester Road were two flags side by side; one was the Union Flag and the other was the flag of the Spanish Republic. The crowd was gathering to see Madge Addy being honoured by the unveiling of a city of Manchester plaque at her last residence in the city. Before the unveiling of Madge's plaque, various dignitaries addressed the assembled crowd. These included the Lord Mayor of Manchester, Eddy Newman, local MP Jeff Smith, and Alison Bunn of the Royal British Legion. Jeff Smith called Madge 'a brave and remarkable woman'. The Lord Mayor ended his address with these words:

> This City Council plaque honours a remarkable local woman and she joins a proud list of Mancunians who have been honoured for their achievements. Many of them like Madge, working class men and women who refused to do nothing

*Epilogue*

and stood up for what they believed and opposed injustice and evil. Thank you all for coming today to remember this remarkable Manchester woman.[1]

After the speeches, the flags were pulled away to uncover the plaque, which was greeted with sustained clapping and enthusiastic exclamations from the young Spaniards of *no pasaran*, the battle cry of the Spanish Republicans.

After the unveiling the event continued in the local library, which from the outside would have looked no different to Madge except for it being much cleaner and whiter in colour than in the 1930s. In the library function room, there was food for the attendees, an exhibition about the Spanish Civil War, and talks and songs from the Spanish Civil War and the Second World War. The success of the day and the enthusiasm to find out more about Madge led to a major decision that the plaque to honour her life was a great achievement, but that her full story needed to be written.

Madge's underground activities had ended in September 1944, when the Billet and Alexandre networks were closed down after the Germans had been driven out of France. In September 1944, both Wilhelm and Madge were living in Paris at the same address, although Madge was referred to as a single or unmarried woman. By April 1945, Madge is back in Marseille living at 5 Allée des Fleurs, Bois Luzy; she had lived with Wilhelm during the occupation years at 48 Rue Boudouresque. At first, Madge was prevented from leaving Marseille by a prohibition order. This meant she could not leave Marseille for three months until the new French authorities under De Gaulle knew who she was and what she had done during the occupation. She wished to travel to Paris to join Wilhelm, who was getting his affairs in order; the purpose of the trip could have been to finalise their separation. Her request to visit Paris was eventually granted.[2]

When the war in Europe was over Madge left France to visit her family in Manchester. Nothing is known of what transpired during this visit. Her brothers and sister would have found the second-youngest member of the Addy family a much-changed woman with life experiences to which none of them could really relate. It is hard to judge if the visit was a happy one; her two nephews, Robert and Francis, missed her visit to Manchester as they were still serving in the armed forces. But neither of them can recall Madge visiting her family in Manchester again. Her elder sister, Florence, had not been happy about her romance with Wilhelm; if Madge had mentioned her blossoming romance with Thorkild Hansen, a Dane, this may have caused further friction with the family, who expected Madge to continue to live in France rather than returning to Manchester.[3]

With the Spanish Civil War coming to an end and most British volunteers back in Britain, leading members of the volunteers who had served in Spain met and on 5 March 1939 set up the IBA. This was open to volunteers who had served in the International Brigades and medical services. The aim was to continue to support the Spanish Republic and Resistance groups to the Franco regime in any way possible. This took the form of publishing pamphlets about Spain, campaigning to release anti-Fascist prisoners and protesting about the Franco regime. Madge never joined the IBA; she was actively involved in opposing Fascism in Spain and France from 1937–1944 and living in France into the 1950s. Perhaps she did not know about it because she was living in France or perhaps she did not wish to join. The IBA did not know about any of her Second World War activities. When Dr Malimson, the Head of the North Manchester SMAC to whom Madge had written many times during her time in Spain, wrote to the IBA in 1947 for a correspondence address for Madge, Nan Green, the hospital administrator in Spain, wrote back saying they had not heard from her since 1939.[4]

After the war, Madge's activities were recognised. She was awarded an OBE in January 1946. The French also honoured her for her wartime exploits, awarding her the *Croix de Guerre* medal with bronze palm, signifying a mention in dispatches. She received various letters of thanks for her Second World War exploits, including one from the British Section for 'Assisting the Evasion of Allied Personnel', and one from the Dutch General Staff, 'for bravery shown during the German occupation' and having assisted Pierre (the alias of Guido Zembsch-Schreve) to set up his escape line, which would have involved helping Dutch SOE agents to escape the clutches of the Gestapo.[5]

During the 1940s and early 1950s, Madge and Thorkild Hansen continued to live in France. Life returned very much to normal; Thorkild worked in various occupations after the war as an import and export manager, an accountant and as an office manager. Madge returned to doing nursing-related work. The relationship between the two of them became serious and they were already seen as man and wife, although at this stage they were not legally married. In November 1950 they were

## Epilogue

invited to a reception in Paris as part of the visit of the King and Queen of Denmark to France. Madge's invitation was addressed to 'Madame Thorkild Hansen'. Up until they were married, they resided in separate dwellings, but always lived within close proximity of each other.[6]

In the early 1950s, Madge and Thorkild decided to leave France and move to Britain. They settled in the Marylebone district of London, Thorkild living in Dorset Square and Madge at Saint Edmund's Terrace. Madge and Thorkild were finally married on 23 December 1955 at Marylebone Registry Office; Thorkild was 55 and Madge was 51. After the wedding they lived together at 56 The Drive in Barnet; a large terraced house quite similar to Madge's pre-war house at 34 Manchester Road. Madge and Thorkild were to live happily at 56 The Drive for the rest of their lives. Thorkild, whose health had never been strong, fell ill in May 1966 with severe breathing difficulties, and was taken into Saint Bartholomew's Hospital suffering from bronchial pneumonia. In the hospital, the strain of his illness was too much for Thorkild's weakened body, and he suffered a stroke and died in hospital on 16 May 1966. Thorkild's death may well have affected Madge greatly. Lonely and isolated, and probably also bored after her truly adventurous life and her previous companionship with amazing men and women, Madge became depressed. It is very possible that in her last years she comforted herself by drinking alcohol. On 4 February 1970 she was discovered dead in her home; the cause of her death was asphyxia due to alcohol intoxication, or in more simple terms, she choked on her own vomit due to drinking large amounts of alcohol. Her death was judged to be accidental. Madge was 66 years of age when she died. It was a sad end to a full and remarkable life, and the way it ended should in no way undermine the amazing exploits she carried out during her lifetime.[7]

Madge died unknown, with her Spanish Civil War and Second World War exploits hidden from the public. When she died, oral history was in its infancy and most histories of the Second World War tended to be mostly about major figures in the war, campaigns or large battles of the conflict. Interest in the Spanish Civil War at this time was very limited. Since Madge's death, interest in the Spanish Civil War and ordinary people's involvement in the Civil War and in the Second World War has expanded massively. Over the years, extracts from Madge's letters have appeared in several books on the Spanish Civil War. Again, she has briefly been mentioned in a few books on Second World War espionage.

But in all cases, there was never more than a fleeting mention. From 2017 interest in Madge grew when a campaign to get her a city of Manchester plaque began.[8]

The local press, the *Manchester Evening News*, was interested in the story and ran a piece on Madge in January 2017, where, although the story was embellished for its readership and she was wrongly called a hairdresser, it was the first instance of Madge appearing in the public eye. A day later a national newspaper, the *Daily Mirror*, ran the same story, calling her an undercover hairdresser; although the story had several inaccuracies, it again helped to move Madge out of the shadows. A year later, in April 2018, the *Manchester Evening News* ran a second article on Madge, carrying similar details but advertising the times and date of the unveiling of a civic plaque in her honour. Interest in Madge climaxed in Manchester with a local television crew from Granada Television interviewing the author outside 34 Manchester Road. The five-minute piece was broadcast on north-west regional television on Thursday, 10 May 2018, and included archive clips from the Spanish Civil War and the Second World War. Madge's great-niece just happened to be watching, and rang her father Robert, the son of Madge's elder brother Francis, who later contacted the author. Madge is no longer a forgotten figure; her image and brief information about can be found easily on the internet.[9]

Madge's story has now finally been told. She can join a select number of remarkable British women who fought Fascism, taking great risks and voluntarily placing themselves in danger for the greater good. Uniquely, Madge served in two wars, as a nurse in Spain and as a *'résistant'* in various roles, opposing the occupying forces in France and working with various organisations, including MI9 and the SOE. She opposed three dictators: Franco, Hitler and Pétain, and worked in highly dangerous and stressful situations for eight long years. She was wounded in Spain, briefly imprisoned by the Nationalist forces and risked arrest many times in France during the Second World War. Madge lived a conventional life in Manchester married to a local man until 1937. The only possible hint of her later daring wartime exploits was the ability to ride a motorbike, an unusual skill for a woman in the 1920s! Her wartime exploits were to lead to national and international honours, an OBE and *Croix de Guerre*, marriage to men from Norway and Denmark, life in two countries – Spain and France – and travel to a third, Portugal. Madge Addy had come a long way from 34 Manchester Road, Chorlton-cum-Hardy, Manchester.

# Notes

**Introduction**

1. For full references and sources of information about Madge's life, see notes for each chapter.

**Chapter 1**

1. Skidelsky, *Oswald Mosley*, Papermac, 1990. 3rd ed.
2. Frederick William Addy Registration of Birth, Macclesfield District, 1856; Census 1891, Bingley, West Riding Yorkshire; Census 1901, Bolton, Lancashire; Census 1911 England and Wales, 58 Rusholme Grove, Manchester; Registration of Marriage, Frederick William Addy and Mary Costello, Macclesfield District, 1882.
3. Mary Costello, Registration of Birth, Macclesfield District, 1866; Census 1911 England and Wales, ibid.; Interview with Robert Francis Addie and Geoffrey Michael Addie, 28/07/2018; Marguerite Nuttall Addy, Nursing Character and Training Reference Document 8452, 1929; Mary Costello, Registration of Death, Chorlton District, 1924.
4. Darling, *Secret Sunday*, William Kimber, 1975, p. 28; Long, *Safe Houses are Dangerous*, William Kimber, 1985, p. 63.
5. Friends of Salford Cemeteries Trust, *Weaste Cemetery Heritage Trial: Mark Addy (1838-1890)*, www.weasteheritagetrail.co.uk/about/explore-the-cemetery/mark-addy-1838-1890/index.htm accessed 07/01/2020.
Manchester and Lancashire Family History Society, *Manchester Worthies: Mr Mark Addy (1838-1889)*, www.mlfhs.org.uk/worthies/addy.php accessed 07/01/2020.

6. Birth Certificate, Marguerite Nuttall Addy, 1904; Census 1911, ibid.; Census 1901, ibid.; Interview with Addie and Addie, ibid.
7. Cronin and Rhodes, *Images of England: Rusholme and Victoria Park*, Tempus, 2000, pp. 7–8; Hylton, *A History of Manchester*, Phillimore, 2010, 2nd ed., p. 150.
8. Census 1911, ibid.; Census 1901, ibid.; Interview with Addie and Addie, ibid.; Nursing Character and Training Reference Document, ibid.; Marriage Certificate 1930, Arthur Wilson Lightfoot and Marguerite Nuttall Addy.
9. Census 1911, ibid.; Census 1901, ibid.; Interview with Addie and Addie, ibid.; Electoral Rolls, Withington 1932–1939; *Grantham Journal* 23/07/1938; Will of Marguerite Nuttall Lightfoot, 27/02/1938.
10. Nursing Character and Training Reference Document, ibid.; *Hope Hospital Centenary 1880–1980: Official Brochure*, Salford Area Health Authority, 1980, pp. 1–4.
11. Postcard shown to the author; Nursing Character and Training Reference Document ibid.; Register of Nurses 1927–1931.
12. Register of Nurses, ibid.; Marriage Certificate 1930, ibid.; Electoral Rolls, Withington, ibid.; Interview Addie and Addie, ibid.; Manchester Trade Directory, 1934; *Daily Worker* 29/11/1938.
13. Dickens, *Chorlton-Cum-Hardy: Through Time*, Amberley Publishing, 2018, pp. 3–4; Hylton, ibid., pp. 211–212.
14. Dickens, ibid., pp. 87–88; Simpson, *The Quirks of Chorlton-Cum-Hardy: A History of its People and Places*, Topper Publishing, 2017, pp. 117, 124–127, 130–133.
15. Hall, *'Disciplina Camaradas': Four English Volunteers in Spain 1936–39*, Gosling Press, 1996.
16. British Broadcasting Corporation, *Fight to Save Manchester Venue Where Bee Gees First Sang*, www.bbc.co.uk/news/uk-england-manchester-50318830 accessed 18/03/2020.
17. Dickens, ibid., p. 88; Interview Addie and Addie, ibid.
18. Laity (ed.), *Left Book Club Anthology*, Victor Gollancz, 2001.
19. Interview Addie and Addie, ibid.
20. Barry, *From Manchester to Spain*, Salford, Working Class Movement Library, 2009, pp. 10, 52–56.
21. Ibid., pp. 35–43.

## Chapter 2

1. Most information for this chapter was from various works but mainly, Carr, *Spain 1808–1975*, Oxford University Press, 1982; Payne, *Spain's First Democracy: The Second Republic 1931–36*, University of Wisconsin, 1993, 2nd ed.; Thomas, *The Spanish Civil War*, Penguin Books, 1986, 3rd ed.; Beevor, *The Battle for Spain: the Spanish Civil War 1936–39*, Weidenfeld & Nicolson, 2006; Graham, *The Spanish Republic at War 1936–1939*, Cambridge University Press, 2002.
2. Useful books about the Second Republic 1931–1936 include, Carr, ibid.; Payne, ibid.; Brenan, *The Spanish Labyrinth: An Account of the Social and Political Background of the Spanish Civil War*, Cambridge University Press, 1988, first published 1943, 2nd ed. 1950; Preston, *The Coming of the Spanish Civil War: Reform, Reaction and Revolution in the Second Republic*, Methuen, 1978; Jackson, *The Spanish Republic and the Civil War 1931–39*, Princeton University Press, 1967.
3. Payne, ibid., pp. 110, 121, 179.
4. Preston, *Doves of War: Four Women of Spain*, HarperCollins, 2002, pp. 297–408.
5. Low, *La Pasionaria: The Spanish Firebrand*, Hutchinson, 1992.
6. Fredericks, 'Feminism: The Essential Ingredient in Federica Montseny's Anarchist Theory' in Slaughter and Kern (eds.), *European Women on the Left: Socialism, Feminism and Problems Faced by Political Women, 1880 to the Present*, Greenwood Press, 1981, pp. 125–146.
7. Books on Spanish Anarchists include: Bookchin, *The Spanish Anarchists: The Heroic Years 1868–1936*, Free Life Editions, 1977; and Casanova, *Anarchism, the Republic and Civil War in Spain 1931–39*, Routledge, 2004.
8. Preston, *Franco: A Biography*, HarperCollins, 1993; Ellwood, *Franco*, Longman, 1994.
9. Graham, *Socialism and War: The Spanish Socialist Party in Power and Crisis 1936–39*, Cambridge University Press, 1991.
10. Graham, *The Spanish Republic at War 1936–39*, ibid.
11. Balcells and Walker, *Catalan Nationalism: Past and Present*, Macmillan, 1996; Payne, *Basque Nationalism*, University of Nevada Press, 1975.

12. Alexander and Graham (eds.) *The French and Spanish Popular Fronts: Comparative Perspectives*, Cambridge University Press, 1989; Graham and Preston (eds.) *The Popular Front in Europe*, Macmillan, 1987.
13. Brenan, ibid., pp. 298–315, Preston, *The Coming of the Spanish Civil War*, ibid., pp. 177–202; Jackson, ibid., pp. 184–217.
14. Ellwood, *Spanish Fascism in the Franco Era: Falange Espanola de las JONs 1936–76*, Macmillan, 1987.
15. Blinkhorn, *Carlism and Crisis in Spain 1931–39*, Cambridge University Press, 1975.
16. Carr, ibid., pp. 640–651; Payne, ibid., pp. 321–370; Thomas, ibid., pp. 156–197; Beevor, ibid., pp. 34–52.
17. Thomas, ibid., p. 985. Estimates 1,264 aircraft, 350 tanks, 2,000 artillery pieces and 167,000 foreign soldiers. Edaile, *The Spanish Civil War: A Military History*, Routledge, 2019, p. 342. Puts foreign aid to the Nationalists as 1,544 aircraft, 284 armoured vehicles and 1,991 artillery pieces. Clifford, *The People's Army in the Spanish Civil War: A Military History of the Republic and International Brigades*, Pen & Sword, 2020, p. 279. Agrees with Edaile on quantities of aid to the Nationalists.
18. Procter, *Hitler's Luftwaffe in the Spanish Civil War*, Greenwood Press, 1983; Whealey, *Hitler and Spain: the Nazi Role in the Spanish Civil War*, University Press of Kentucky, 1989.
19. Coverdale, *Italian Intervention in the Spanish Civil War*, Princeton University Press, 1975.
20. Beevor, ibid., p. 138.
21. Alba and Schwartz, *Spanish Marxism Versus Soviet Communism: A History of the P.O.U.M.*, Transaction Book, 1988.
22. Quoted in Orwell, *Homage to Catalonia and Looking Back on the Spanish War*, Penguin, 1988, first published 1938, p. 9.
23. Ibid.; Hall, *'In Spain with Orwell': George Orwell and the Independent Labour Party Volunteers in the Spanish Civil War, 1936–1939*, Tippermiur Books Ltd, 2013.
24. Lines, *Women in Combat in the Spanish Civil War*, Lexington Books, 2012; Hall, *Revolutionary Warfare: Spain 1936–37*, Gosling Press, 1996, pp. 38–41.
25. Lines, ibid., pp. 75–76, 81–82.

*Notes*

26. Thomas, ibid., pp. 982–984. Estimates around 35,000 in International Brigades; the maximum number of foreign volunteers at any one time was 18,000. 10,000 came from France, 5,000 from Germany, 3,350 from Italy, 2,800 from the USA and 2,000 from Britain and Ireland. Losses in each national group was high. Brigades were roughly organised by language so, for example, 15th International Brigade was English speaking and included British, Irish, American and Canadian volunteers.
27. Ibid., p. 984. Estimated military aid to the Republic 1,320 planes, 900 tanks, 1,550 artillery pieces and 52–53,000 foreign volunteers. Esdaile, ibid., p. 346. 854 planes, 535 armoured vehicles and 1,180 artillery pieces. Clifford, ibid., p. 279. Agrees with Esdaile but has artillery numbers at 2,420. Howson, *Arms for Spain: The Untold Story of the Spanish Civil War*, John Murray, 1998.
28. Paz, *Durutti in the Spanish Revolution*, AK Press, 2007.
29. Hills, *The Battle for Madrid*, Vantage Books, 1976; Colodny, *The Struggle for Madrid: The Central Epic of the Spanish Conflict 1936–37*, Paine-Whitman, 1958; Mathieson, *Frontline Madrid: Battlefield Tours of the Spanish Civil War*, Signal Books, 2014.
30. Ellwood, ibid, pp. 41–45.
31. Jackson, *Juan Negrin: Physiologist, Socialist and Spanish Republican War Leader*, Sussex Academic Press, 2010.
32. Graham, *The Spanish Republic at War*, ibid., pp. 237–238, 254–315.
33. Coverdale, ibid., pp. 205–262.
34. Thomas and Witts, *Guernica: The Crucible of World War II*, Stein and Day, 1975; Steer, *The Tree of Gernika: A Field Study of Modern War*, Hodder and Stoughton, 1938; Rankin, *Telegram from Guernica: The Extraordinary Life of George Steer War Correspondent*, Faber and Faber, 2003, pp. 114–148.
35. Clifford, ibid, pp. 72–115.
36. Ibid., pp. 116–171.
37. Ibid., pp. 172–229.
38. Henry, *The Ebro 1938: Death Knell of the Republic*, Osprey Publishing, 1999.
39. Low, ibid., pp. 108–110.
40. Preston, *The Last Days of the Spanish Republic*, William Collins, 2016.

## Chapter 3

1. Blakeway, *The Last Dance: 1936: The Year of Change*, John Murray, 2010; Brandon, *The Dark Valley: A Panorama of the 1930s*, Jonathan Cape, 2000; Stevenson and Cook, *The Slump*, Quartet Books, 1979; Gardiner, *The Thirties: An Intimidate History*, HarperPress, 2011.
2. Buchanan, *Britain and the Spanish Civil War*, Cambridge University Press, 1997; Watkins, *Britain Divided: The Effect of the Spanish Civil War on British Political Opinion*, Thomas Nelson and Sons Ltd, 1963; Fyrth, *The Signal was Spain: The Aid Spain Movement in Britain 1936–39,* Lawrence and Wishart, 1986; Mason, *Democracy, Deeds and Dilemmas: Support for the Spanish Republic within British Civil Society, 1936–1939*, Sussex Academic Press, 2017.
3. Shelmerdine, *British Representations of the Spanish Civil War*, Manchester University Press, 2006; Buchanan, *The Impact of the Spanish Civil War on Britain: War, Loss and Memory*, Sussex Academic Press, 2007, pp. 1–22.
4. Quoted in Shelmerdine, ibid., p. 6.
5. Ibid., p. 177.
6. Fyrth, ibid., pp. 198–219; Buchanan, *Britain and the Spanish Civil War*, ibid., pp. 93–120.
7. Shelmerdine, ibid., pp. 175–176.
8. Quoted in Fyrth, ibid., p. 21.
9. Ibid., pp. 22–23, 207–210, 261; Mason, ibid., pp. 93–96, 102–105.
10. Skidelsky, *Oswald Mosley*, ibid.
11. Quoted in Buchanan, *Britain and the Spanish Civil War*, ibid., p. 1.
12. Thorpe, *Britain in the 1930s: The Deceptive Decade*, Blackwell, 1992, pp. 7–22.
13. Buchanan, *Britain and the Spanish Civil War*, ibid., pp. 37–62; Edwards, *The British Government and the Spanish Civil War 1936–39*, Macmillan, 1979; Alberca, *Gibraltar and the Spanish Civil War 1936–39: Local, National and International Perspectives*, Bloomsbury, 2015.
14. Buchanan, ibid., p. 37.
15. Quoted in Edwards, ibid., p. 137.
16. Buchanan, *Britain and the Spanish Civil War*, ibid., pp. 54–61.
17. Ibid., pp. 38, 56.
18. Alberca, ibid., pp. 45–46.

19. Edwards, ibid., p. 131.
20. Buchanan, *Britain and the Spanish Civil War*, ibid., pp. 40–41, 52–53, 59, 61–62.
21. Tom Buchanan, *The Spanish Civil War and the British Labour Movement*, Cambridge University Press, 1991, pp. 1–36.
22. Quoted in ibid., p. 62.
23. Ibid., pp. 37–72.
24. Ibid., pp. 73–106.
25. Ibid., p. 99.
26. Ibid., pp. 137, 226–7.
27. Quoted in Watkins, ibid., p. 194.
28. Morgan, *J. Ramsay MacDonald*, Manchester University Press, 1987.
29. Butler and Butler, *British Political Facts 1900–1985*, Macmillan, 1986, pp. 225–226; Vickers, *The Labour Party and the World Volume 1: The Evolution of Labour's Foreign Policy 1900–51*, Manchester University Press, 2004, pp. 119–128; Buchanan, *Britain and the Spanish Civil War*, ibid., pp. 78–83.
30. Buchanan, ibid., p. 81; Vickers, ibid., pp. 125–126.
31. Beckett, *Clem Attlee*, Politico's Publishing, 2000, pp. 134–135.
32. Baxell, *British Volunteers in the Spanish Civil War: The British Battalion in the International Brigades 1936–39*, Routledge, 2004, p. 15; Jackson, *British Women and the Spanish Civil War*, Routledge, 2002, pp. 175–176.
33. Buchanan, *Britain and the Spanish Civil War*, ibid., pp. 121–145; Jackson, 'The British International Brigades as Labour Party Dissidents', *International Journal of Iberian Studies* 18(1), 2005.
34. Buchanan, ibid., pp. 80–83; Jackson, ibid., pp. 15–17; Vickers, ibid., pp. 125–126.
35. Mason, ibid., pp. 83–85, 98–101.
36. Branson, *History of the Communist Party of Great Britain 1927–1941*, Lawrence & Wishart, 1985, pp. 220–239; Thompson, *The Good Old Cause: British Communism 1920–1991*, Pluto Press, 1992, p. 218; Beckett, *Enemy Within: The Rise and Fall of the British Communist Party*, John Murray, 1995, pp. 46–59.
37. Laity (ed), ibid., pp. ix–xxxi.
38. Morgan, *Harry Pollitt*, Manchester University Press, 1993, pp. 89–118.

39. Fyrth, ibid., pp. 198–291.
40. Buchanan, *Britain and the Spanish Civil War*, ibid., p. 158.
41. Watkins, ibid., p. 194.
42. Baxell, ibid., pp. 14–15; Baxell, *Unlikely Warriors: The British in the Spanish Civil War and the Struggle against Fascism*, Aurum Press, 2012, p. 6; Alexander, *British Volunteers for Liberty: Spain 1936–1939*, Lawrence & Wishart, 1982, pp. 29–39.
43. Baxell, *British Volunteers in the Spanish Civil War*, ibid., pp. 107–129; Alexander, ibid., pp. 183–195, 237–244; Baxell, *Unlikely Warriors*, ibid., pp. 340–374.
44. Baxell, *British Volunteers in the Spanish Civil War*, ibid., pp. 150–151.
45. Thompson, ibid., p. 218; Branson, ibid., p. 56.
46. McGarry, *Eoin O'Duffy: A Self-Made Hero*, Oxford University Press, 2005.
47. Kemp, *Mine Were of Trouble*, Cassell, 1957; Thomas and Stradling, *Brother Against Brother: Experiences of a British Volunteer in the Spanish Civil War*, Sutton Publishing, 1998, pp. 35–154; Preston, *Doves of War*, ibid., pp. 11–120.
48. Thomas, ibid., pp. 204, 212–214.
49. Buchanan, *Britain and the Spanish Civil War*, ibid., pp. 24–29; Fyrth, ibid., pp. 37–40.
50. Buchanan, ibid., pp. 24–26.
51. Gibson, *The Assassination of Federico Garcia Lorca*, Penguin Books, 1983.
52. Buchanan, *Britain and the Spanish Civil War*, ibid., pp. 32, 146–168.
53. Ibid., pp. 169–188; Mason, ibid., pp. 112–143.
54. Fyrth, ibid., pp. 158–180; Mendlesohn, *Quaker Relief Work in the Spanish Civil War*, Edwin Mellen Press Ltd, 2002.
55. Buchanan, *Britain and the Spanish Civil War*, ibid., pp. 33, 179–80; Fyrth, ibid., pp. 192–197.

## Chapter 4

1. Fyrth, ibid., pp. 198–219; Buchanan, *Britain and the Spanish Civil War*, ibid., pp. 93–120; Mason, ibid., pp. 32–33.
2. Palfreeman, *Salud: British Volunteers in the Republican Medical Service During the Spanish Civil War, 1936–39*, Sussex Academic Press, 2012, p. 11.

## Notes

3. Fyrth, ibid., p. 201; Palfreeman, ibid., pp. 11–13; Buchanan, *Britain and the Spanish Civil War*, ibid., pp. 97–98.
4. Fyrth, ibid., p. 215; Jackson, *British Women and the Spanish Civil War*, ibid., pp. 75–76.
5. Jackson, ibid., pp. 218–219.
6. Fyrth, ibid., pp. 45–48; Palfreeman, ibid., pp. 239–240; Buchanan, *Britain and the Spanish Civil War*, ibid., pp. 101–102.
7. Palfreeman, ibid., p. 257; Bill and Newens, *Leah Manning*, Leah Manning Trust, 1991, pp. 42–47.
8. Buchanan, *Britain and the Spanish Civil War*, ibid., pp. 104–105.
9. Fyrth, ibid., p. 47; Palfreeman, ibid., pp. 24–25.
10. Palfreeman, ibid., p. 26.
11. Jackson, *British Women and the Spanish Civil War*, ibid., pp. 232–233.
12. Ibid., p. 233.
13. Fyrth, ibid., pp. 220–222.
14. Ibid., pp. 222–237; Buchanan, *Britain and the Spanish Civil War*, ibid., pp. 109–113.
15. Palfreeman, ibid., pp. 12–13.
16. Fyrth, ibid., pp. 238–240; Jackson, *British Women and the Spanish Civil War*, ibid., p. 71.
17. Fyrth, ibid., pp. 240–242; Buchanan, *Britain and the Spanish Civil War*, ibid., pp. 114–116.
18. Palfreeman, ibid., p. 29.
19. Ibid., pp. 28–37; Fyrth, ibid., pp. 43–52.
20. Palfreeman, ibid., p. 255; Buchanan, *Britain and the Spanish Civil War*, ibid., pp. 103, 105.
21. Fyrth, ibid., pp. 52–54; Palfreeman, ibid., pp. 37–39.
22. Palfreeman, ibid., pp. 38–39; Jackson, *'For us it was Heaven': The Passion, Grief and Fortitude of Patience Darton: From the Spanish Civil War to Mao's China*, Sussex Academic Press, 2012.
23. Fyrth, ibid., p. 54; Palfreeman, ibid., p. 42.
24. Fyrth, ibid., pp. 55–61; Palfreeman, ibid., pp. 40–48.
25. Palfreeman, *Aristocrats, Adventurers and Ambulances: British Medical Units in the Spanish Civil War*, Sussex Academic Press, 2014, pp. 11–122.
26. Ibid., pp. 123–203.
27. Fyrth, ibid., pp. 61–82; Palfreeman, *Salud*, ibid., pp. 49–90.
28. Fyrth, ibid., pp. 83–122; Palfreeman, ibid., pp. 91–151.
29. Fyrth, ibid., pp. 123–139; Palfreeman, ibid., pp. 152–170.

30. Fyrth, ibid., p. 96; Palfreeman, ibid., p. 167.
31. Coni, 'Medicine and the Spanish Civil War', *Journal of the Royal Society of Medicine*, 95(3), 2002, p. 147.
32. Ibid., p. 148, Fyrth, ibid., pp. 146–9; Palfreeman, *Salud*, ibid., p. 113.
33. Allan and Gordon, *The Scalpel, the Sword: The Story of Dr Norman Bethune*, Monthly Review Press, 1973.
34. Coni, ibid., p. 148; Fyrth, ibid., pp. 150–153; Palfreeman, *Salud*, ibid. pp. 89–90.
35. Coni, ibid., p. 149; Fyrth, ibid., p. 142–143; Palfreeman, ibid., p. 114.
36. Palfreeman, ibid., pp. 260–266, 189–205.
37. Ibid., pp. 268–269.
38. Ibid., pp. 266–267.
39. Ibid., pp. 186–189.
40. Fyrth, ibid., p. 45.
41. Palfreeman, *Salud*, ibid., p. 222.
42. Quoted in ibid., p. 223.
43. Ibid., pp. 222–223; Fyrth, ibid., pp. 86–87, 104, 150.
44. Fyrth, ibid., pp. 101, 107.
45. Ibid., pp. 104–105.
46. Ibid., p. 105.
47. Ibid., p. 103.
48. Quoted in Fyvel, *English Penny*, Arthur H. Stockwell Ltd., 1992, p. 35.
49. Imperial War Museum, *The Spanish Civil War Collection: Sound Archive Oral History Recordings*, Trustees of the Imperial War Museum, 1996, p. 75.
50. Palfreeman, *Salud*, ibid., p. 73.
51. Ibid., p. 228.
52. Ibid., p. 119.
53. Quoted in Imperial War Museum, ibid., p. 192.
54. Quoted in Palfreeman, Salud, ibid., p. 95.
55. Ibid., pp. 95–96.
56. Quoted in ibid., p. 90.
57. Imperial War Museum, ibid., p. 220.
58. Ibid., p. 75.
59. Fyrth, ibid., pp. 136–137.
60. Palfreeman, *Salud*, ibid., p. 247; Jackson, *Britain and the Spanish Civil War*, ibid., p. 230; Murphy, *Molly Murphy: Suffragette and Socialist*, Institute of Social Research, Salford University, 1998.

*Notes*

61. Palfreeman, ibid., pp. 248–249; Jackson, ibid., p. 231; Fyvel, ibid.
62. Palfreeman, ibid., p. 251; Jackson, ibid., pp. 234–235.
63. Quoted in Palfreeman, ibid., p. 228.
64. Quoted in ibid., p. 230.

# Chapter 5

1. Marx Memorial Library, Box D-1/A5.
2. Palfreeman, *Salud*, ibid., p. 242; Jackson, 'Madge Addy: Forgotten Heroine of the Wars in Spain and France', *IBMT Newsletter*, 43(3), 2016, p. 19; Jackson, Angela, *From Foodships to the Frontline: A Forgotten Manchester Heroine of the Spanish Civil War*, http://www.international-brigades.org.uk/content/foodships-frontlines-forgotten-manchester-heroine-spanish-civil-war, accessed 17/03/2017; *Daily Herald* 28/11/1938, *Daily Worker* 29/11/1938.
3. On the reverse of a photograph of medical staff at Uclés which includes Madge Addy it is dated February 1938. Will 27/02/1938, ibid.; Baxell, Richard, *List of British Volunteers in Spain*, http://www.richardbaxell.info/volunteers/, accessed 20/07/19; Warwick University, Trade Union Congress Archives at the Modern Records Centre, Spanish Medical Aid Committee minutes 14/07/39.
4. Warwick Univ., SMAC minutes 07/1938, SMAC Bulletin 08/1938; *Grantham Journal* 23/07/1938, *Daily Herald* 28/11/1938; Baxell, ibid.; Palfreeman, ibid., pp. 160, 242.
5. *Daily Worker* 26/11/1938; Fyrth, ibid., pp. 136–137.
6. Fyrth, ibid., pp. 136–137.
7. Ibid., pp. 136–137; *Manchester Evening News* 30/06/1939; *Yorkshire Evening Post* 30/06/1939; *Nottingham Journal* 01/07/1939; Warwick Univ., SMAC minutes 14/07/1939; Baxell, ibid.; Palfreeman, ibid., pp. 160, 242.
8. MML, 17/01/1939, Box D-1/A11.
9. Fyrth and Alexander (eds.), ibid., pp. 15, 85; Buchanan, *Impact of the Spanish Civil War on Britain*, ibid., p. 52; Fyrth, ibid., pp. 87, 104–105.
10. Corkill and Rawnsley (eds.), *Road to Spain: Anti-Fascists at War 1936–39*, Borderline Press, 1981, pp. 125–126.
11. Green, *A Chronicle of Small Beer: The Memoirs of Nan Green*, Trent Editions, 2004, p. 84; Buchanan, ibid., p. 63.

12. Interview Addie and Addie, ibid.
13. MML, Madge Addy letter, 07/10/1938, Box D-1/A8.
14. Madge Addy letters; SMAC Minutes; SMAC Bulletin; *Manchester Evening News* 17/02/1939; *Grantham Journal* 23/07/1938.
15. Fyrth, ibid., pp. 199–200.
16. Ibid., pp. 119–120; Palfreeman, ibid., p. 157.
17. Quoted in Green, ibid., p. 85.
18. Ibid., Palfreeman, ibid., pp. 255, 159; MML, Secretary IBA to Dr Malimson letter of reply 29/09/1947.
19. Quoted in Fyrth and Alexander (eds), ibid., p. 93.
20. Quoted in Palfreeman, ibid., p. 158.
21. Ibid., pp. 246, 256.
22. Ibid., pp. 158–159, Warwick Univ., Madge Addy letters 20/02/1939.
23. MML, MA letter 23/11/1938, Box D-1/A10.
24. Warwick Univ., SMAC minutes 07/1938.
25. MML, MA letters 31/08/1938, Box D-1/A6.
26. MML, MA letters 17/10/1938, Box D-1/A9.
27. Warwick Univ., MA letters 20/02/1939.
28. MML, MA letters 17/01/1939, Box D-1/A11.
29. MML, MA letters 17/10/1938, Box D-1/A9.
30. MML, MA letters 07/10/1938, Box D-1/A8.
31. *Daily Worker* 26/11/1939.
32. Warwick Univ., MA letters 01/03/1939.
33. Warwick Univ., MA letters 20/2/1939.
34. MML, MA letters 16/09/1938 box D-1/A7.
35. Warwick Univ., MA letters 20/02/1939, 24/02/1939.
36. Information supplied by Máximo Molina Gutiérrez, local Uclés historian.
37. Ibid., MML, MA letters 23/11/1938 Box D-1/A10.
38. MML, MA letters 17/01/1939 Box D-1/A11.
39. *Daily Herald* 29/11/1938; *Daily Worker* 26/11/1939; Warwick Univ., SMAC minutes 30/11/1938.
40. MML, MA letters 16/09/1938, Box D-1/A7.
41. MML, MA letters 17/01/1939, Box D-1/A11.
42. Warwick Univ., MA letters 24/02/1939.
43. *Yorkshire Evening Post* 30/06/1939.
44. Palfreeman, ibid., p. 244; Jackson, *'For us it was Heaven'*, ibid., p. 46.

## Notes

45. Palfreeman, ibid., pp. 243–244; Jackson, *'For Us it Was Heaven'*, ibid., p. 131; Fyrth, ibid., p. 296.
46. Warwick Univ., MA letters 02/03/1939.
47. MML, MA letters 17/10/1938, Box D-1/A9 MML, MA letters 16/09/1938, Box D-1/A7; Palfreeman, ibid., pp. 244, 249, 251–252; Fyrth, ibid., pp. 137–138.
48. Palfreeman, ibid., pp. 241–242.
49. Warwick Univ., SMAC Bulletin 08/1938.
50. *Manchester Evening News* 17/02/1939.
51. MML, MA letters 02/1939, Box D-1/A12.
52. *Grantham Journal* 23/07/1938.
53. MML, MA letters 17/10/1938, Box D-1/A9.
54. Warwick Univ., MA letters 20/02/1939.
55. Quoted in *Daily Workers* 26/11/1938, 16/03/1939.
56. MML, MA letters 31/08/1938, Box D-1/A6.
57. Ibid.
58. Warwick Univ., MA letters 20/02/1939.
59. Warwick Univ., SMAC Minutes 21/09/1938, 22/02/1939; MML, MA letters 17/01/1939, Box D-1/A11.
60. Quoted in *Grantham Journal* 23/07/1938.
61. *Daily Herald* 28/11/1938.
62. MML, MA letters 31/08/1938, Box D-1/A6.
63. Quoted in *Grantham Journal* 23/07/1938.
64. Quoted in *Daily Herald* 28/11/1938.
65. Warwick Univ., SMAC Bulletin, 08/1938.
66. *Daily Worker* 16/03/1939.
67. MML, MA letters 28/07/1938, Box D-1/A5.
68. Simpson, Andrew, *On the Trial of a Bullet Holed Ambulance Somewhere in Stalybridge* https://chorltonhistory.blogspot.com/search/label/Madge%20Addy, accessed 24/4/2019; Quoted in Corkill and Rawnsley (eds.), ibid., pp. 132–133.
69. Palfreeman, ibid., p. 253.
70. MML, MA letters 31/08/1938, Box D-1/A6.
71. MML, MA letters 27/07/1938, Box D-1/A4.
72. MML, MA letters 31/08/1938, Box D-1/A6.
73. MML, MA letters 27/07/1938, Box D-1/A4.
74. MML, MA letters 27/07/1938 Box D-1/A3.
75. MML, MA letters 07/10/1938 Box D-1/A8.

76. MML, MA letters 31/08/1938 Box D-1/A6.
77. Information provided by Ole Kleppe, grandson Wilhelm Holst. Wilhelm Holst has two SOE files from the Second World War, The National Archives, HS 9/735 and HS 9/734/3.
78. TNA, HS 9/735 Mr Gleditch's Report on Wilhelm Holst, 29/4/1941.
79. *Arbeiderbladet*, 28/07/1938 (translated by Kleppe).
80. TNA, HS9/735 Gleditch ibid.; *Fram*, 07/1939 (translated by Kleppe).
81. MML, MA letters 27/07/1938, Box D-1/A3.
82. MML, MA letters 27/03/1938, Box D-1/A4.
83. Fyrth, ibid., p. 137.
84. Warwick Univ., MA letters 14/03/1939.
85. Warwick Univ., SMAC Minutes 15/03/1939.
86. Fyrth, ibid., p. 137.
87. *Manchester Evening News* 30/06/1939.
88. *Manchester Guardian* 01/07/1939.
89. Warwick Univ., SMAC Minutes 14/07/1939.
90. Quoted in *Yorkshire Evening Post* 30/06/1939; *Nottingham Journal* 01/07/1939.
91. Warwick Univ., SMAC Minutes 19/07/1939.
92. Warwick Univ., SMAC Minutes 21/08/1939; Dix Noonan Webb, *Ron Penhall Collection*, www.dnw.co.uk/auction-archive/lot-archive/lot.php?department=Medals&lot_uid=130474, accessed 30/11/2019. Madge's account of her time in Uclés has unfortunately been lost since it was first sold along with OBE in 1971.
93. MML, Letter Dr Malimson to IBA 24/09/1947; Secretary IBA letter of reply 29/09/1947.

## Chapter 6

1. Stein, *Beyond Death and Exile: The Spanish Republicans in France 1939–1955*, Harvard University Press, 1979, pp. 23–24.
2. Ibid., pp. 27–28.
3. Ibid., pp. 19–38; Soo, *The Routes to Exile: France and the Spanish Civil War 1939–2009*, Manchester University Press, 2017, pp. 25–56; Fyrth and Alexander (eds.), ibid., pp. 327–332; de Palencia, *Smouldering Freedom: the Story of the Spanish Republicans in Exile*, Victor Gollancz, 1946.

## Notes

4. Fyrth, ibid., pp. 292–303; Fyrth and Alexander (eds.), ibid., pp. 334–336; Jackson, *British Women and the Spanish Civil War*, ibid., pp. 160–172; Fagen, *Exiles and Citizens: Spanish Republicans in Mexico*, University of Texas Press, 1973.
5. Stein, ibid., p. 46.
6. Quoted in Fyrth and Alexander (eds.), ibid., p. 333.
7. Quoted in Jackson, *British Women and the Spanish Civil War,* ibid., p. 165.
8. Stein, ibid., p. 68.
9. Ibid., pp. 39–75; Fyrth, ibid., pp. 293–295; Soo, ibid., pp. 57–92.
10. Stein, ibid., pp. 76–91.
11. Ibid., pp. 92–106; Soo, ibid., pp. 93–151.
12. Stein, ibid., pp. 107–123.
13. Ibid., p. 247.
14. Mesquida, *La Nueve 24 August 1944: The Spanish Republicans Who Liberated Paris*, Christie Books, 2015.
15. Stein, ibid., pp. 123–180; Soo, ibid., pp. 152–190; Wingeate Pike, *In the Service of Stalin: The Spanish Communists in Exile 1939–1945*, Clarendon Press, 1993.
16. Stein, ibid., p. 227.
17. Ibid., pp. 181–236; Soo, ibid., pp. 191–252.
18. Quoted in Stein, ibid., p. 234.
19. Henig, *The Origins of the Second World War 1933–41*, Routledge, 2005, 2nd ed, pp. 5–16; Bell, *The Origins of the Second World War in Europe*, Longman, 1997, pp. 19–25; for some useful further reading on the origins of the Second World War and the major events in the 1930s see: Wheatcroft and Overy, *The Road to War: The Origins of World War II*, Vantage, 2009, Brandon, *The Dark Valley: A Panorama of the 1930s*, Johnathan Cape, 2000; Gilbert, *The Illustrated London News Marching to War 1933–39*, Bracken Books, 1989.
20. Henig, ibid., p. 28; Bell, ibid., pp. 254–255.
21. Henig, ibid., pp. 29–30; Bell, ibid., p. 249.
22. Henig, ibid., pp. 37–40; Bell, ibid., pp. 230–233.
23. Henig, ibid., pp. 39–42; Bell, ibid., pp. 233–238.
24. Henig, ibid., pp. 24–26, 28, 30, 32, 34, 41.
25. Bell, ibid., pp. 159–160, 167–168, 170–171, 209–212; Taylor, *The Origins of the Second World War*, Penguin, 1964, first published 1961.

26. Henig, ibid., pp. 35–37, 60–62.
27. Ibid., pp. 49–50; Bell, ibid., pp. 254–258.
28. Henig, ibid., pp. 50–56; Bell, ibid., pp. 258–289.
29. Henig, ibid., pp. 56–59; Bell, ibid., pp. 292–301.
30. Cobban, *A History of France: Volume 3: France of the Republics 1871–1962*, Penguin, 1975, first published 1965, pp. 142–149. , Hastings, *All Hell Let Loose: The World at War 1939–1945*, Harper Press, 2011, p. 74; Weber, *The Hollow Years: France in the 1930s*, Sinclair-Stevenson, 1995.
31. Cobban, ibid., pp. 149–159; Danos and Gibelin, *June 36: Class Struggle and the Popular Front in France*, Bookmarks, 1986; Levy, 'The French Popular Front 1936–37' in Graham and Preston (eds.) *The Popular Front in Europe*, Macmillan Press, 1987, pp. 58–83.
32. Cobban, ibid., pp. 159–176; Thomas, *Britain, France and Appeasement: Anglo-French Relations in the Popular Front Era*, Berg, 1996; Weber, ibid., pp. 257–279.
33. Quoted in Hastings, ibid., p. 17.
34. Ibid., pp. 1–24; Deighton, *Blitzkrieg: From the Rise of Hitler to the Fall of Dunkirk*, Triad Granada, 1980, pp. 107–114.
35. Hastings, ibid., pp. 25–42.
36. Ibid., pp. 43–53; Deighton, ibid., pp. 115–129.
37. Hastings, ibid., pp. 53–64; Deighton, ibid., pp. 256–334; Horne, *To Lose a Battle: France 1940*, Penguin, 2007; Jackson, *Fall of France: The Nazi Invasion*, Oxford University Press, 2003.
38. Hastings, ibid., pp. 64–77; Deighton, ibid., pp. 334–360.

## Chapter 7

1. Kedward, *Occupied France: Collaboration and Resistance 1940–1944*, Blackwell, 2000, pp. 1–4; Ousby, *Occupation: The Ordeal of France 1940–1944*, Pimlico, 1999; Jackson, *France: The Dark Years 1940–1944*, Oxford University Press, 2003; Paxton, *Vichy France: Old Guard and New Order 1940–1944*, Columbia University Press, 2001.
2. Quoted in Kedward, ibid., p. 4.
3. Ibid., pp. 4–16; Foot, *SOE in France: An Account of the Work of the British Special Operations Executive in France 1940–1944*, HMSO,

## Notes

1966, pp. 115–125; Neave, *Saturday at M.I.9: The Classic Account of the WW2 Allied Escape Organisation*, Pen & Sword, 2010, first published in 1969, p. 305.
4. Kedward, ibid., pp. 17–21.
5. Ibid., pp. 21–25.
6. Quoted in Weitz, *Sisters in the Resistance: How Women Fought to Free France 1940–1945*, John Wiley, 1995, p. 44.
7. Kedward, ibid., pp. 6–7, 25–26; ibid., pp. 44–57.
8. Kedward, ibid.., pp. 26– 31.
9. Ibid., pp. 32–37, 41.
10. Ibid., pp. 37–45.
11. Ibid., pp. 46–50; Ousby, ibid., p. 207; Cobb, *The Resistance: the French Fight Against the Nazis*, Simon and Schuster, 2010.
12. Kedward, ibid., pp. 51–54.
13. Ibid., pp. 55–60; Ousby, ibid., p. 240.
14. Kedward, ibid., pp. 61–65.
15. Ibid., pp. 65–69; Cullen and Stacey, *World War II Vichy French Security Troops*, Osprey Publishing, 2016.
16. Weitz, ibid., pp. 286–307.
17. Ibid., pp. 308–311.
18. Kedward, ibid., pp. 69–73; Cobb, ibid., pp. 170–194.
19. Kedward, ibid., pp. 74–80.
20. Foot, ibid.; Foot and Langley, *MI9: Escape and Evasion 1939–1945*, Biteback Publishing, 2011; Hastings, *The Secret War: Spies, Codes and Guerrillas 1939–45*, William Collins, 2015; Jeffrey, *MI6: The History of the Secret Intelligence Service 1909–1949*, Bloomsbury, 2011; Andrew, *Defence of the Realm: Authorised History of MI5*, Penguin, 2010; War Office, *The British Spy Manual: The Authentic Special Operations Executive (SOE) Guide for WWII*, Imperial War Museum, 2014.
21. Jeffrey, ibid.; Andrew, ibid.
22. Foot and Langley, ibid., pp. 26–27.
23. Foot, ibid., pp. 1–11; Hastings, ibid., pp. 260–261; Escott, *The Heroines of SOE: Britain's Secret Women in France F Section*, History Press, 2010, pp. 7–11; War Office, ibid., p. 8.
24. War Office, ibid., p. 14; Hastings, ibid., pp. 250, 262–282; Foot, ibid., pp. 33, 147.
25. Foot, ibid., pp. 40–53.

26. Ibid., pp. 50, 53–59; Escott, ibid., pp. 15–23.
27. Foot, ibid., pp. 60–101; Escott, ibid., pp. 23–26.
28. Foot, ibid.; pp. 101–110; Escott, ibid., pp. 26–27.
29. Foot, ibid., pp. 50, 118–125; Escott, ibid., pp. 216–227.
30. War Office, ibid., pp. 215–219.
31. Ibid., pp. 197, 199, 204.
32. Ibid., p. 130.
33. Foot, ibid., pp. 46–48; Escott, ibid., pp. 11–13.
34. Foot, ibid., pp. 465–469; Escott, ibid., p. 230.
35. Escott, ibid., pp. 34–38.
36. Ibid., pp. 39–43.
37. Ibid., pp. 44–48.
38. Ibid., pp. 228–230, Foot, ibid., p. 20; Hastings, ibid., pp. 281–282.
39. Quoted in Hastings, ibid., p. 281.

## Chapter 8

1. Foot and Langley, ibid., p. 37.
2. Langley, *Fight Another Day*, Magnum Books, 1980, p. 190; Darling, ibid., p. 19.
3. Darling, ibid., p. 28.
4. TNA, HS 9/735, Gleditch, ibid.
5. TNA, ibid., HS 9/735, Letter from Major Finn Nagell 21/09/1942.
6. TNA, HS 9/735, Holst letter to Nini 04/03/1941.
7. TNA, IS9 Recommendations WO 208/5451.
8. Langley, ibid., p. 99; Caskie, *The Tartan Pimpernel*, Fontana Books, 1967, pp. 25–32; Foot and Langley, ibid., pp. 62–63; Long, ibid., pp. 17–20.
9. Langley, ibid., p. 100; Caskie, ibid., pp. 33–43; Long, ibid., pp. 20–21; Foot and Langley, ibid., pp. 63–64.
10. Caskie, ibid., pp. 1–31; Donald Caskie has a file at the TNA, TNA, FO 916/637 and recommendation for an award FO 371/49176.
11. Ibid., pp. 32–108.
12. Ibid., pp. 109–256; Long, ibid., pp. 200–201.
13. Quoted in Caskie, ibid., p. 67.
14. TNA, IS9 Recommendations, WO 208/5451, Recommendation supporting letter Reverend Caskie and Mrs Holst.

15. TNA, WO208/3312/1075; Langley, ibid., pp,102–112; Foot and Langley, ibid., pp. 64–65; Neave, ibid., p. 78; Long, ibid., pp. 21–23; Ottis, *Silent Heroes: Downed Airmen and the French Underground*, University Press of Kentucky, 2001, pp. 76–78.
16. Foot and Langley, ibid., pp. 71–77, 148–149; Long, ibid., pp. 72, 171–174, 198–199; Ottis, ibid., pp. 78–81, 85–86, 105–109; Neave, ibid., pp. 79–80, 110–116; Brome, *The Way Back: The Story of Lieutenant-Commander Pat O'Leary*, Pan Books, 1957, pp. 31–34, 133–139.
17. TNA, IS9 Recommendations WO 208/5451; Darling, ibid., p. 28.
18. TNA, IS9, ibid.
19. TNA, ibid., TNA; Dix Noonan Webb, ibid..
20. Long, ibid., pp. 26–29, 36, 98–99, 138, 149–152, 183–196; Rodocanachi, Fanny, *Dr George Rodocanachi (1875–1944)*, www.christopherlong.co.uk/per/rodocanachigeorge.html, accessed 01/12/2019.
21. Ibid., pp. 39, 105, 169–171, 196–197; Ottis, ibid., p. 86.
22. Long, ibid., pp. 83,199; Ottis, ibid., pp. 101–105, 118.
23. Long ibid., pp. 53–68, 95–96,180–182, 201; Ottis, ibid., pp. 101–104, 111–144, Neave, ibid., pp. 49–54, 314–315.
24. Fitzsimons, *Nancy Wake: The Inspiring Story of One of the War's Greatest Heroines*, HarperCollins, 2002, pp. 1–82; Escott, ibid., pp. 185–186; see also Braddon, *Nancy Wake: The Story of a Very Brave Woman*, W.W. Norton, 1957, and Nancy Wake, *The White Mouse*, Sun Books, 1985.
25. Fitzsimons, ibid., pp. 83–165; Escott, ibid., pp. 186–187; Long, ibid., pp. 74–76.
26. Quoted in Escott, ibid., p. 189.
27. Fitzsimons, ibid., pp. 188–300; ibid., pp. 187–189; Long, ibid., p. 198; TNA, HS 9/1545.
28. Long, ibid., pp. 31–32, 48–51, 88, 96, 197–198.
29. Quoted in Darling, ibid., p. 28.
30. Quoted in Long, ibid., p. 109.
31. Quoted in Langley, ibid., p. 111.
32. Quoted in Ottis, ibid., p. 79.
33. TNA, HS 9/735, HS 9/734/3, HS 9/659/3, HS 9/658/7; Darling, ibid., p. 28.
34. Darling, ibid., p. 15.

35. Foot and Langley, ibid., pp. 36–38.
36. Ibid., p. 65; Ottis, ibid., pp. 8–10; and in detail Neave, ibid., Langley, ibid.
37. Langley and Foot, ibid.
38. Darling, ibid., pp. 1–47; Long., ibid., pp. 63–64, 203; Ottis, ibid., p. 78.
39. Quoted in Darling, ibid., p. 28.
40. Ibid., p. 28; Foot, ibid., p. 157; Foot and Langley, ibid., pp. 71–72; Long, ibid., p. 63; TNA, HS 9/735, HS 9/734/3.
41. Darling, ibid., pp. 28, 118. Dix Noonan Webb, ibid.; TNA, IS9, ibid.
42. Darling, ibid., p. 28; TNA, IS9, ibid.; HS 9/735 General Instructions for Writing in Secret Inks and Special Instructions for making Secret Ink from Tablets of Pyramidon Headache Cure.
43. Quoted in Long, ibid., p. 63.
44. Quoted in Darling, ibid., p. 46.
45. Quoted in Langley, ibid., p. 146.
46. Darling, ibid., p. 28; Dix Noonan Webb, ibid.; TNA, IS9, ibid., Recommendation supporting letter Reverend Caskie and Mrs Holst.
47. Ottis, ibid., pp. 76–118; Long, ibid.; Langley., ibid., pp. 99–124, 146–158; Brome, ibid.
48. TNA, IS9, ibid.
49. Ibid; Dixon Noonan Webb, ibid.; Darling, ibid., p. 28.
50. Brome, ibid., pp. 13–22; Long, ibid., pp. 69–70.
51. Brome, ibid., pp. 23–47; Long, ibid., pp. 77–80.
52. Quoted in Brome, ibid., pp. 64–65.
53. Ibid., pp. 40–50; Long, ibid., pp. 88–89, 110–113.
54. Brome, ibid., pp. 80–86; Long, ibid., pp. 146–147.
55. Quoted in Long, ibid., p. 174.
56. Brome, ibid.; pp. 10, 74–80, 104, 126–127, 133–141, 167–168, 187; ibid., pp. 135, 171–174, 177–178; Fitzsimons, ibid., pp. 141–142.
57. Brome, ibid., pp. 169–251; Long, ibid., p. 196.
58. Dixon, Noonan and Webb, ibid.; TNA, WO 373/184/164, HS 9/1329/2; Zembsch-Schreve, *Pierre Lalande: Special Agent: The Wartime Memoirs of Guido Zembsch-Schreve*, Leo Cooper, 1996, p. 76.
59. TNA, HS 9/1329/2 History Sheet, Form T1; ibid., pp. 12–15.
60. TNA, ibid.; ibid., pp. 16–60.
61. TNA, HS 9/1329/2 Form T2, Preliminary Report.
62. TNA, HS 9/1329/2 Form T2, WO/373/184/164.

63. Zembsch-Schreve, ibid., p. 76.
64. Ibid., p. 76.
65. Ibid., pp. 76–94.
66. Ibid., pp. 100–106.
67. Quoted in ibid., p. 106.
68. TNA, HS 9/1329/2 Organisation of Pierre-Jacques Line; Foot, ibid., pp. 94–96.
69. Ibid., pp. 107–189; TNA, WO 373/184/164.
70. Quoted in Darling, ibid., p. 28.
71. TNA, HS 9/734/3, DF301.
72. TNA, HS 9/735 no.38, 14/04/1941, HS 9/735 letter 09/04/1941 To F from DF, Service Historique de la Défense (SHD) Archives, Vincennes, GR 16P/3056 Réseaux Alexandre P2.
73. Quoted in Darling, ibid., p. 28.
74. TNA, HS 9/735 Nini, ibid.; HS 9/735 letter 09/04/1941 To F from DF, ibid.; HS 9/735 Gleditch ibid.; Kleppe, ibid.
75. SHD, GR 16P/3056 Réseaux Alexandre, ibid., GR 16P/3056 Attestation D'Appartenance Aux Forces Françaises Combattantes, Madame Marguerite Addy épouse Holst.
76. TNA, HS 9/735, Letter to Captain Liger, 30/04/1945.
77. SHD, GR 16P/3056 Réseaux Alexandre, ibid.; TNA, IS9 ibid.; HS 9/735, Letter to Captain Liger, ibid.; Kleppe, ibid.
78. Foot, ibid., p. 157; Foot and Langley, ibid., p. 71, Darling, ibid., p. 28; Long, ibid., p. 63; TNA, HS 9/735, Gleditch ibid.
79. TNA, HS 9/735, ibid.; Kleppe, ibid.
80. SHD, GR 16P/3056 Réseaux Alexandre, ibid., GR 16P/3056 Billet (Alexandre) Fiche de Renseignements; Foot, op cit., p157, Foot and Langley, ibid., p. 71.
81. Quoted in Foot, ibid., p. 157.
82. TNA, HS 9/735 no.38, ibid.; HS 9/735 Letter from Major Finn Nagell 21/09/1942, ibid.; HS 9/734/3 letter from R. Jaraandstand.
83. TNA, HS 9/734/3 Letter no.60, 06/04/1945; HS 9/734/3 Jaraandstand, ibid.; HS 9/658/7 Letter 26/01/1945 Major Lynch.
84. Kleppe, ibid.
85. TNA, HS 9/658/7 Curriculum Vitae.
86. TNA, HS 9/658/7 DF/REC/7777 25/01/1945; Darling, ibid., p. 28.
87. TNA, HS 9/658/7 CV, ibid., Zembsch-Schreve, ibid., pp. 78, 88, 94, 102–103.

88. TNA, HS 9/658/7 ibid., HS 9/658/7 Recommendation for King's Medal for Courage.
89. TNA, HS 9/658/7 Recommendation, ibid.
90. Dix, Noonan and Webb, ibid.

## Epilogue

1. Speech written for the Lord Mayor by the author, Chris Hall.
2. SHD, GR 16P/3056 Réseaux Alexandre, ibid., TNA, HS 9/735, Captain Liger, ibid.
3. Interview with Addie and Addie, ibid.
4. Alexander, *No to Franco: The Struggle Never Stopped 1939–1975*, Bill Alexander, 1992; MML, Malimson letters, ibid.
5. TNA, IS9, ibid.; Dix, Noonan and Webb, ibid.; these letters were sold with Madge's and Thorkild's medals after their deaths at Sotheby's in 1971 and have now been lost.
6. Dix, Noonan and Webb, ibid.; Marriage Certificate Thorkild Hansen and Marguerite Addy, Marylebone Registry Office, 23/12/1955; Death Certificate Thorkild Hansen, City of London, 16/05/1966; Death Certificate Marguerite Hansen, London Borough of Barnet, 04/02/1970.
7. Marriage Certificate, ibid.; Death Certificate Thorkild Hansen, ibid.; Death Certificate Marguerite Hansen, ibid.
8. See Fyrth, ibid.; Palfreeman, *Salud*, ibid.; Jackson, *British Women and the Spanish Civil War*, ibid.; Fyrth and Alexander (eds), ibid.; Foot and Langley, ibid.; Long, ibid.; Darling, ibid..
9. *Manchester Evening News*, 11/01/2017, 'Spy Madge risked her life in fight against Nazis' by Paul Britton; *Daily Mirror*, 12/01/2017, 'Undercover hairdresser who helped win the war' by Stephen White; *Manchester Evening News*, 02/04/2018, 'The Chorlton hairdresser who turned wartime spy' by Paul Britton.

# Bibliography

**Primary Sources**

Birth Certificate Marguerite Nuttall Addy, 1904.
Birth, Registration of, Frederick William Addy, Macclesfield District, 1856.
Birth, Registration of, Mary Costello, Macclesfield District, 1866.
Census 1891.
Census 1901.
Census 1911.
Death, Registration of, Mary Costello, Chorlton District, 1924.
Death Certificate, Marguerite Hansen, London Borough of Barnet, 1970.
Death Certificate, Thorkild Hansen, City of London, 1966.
Electoral Rolls, Withington 1932–1939.
Manchester Trade Directory, 1934.
Marriage Certificate, Thorkild Hansen and Marguerite Addy, Marylebone Registry Office, 1955.
Marriage Certificate, Arthur Wilson Lightfoot and Marguerite Nuttall Addy, 1930.
Marriage, Registration of, Frederick William Addy and Mary Costello, Macclesfield District, 1882.
Marx Memorial Library, Spanish Collection, Box D-1, Madge Addy letters from Spain and letter from Dr Malimson and reply from IBA.
Nurses, Register of, 1927–1931.
Nursing Character and Training Reference, Marguerite Nuttall Addy, Document 8452, 1929.
Service Historique de la Défense Archives, Vincennes, GR 16P/3056 includes material on Madge Addy.
The National Archives (TNA) FO 371/49176 Donald Caskie.
TNA, FO 916/637 Donald Caskie.
TNA, HS 9/1329/2 Guido Zembsch-Schreve.

TNA, HS 9/1545 Nancy Wake.
TNA, HS 9/658/7 Thorkild Hansen.
TNA, HS 9/659/3 Thorkild Hansen.
TNA, HS 9/734/3 Wilhelm Holst.
TNA, HS 9/735 Wilhelm Holst.
TNA, IS9 Recommendations WO 208/5451. Includes correspondence relating to Madge Addy's OBE.
TNA, WO 208/3312/1075 Ian Garrow.
TNA, WO 373/184/164 Guido Zembsch-Schreve.
Warwick University, Trade Union Congress Archives at the Modern Records Centre, SMAC minutes, SMAC Bulletin, Madge Addy letters from Spain.
Will of Marguerite Nuttall Lightfoot, 1938.


## Scholarship and secondary material

Alba, Victor and Schwartz, Stephen, *Spanish Marxism versus Soviet Communism: A History of the P. O.U.M.*, Transaction Book, 1988.
Alberca, Julio Ponce, *Gibraltar and the Spanish Civil War 1936–39: Local, National and International Perspectives*, Bloomsbury, 2015.
Alexander, Bill, *British Volunteers for Liberty: Spain 1936–39*, Lawrence & Wishart, 1982.
Alexander, Bill, *No to Franco: The Struggle Never Stopped 1939–1975*, Bill Alexander, 1992.
Alexander, Martin S. (ed.) and Graham, Helen (ed.), *The French and Spanish Popular Fronts: Comparative Perspectives*, Cambridge University Press, 1989.
Allan, Ted and Gordon, Sydney, *The Scalpel, the Sword: The Story of Dr. Norman Bethune*, Monthly Review Press, 1973.
Andrew, Christopher, *Defence of the Realm: Authorised History of MI5*, Penguin, 2010.
Balcells, Albert and Walker, Geoffrey J, *Catalan Nationalism: Past and Present*, Macmillan, 1996.
Barry, Bernard, *From Manchester to Spain*, Salford, Working Class Movement Library, 2009.
Baxell, Richard, *British Volunteers in the Spanish Civil War: The British Battalion in the International Brigades 1936–39*, Routledge, 2004.

# Bibliography

Baxell, Richard, *Unlikely Warriors: The British in the Spanish Civil War and the Struggle against Fascism*, Aurum Press, 2012.

Beckett, Francis, *Clem Attlee*, Politico's Publishing, 2000.

Beckett, Francis, *Enemy Within: The Rise and Fall of the British Communist Party*, John Murray, 1995.

Beevor, Anthony, *The Battle for Spain: The Spanish Civil War 1936–39*, Weidenfeld & Nicolson, 2006.

Bell, P. M. H., *The Origins of the Second World War in Europe*, Longman, 1997.

Bill, Ron and Newens, Stan, *Leah Manning*, Leah Manning Trust, 1991.

Blakeway, Denys, *The Last Dance: 1936: The Year of Change*, John Murray, 2010.

Blinkhorn, Martin, *Carlism and Crisis in Spain 1931–39*, Cambridge University Press, 1975.

Bookchin, Murray, *The Spanish Anarchists: The Heroic Years 1868–1936*, Free Life Editions, 1977.

Braddon, Russell, *Nancy Wake: The Story of a Very Brave Woman*, W.W. Norton, 1957.

Brandon, Piers, *The Dark Valley: A Panorama of the 1930s*, Jonathan Cape, 2000.

Branson, Noreen, *History of the Communist Party of Great Britain 1927–1941*, Lawrence & Wishart, 1985.

Brenan, Gerald, *The Spanish Labyrinth: An Account of the Social and Political Background of the Spanish Civil War*, Cambridge University Press, 1988. First published 1943, 2nd ed. 1950.

Brome, Vincent, *The Way Back: The Story of Lieutenant-Commander Pat O'Leary*, Pan Books, 1957.

Buchanan, Tom, *Britain and the Spanish Civil War*, Cambridge University Press, 1997.

Buchanan, Tom, *The Impact of the Spanish Civil War on Britain: War, Loss and Memory*, Sussex Academic Press, 2007.

Buchanan, Tom, *The Spanish Civil War and the British Labour Movement*, Cambridge University Press, 1991.

Butler, David and Butler, Gareth, *British Political Facts 1900–1985*, Macmillan, 1986.

Carr, Raymond, *Spain 1808–1975*, Oxford University Press, 1982.

Casanova, Julian, *Anarchism, the Republic and Civil War in Spain 1931–39*, Routledge, 2004.

Caskie, Donald, *The Tartan Pimpernel*, Fontana Books, 1967.

Clifford, Alexander, *The People's Army in the Spanish Civil War: A Military History of the Republic and International Brigades*, Pen & Sword, 2020.

Cobb, Matthew, *The Resistance: the French Fight Against the Nazis*, Simon and Schuster, 2010.

Cobban, Alfred, *A History of France: Volume 3: France of the Republics 1871–1962*, Penguin, 1975. First published 1965.

Colodny, Robert G., *The Struggle for Madrid: The Central Epic of the Spanish Conflict 1936–37*, Paine-Whitman, 1958.

Coni, Nicholas, 'Medicine and the Spanish Civil War', *Journal of the Royal Society of Medicine*, 95(3), 2002, pp. 147–150.

Corkill, David and Rawnsley, Stuart J. (eds.), *Road to Spain: Anti-Fascists at War 1936– 1939*, Borderline Press, 1981.

Coverdale, John F., *Italian Intervention in the Spanish Civil War*, Princeton University Press, 1975.

Cronin, Jill and Rhodes, Frank, *Images of England: Rusholme and Victoria Park*, Tempus, 2000.

Cullen, Stephen M. and Stacey, Mark, *World War II Vichy French Security Troops*, Osprey Publishing, 2016.

Danos, Jacques and Gibelin, Marcel, *June 36: Class Struggle and the Popular Front in France*, Bookmarks, 1986.

Darling, Donald, *Secret Sunday*, William Kimber, 1975.

Deighton, Len, *Blitzkrieg: From the Rise of Hitler to the Fall of Dunkirk*, Triad Granada, 1980.

Dickens, Steven, *Chorlton-Cum-Hardy: Through Time*, Amberley Publishing, 2018.

Edaile, Charles J., *The Spanish Civil War: A Military History*, Routledge, 2019.

Edwards, Jill, *The British Government and the Spanish Civil War 1936–39*, Macmillan, 1979.

Ellwood, Sheelagh M., *Franco*, Longman, 1994.

Ellwood, Sheelagh M., *Spanish Fascism in the Franco Era: Falange Espanola de las JONs 1936–76*, Macmillan, 1987.

Escott, Beryl E., *The Heroines of SOE: Britain's Secret Women in France F Section*, History Press, 2010.

Fagen, Patricia W., *Exiles and Citizens: Spanish Republicans in Mexico*, University of Texas Press, 1973.

## Bibliography

Fitzsimons, Peter, *Nancy Wake: The Inspiring Story of One of the War's Greatest Heroines*, HarperCollins, 2002.

Foot, M. R. D. and Langley, J. M., *MI9: Escape and Evasion 1939–1945*, Biteback Publishing, 2011.

Foot, M. R. D., *SOE in France: An Account of the Work of the British Special Operations Executive in France 1940–1944*, HMSO, 1966.

Fredericks, Shirley, 'Feminism: The Essential Ingredient in Federica Montseny's Anarchist Theory', in Slaughter and Kern Robert (eds.), *European Women on the Left: Socialism, Feminism and Problems Faced by Political Women, 1880 to the Present*, Greenwood Press, 1981.

Fyrth, Jim, *The Signal Was Spain: The Aid Spain Movement in Britain 1936–39*, Lawrence and Wishart, 1986.

Fyvel, Penelope, *English Penny*, Arthur H. Stockwell Ltd, 1992.

Gardiner, Juliet, *The Thirties: An Intimate History*, Harper Press, 2011.

Gibson, Ian, *The Assassination of Federico Garcia Lorca*, Penguin Books, 1983.

Gilbert, Martin, *The Illustrated London News Marching to War 1933–39*, Bracken Books, 1989.

Graham, Helen and Preston, Paul (eds.), *The Popular Front in Europe*, Macmillan, 1987.

Graham, Helen, *Socialism and War: The Spanish Socialist Party in Power and Crisis 1936–39*, Cambridge University Press, 1991.

Graham, Helen, *The Spanish Republic at War 1936–39*, Cambridge University Press, 2002.

Green, Nan, *A Chronicle of Small Beer: The Memoirs of Nan Green*, Trent Editions, 2004.

Hall, Christopher, *'Disciplina Camaradas': Four English Volunteers in Spain 1936–39*, Gosling Press, 1996.

Hall, Christopher, *'In Spain with Orwell': George Orwell and the Independent Labour Party Volunteers in the Spanish Civil War, 1936–1939*, Tippermiur Books Ltd, 2013.

Hall, Christopher, *Revolutionary Warfare: Spain 1936–37*, Gosling Press, 1996.

Hastings, Max, *All Hell Let Loose: The World at War 1939–1945*, Harper Press, 2011.

Hastings, Max, *The Secret War: Spies, Codes and Guerrillas 1939–45*, William Collins, 2015.

Henig, Ruth, *The Origins of the Second World War 1933–41*, Routledge, 2005.
Henry, Chris, *The Ebro 1938: Death Knell of the Republic*, Osprey Publishing, 1999.
Hills, George, *The Battle for Madrid*, Vantage Books, 1976.
*Hope Hospital Centenary 1880–1980: Official Brochure*, Salford Area Health Authority, 1980.
Horne, Alistair, *To Lose a Battle: France 1940*, Penguin, 2007.
Howson, Gerald, *Arms for Spain: The Untold Story of the Spanish Civil War*, John Murray, 1998.
Hylton, Stuart, *A History of Manchester*, Phillimore, 2010.
Imperial War Museum, *The Spanish Civil War Collection: Sound Archive Oral History Recordings*, Trustees of the Imperial War Museum, 1996.
Jackson, Angela, *British Women and the Spanish Civil War*, Routledge, 2002.
Jackson, Angela, *'For us it was Heaven': The Passion, Grief and Fortitude of Patience Darton: From the Spanish Civil War to Mao's China*, Sussex Academic Press, 2012.
Jackson, Angela, 'Madge Addy: Forgotten Heroine of the Wars in Spain and France', *IBMT Newsletter*, 43(3), 2016, pp. 19.
Jackson, Gabriel, *Juan Negrin: Physiologist, Socialist and Spanish Republican War Leader*, Sussex Academic Press, 2010.
Jackson, Gabriel, *The Spanish Republic and the Civil War 1931–39*, Princeton University Press, 1967.
Jackson, Julian, *Fall of France: The Nazi Invasion*, Oxford University Press, 2003.
Jackson, Julian, *France: The Dark Years 1940–1944*, Oxford University Press, 2003.
Jackson, Sarah, 'The British International Brigades as Labour Party Dissidents', *International Journal of Iberian Studies*, 18(1), 2005, pp. 3–21.
Jeffrey, Keith, *MI6: The History of the Secret Intelligence Service 1909–1949*, Bloomsbury, 2011.
Kedward, H. R., *Occupied France: Collaboration and Resistance 1940–1944*, Blackwell, 2000.
Kemp, Peter, *Mine Were of Trouble*, Cassell, 1957.
Laity, Paul (ed.), *Left Book Club Anthology*, Victor Gollancz, 2001.
Langley, J. M., *Fight Another Day*, Magnum Books, 1980.

*Bibliography*

Levy, David A. L., 'The French Popular Front 1936–37', in Graham and Preston (eds.), *The Popular Front in Europe*, Macmillan Press, 1987.

Lines, Lisa, *Women in Combat in the Spanish Civil War*, Lexington Books, 2012.

Long, Helen, *Safe Houses are Dangerous*, William Kimber, 1985.

Low, Robert, *La Pasionaria: The Spanish Firebrand*, Hutchinson, 1992.

Mason, Emily, *Democracy, Deeds and Dilemmas: Support for the Spanish Republic within British Civil Society, 1936–1939*, Sussex Academic Press, 2017.

Mathieson, David, *Frontline Madrid: Battlefield Tours of the Spanish Civil War*, Signal Books, 2014.

McGarry, Fearghal, *Eoin O'Duffy: A Self-Made Hero*, Oxford University Press, 2005.

Mendlesohn, Farah, *Quaker Relief Work in the Spanish Civil War*, Edwin Mellen Press Ltd, 2002.

Mesquida, Evelyn, *La Nueve 24 August 1944: The Spanish Republicans Who Liberated Paris*, Christie Books, 2015.

Morgan, Austen, *J. Ramsay MacDonald*, Manchester University Press, 1987.

Morgan, Kevin, *Harry Pollitt*, Manchester University Press, 1993.

Murphy, Molly, *Molly Murphy: Suffragette and Socialist*, Institute of Social Research, Salford University, 1998.

Neave, Airey, *Saturday at M.I.9.: The Classic Account of the WWII Allied Escape Organisation*, Pen & Sword, 2010. First published 1969.

Orwell, George, *Homage to Catalonia and Looking Back on the Spanish War*, Penguin, 1988. First published 1938.

Ottis, Sherri Greene, *Silent Heroes: Downed Airmen and the French Underground*, University Press of Kentucky, 2001.

Ousby, Ian, *Occupation: The Ordeal of France 1940–1944*, Pimlico, 1999.

Palencia, Isabel de, *Smouldering Freedom: The Story of the Spanish Republicans in Exile*, Victor Gollancz, 1946.

Palfreeman, Linda, *Aristocrats, Adventurers and Ambulances: British Medical Units in the Spanish Civil War*, Sussex Academic Press, 2014.

Palfreeman, Linda, *Salud: British Volunteers in the Republican Medical Service During the Spanish Civil War, 1936–39*, Sussex Academic Press, 2012.

Paxton, Robert, *Vichy France: Old Guard and New Order 1940–1944*, Columbia University Press, 2001.

Payne, Stanley G., *Basque Nationalism*, University of Nevada Press, 1975.
Payne, Stanley G., *Spain's First Democracy: The Second Republic 1931–36*, University of Wisconsin, 1993.
Paz, Abel, *Durutti in the Spanish Revolution*, AK Press, 2007.
Preston, Paul, *The Coming of the Spanish Civil War: Reform, Reaction and Revolution in the Second Republic*, Methuen, 1978.
Preston, Paul, *Doves of War: Four Women of the Spanish Civil War*, HarperCollins, 2002.
Preston, Paul, *Franco: A Biography*, HarperCollins, 1993.
Preston, Paul, *The Last Days of the Spanish Republic*, William Collins, 2016.
Procter, Raymond L., *Hitler's Luftwaffe in the Spanish Civil War*, Greenwood Press, 1983.
Rankin, Nicholas, *Telegram from Guernica: The Extraordinary Life of George Steer War Correspondent*, Faber and Faber, 2003.
Shelmerdine, Brian, *British Representations of the Spanish Civil War*, Manchester University Press, 2006.
Simpson, Andrew, *The Quirks of Chorlton-Cum-Hardy: A History of its People and Places*, Topper Publishing, 2017.
Skidelsky, Robert, *Oswald Mosley*, Papermac, 1990.
Slaughter, Jane and Kern, Robert (eds.), *European Women on the Left: Socialism, Feminism and Problems Faced by Political Women, 1880 to the Present*, Greenwood Press, 1981.
Soo, Scott, *The Routes to Exile: France and the Spanish Civil War 1939–2009*, Manchester University Press, 2017.
Steer G. L., *The Tree of Gernika: A Field Study of Modern War*, Hodder and Stoughton, 1938.
Stein, Louis, *Beyond Death and Exile: The Spanish Republicans in France 1939–1955*, Harvard University Press, 1979.
Stevenson, John and Cook, Chris, *The Slump*, Quartet Books, 1979.
Taylor, A. J. P., *The Origins of the Second World War*, Penguin, 1964. First published 1961.
Thomas, Frank and Stradling, Robert, *Brother Against Brother: Experiences of a British Volunteer in the Spanish Civil War*, Sutton Publishing, 1998.
Thomas, Gordon and Witts, Max Morgan, *Guernica: The Crucible of World War II*, Stein and Day, 1975.
Thomas, Hugh, *The Spanish Civil War*, Penguin, 1986. 3rd ed.

## Bibliography

Thomas, Martin, *Britain, France and Appeasement: Anglo-French Relations in the Popular Front Era*, Berg, 1996.

Thompson, Willie, *The Good Old Cause: British Communism 1920–1991*, Pluto Press, 1992.

Thorpe, Andrew, *Britain in the 1930s: The Deceptive Decade*, Blackwell, 1992.

Vickers, Rhiannon, *The Labour Party and the World Volume 1: The Evolution of Labour's Foreign Policy 1900–51*, Manchester University Press, 2004.

Wake, Nancy, *The White Mouse*, Sun Books, 1985.

War Office, *The British Spy Manual: The Authentic Special Operations Executive (SOE) Guide for WWII*, Imperial War Museum, 2014.

Watkins, K. W., *Britain Divided: The Effect of the Spanish Civil War on British Political Opinion*, Thomas Nelson and Sons Ltd, 1963.

Weber, Eugen, *The Hollow Years: France in the 1930s*, Sinclair-Stevenson, 1995.

Weitz, Marget Collins, *Sisters in the Resistance: How Women Fought to Free France 1940–1945*, John Wiley, 1995.

Whealey, Robert H., *Hitler and Spain: The Nazi Role in the Spanish Civil War*, University Press of Kentucky, 1989.

Wheatcroft, Andrew and Overy, Richard, *The Road to War: The Origins of World War II*, Vantage, 2009.

Wingeate Pike, David, *In the Service of Stalin: the Spanish Communists in Exile 1939–1945*, Clarendon Press, 1993.

Zembsch-Schreve, Guido, *Pierre Lalande: Special Agent: The Wartime Memoirs of Guido Zembsch-Schreve*, Leo Cooper, 1996.

## Websites

Baxell, Richard, *List of British Volunteers in Spain*, http://www.richardbaxell.info/volunteers/, accessed 20/7/2019.

British Broadcasting Corporation, *Fight to Save Manchester Venue Where Bee Gees First Sang*, www.bbc.co.uk/news/uk-england-manchester-50318830, accessed 18/03/2020.

Dix Noonan Webb, *Ron Penhall Collection*, www.dnw.co.uk/auction-archive/lot-archive/lot.php?department=Medals&lot_uid=130474, accessed 30/11/2019.

Friends of Salford Cemeteries Trust, *Weaste Cemetery Heritage Trial: Mark Addy (1838–1890)*, www.weasteheritagetrail.co.uk/about/explore-the-cemetery/mark-addy-1838-1890/index.htm, accessed 07/01/2020.

Jackson, Angela, *From Foodships to the Frontline: A Forgotten Manchester Heroine of the Spanish Civil War*, http://www.international-brigades.org.uk/content/foodships-front-lines-forgotten-manchester-heroine-spanish-civil-war, accessed 17/03/2017.

Manchester and Lancashire Family History Society, *Manchester Worthies: Mr Mark Addy (1838–1889)*, www.mlfhs.org.uk/worthies/addy.php, accessed 07/01/2017.

Rodocanachi, Fanny, *Dr George Rodocanachi (1875–1944)* www.christopherlong.co.uk/per/rodocanachigeorge.html, accessed 01/12/2019.

Simpson, Andrew, *On the Trail of a Bullet-holed Ambulance Somewhere in Stalybridge*, https://chorltonhistory.blogspot.com/search/label/Madge%20Addy, accessed 24/04/2019.

## Newspapers

*Arbeiderbladet* (translated by Ole Kleppe)
*Daily Herald*
*Daily Mirror*
*Daily Worker*
*Fram* (translated by Ole Kleppe)
*Grantham Journal*
*Manchester Evening News*
*Manchester Guardian*
*Nottingham Journal*
*Yorkshire Evening post*

## Interviews and correspondence

Interview with Madge's nephews, Robert Francis Addie and Geoffrey Michael Addie, 28/07/2018.
Máximo Molina Gutiérrez, local Uclés historian 2019–2020.
Ole Kleppe, grandson of Wilhelm Holst, 2018–2020.

# Illustration Sources

1–5, 7 Addie family.
6 and 31, author.
8–9, Lloyds Collection.
10–11, Mike Arnott.
12–19, Ángel y Santiago García Langa.
20–22 and 25–29, Ole Kleppe.
23–24, The National Archives.
30, Dominic Winter Auctioneers.

# Index

Abyssinia, 110, 132
Addie, Geoffrey, 1–2, 5, 8, 175, 178
Addie, Robert, 1–2, 5, 8, 10, 175, 178
Addison, Christopher, 50
Addy, Edward, 3, 5
Addy, Florence, 3–4, 94–95, 175–176
Addy, Francis, 1, 3–5, 10
Addy, Frederick William, 2–3
Addy, Henry, 2–4
Addy, Joseph, 3–4
Addy, Madge
  Early life, 1–11
    34 Manchester Road, Chorlton-cum-Hardy, 1, 7–9, 174–175, 178
    Childhood and family 2–5, see Addy, Edward; Addy, Florence; Addy, Francis; Addy, Frederick William; Addy, Henry; Addy, Joseph; Addy, Mary; Addy, Thomas
    First marriage, see Lightfoot, Arthur
    Nursing in Manchester, 5–7
  Personal qualities, 10–11, 71–72, 96–97, 156, 159, 166
    Appearance, 166

Bravery and calmness, 141, 156, 166
Political views, 10–11, 71–72
Views on death, 96–97
Nurse in the Spanish Civil War, 69–101
  Aragon, 70
  Blood transfusions, 79–80
  Bombing raids, 72, 85–86
  British medical staff, 84, 92
    see Nurses (British); Jones, Louise
  End of the Civil War, 69–71, 81, 96–99
  Illness, 70, 86
  Leave, 70, 76, 81–82, 85, 87–88, 90, 92–93, 95
  Letters, 70–72, 76–84, 86–89, 91–94, 96–98
  Lousy, 78
  Love affair see Holst, Wilhelm
  Manchester Ward, 73, 79
  Organising/appealing for Medical Aid, 70, 76–77, 80, 86–93
  Patients, 76–78, 86–87
  Post–Civil War Spain, 99–100

212

SMAC *see* Davson, Rosita; Jeger, George; Malimson, Nat; Manning, Leah
Spanish Medical Staff, 71, 75–78, 80–83, 94, 97–98
*Stanleigh*, 87, 92–93, 96
Teaching English, 70, 81–82
Training Spanish nurses, 70, 74–75, 80–82, 87
Transporting refugees 70, 72, 85–86
Uclés *see* Uclés Hospital
Wounded, 70, 85, 90, 92, 178
Between the Civil War and Second World War, 83, 100–102, 109, 120, 142
Paris helping Spanish Republican Refugees, 101–102, 109, 120, 142
Return to Britain, 83, 100–101, 109
Marriage (second) *see* Holst, Wilhelm
SMAC Committee Member, 100
Second World War Secret Agent, 139–173
Alias, 141, 168
British Intelligence *see* Darling, Donald; Hansen, Thorkild; Holst, Wilhelm; Humphreys, Leslie; MI9; O'Leary, Patrick; SOE; Zembsch-Schreve, Guido
Amateur resister, 141, 146, 150–151, 166, 178
Courier to Portugal, 139–141, 154–156, 159, 167, 172–173, 178
Escape lines *see* Garrow-O'Leary Line and Pierre-Jacques Line
French language skills, 133, 166
House in Marseille (safe house), 140, 146, 167
Lieutenant, 140, 168, 172
Marseille group *see* Garrow, Ian; Nouveau, Louis; Nouveau, Renee; Prassinos, Mario; Rodocanachi, Fanny; Rodocanachi, George; Wake, Nancy; Zafiri, George
Norwegian passport, 139, 155, 167
P2 Agent, 141, 166, 168
Secret inks, 140, 155–156, 159, 172
Secretary/secret correspondence, 140, 166–168
SOE networks *see* Alexandre network, Billet network
Post-war, 174–178
Death, 177
Family (visit), 175–176
King and Queen of Denmark, 177
London, 177
Manchester Commemorative Plaque, 174–175, 178
Marriage (third) *see* Hansen, Thorkild
Medals, 140, 144, 146, 176, 178
Post-war France, 175–177
Addy, Mark, 3
Addy (née Costello), Mary, 2–3
Addy, Thomas, 3–5

Aid Spain Movement, 1–2, 10–11, 29–31, 37, 39–43, 46, 48–50, 52, 62, 66, 70, 85, 88–90
Alexandre network, 140, 155, 166–169
Alfonso XIII, 12–13
Appeasement, 28–29, 32–34, 39, 109–113, 116
Aran Valley, 108
Army of Africa, 15, 17, 19–20, 22, 34, 44
Atholl, Katherine, Duchess of, 39, 49, 52
Attlee, Clement, 39
Asturias Uprising, 15
Austria, 110, 112–113
Ayres, Frank, 74

Baldwin, Stanley, 32
Basque refugee children, 29, 37, 42, 46, 49, 51–52, 89–90
Bates, Winifred, 62
BBC, 126, 130, 145, 149, 160
Bebb, Cecil, 44
Belgium, 107, 109, 118–119, 158–159, 162–163, 165, 172
Belsen, 137
Bethune, Norman, 58
Bevin, Ernest, 35–36
Billet network, 140, 154–155, 166–169, 175
Bletchley Park, 131
Blum, Leon, 33, 38, 115
Bradsworth, Colin, 59
Britain and the Spanish Civil War, 28–47
Britain and the Spanish Republic, 28–47

British and Irish Intellectuals and Spanish Civil War, 44–45
British Church and Spanish Civil War, 45–47, 52
British Communists *see* CPGB and YCL
British Fascists *see* BUF
British Mass Media and Spanish Civil War, 44, 47
British Medical Unit (1st), 51, 53–54, 59–60, 62, 68
British and Allied POW/evaders, 142–145, 147–149, 151–153, 156–158, 160, 171
British Trade Unions and Spanish Civil War, 28, 33, 35–38, 42
Broggi, Moises, 68
Brook, Charles, 50
Brown, Isabel, 50
Buchenwald, 147–148, 166
BUF, 2, 31, 42, 131
Bury, Harry, 59, 84

Cabellero, Largo, 20, 23
Carlists, 16, 23
Casado Junta, 27, 97–98
Caskie, Donald, 142–145, 150
Catalan Communists *see* PSUC
Caudwell, Christopher, 45
Causes of the Second World War, 109–114
*Central Sanitaria Internacional see* CSI
Chamberlain, Neville, 32–33, 113, 116. 118
Channel Islands, 163
Charlet, Blanche, 137–138
China, 112

*Index*

Chorlton-cum-Hardy, 1, 7–9
Churchill, Randolph, 30
Churchill, Winston, 118, 132, 166
Circuit or network, 134–135
Citrine, Walter, 35–36
CNT-FAI, 14–15, 17–18, 22–23, 53, 106
Colin, Max, 56–57
Collier, Dorothy, 59
Comet escape line, 158
Conservative Party, 28–29, 31–32, 34–35, 38
Co-operative Movement, 40
Cochrane, Archie, 59–60
Colditz, 152
Cole, Harold, 158, 160–162
Commandoes, 163
Communist Resistance, 124–125, 127, 129, 133
Companys, Luis, 107
Concentration camps (French), 102–106
Cornford, John, 45
CPGB, 1, 28, 30, 33, 37, 39–41, 45, 67, 71–72, 74, 131
Cripps, Stafford, 38–39
Crockatt, Norman, 132
Crome, Len, 59
CSI, 56, 96, 142
Czechoslovakia, 113–114

Dachau, 162
D-Day, 127, 130, 133
Daladier, Edouard, 116
Dalton, Hugh, 132
Dansey, Claude, 140, 152
Darlan, Francois, 124
Darling, Donald, 150–156, 158, 161–162, 166–167, 171
Darton, Patience, 53, 62, 65, 83–84, 100
Davson, Rosita, 53
Denmark, 164, 171, 178
Dissart, Francoise, 159
Dobson, Harry, 43
Dollfuss, Engelbert, 110
Dunkirk, 119, 152
Duran-Jorda, Frederico, 59
Durruti, Buenaventura, 22

Eden, Anthony, 32–33, 36, 108, 110
Eisenhower, Dwight D., 130
Escape lines, 107, 132, 137, 140–141, 143, 152–153
Etchebehere, Mika, 19

F Section, 132
*Falange*, 16, 23, 69–70
Fall of France, 118–120
FANY, 136
Faringdon, Lord, 90–91
FFC, 168–169
FFI, 127
Findlay, Margaret, 66
Fiocca, Henri, 149
First Aid Nursing Yeomanry *see* FANY
*Forces françaises combattantes see* FFC
*Forces françaises de l'intérieur see* FFI
Fox, Ralph, 45
France, 33, 36, 38, 101–110, 114–120, 139–177

215

France (German Occupied Zone), 121–130, 138, 139–173
Franco, Francisco, 15, 17, 19–20, 22, 24–25, 44, 102, 105–108, 116, 152–153, 176, 178
Free French, 104, 107–108, 124, 126–127, 130, 147, 168
French fascists, 114–115, 124–128, 130
French Resistance, 107–108, 124–131, 133–134, 149, 160, 165, 168–169, 172
Fresnes Prison, 137

Gallagher, Willie, 41
Garrow, Ian, 140–142, 144–148, 150–151, 153–157, 159–161, 166, 168, 173
Garrow-O'Leary Line, 140–141, 143–147, 149, 151, 156–162
Gaulle, Charles de, 125, 127–128, 130, 147, 175
German counterespionage, 122, 133–135, 137, 144–145, 147–150, 156–158, 160–161, 166
Germany, 17, 24, 31, 33, 38, 41, 102, 107, 109–114, 116–120, 139–173
Gibraltar, 29, 32, 34, 149, 152, 154–155, 157–159, 161
Gorgopotamos Railway Viaduct, 132
Granen Hospital, 53–54
Green, Nan, 64–65, 71, 73–74, 84, 100, 104, 176
Green, George, 74
Gubbins, Colin, 166, 172

Guerisse, Albert-Marie *see* O'Leary, Patrick
Guernica bombing, 24, 44
*Guernica* painting, 11, 52
Guezennec, Lucienne, 129
Gulbenkian, Nubar, 153–154

Haden-Guest, David, 45, 150
Haden-Guest, Elizabeth, 150
Hall, Virginia, 136–137
Hansen, Thorkild, 120, 140–141, 151, 163–165, 168, 171–173, 176–178
Hayes, Miss, 6
Heydrich, Reinhard, 132
Hibbert, Phyllis, 64, 68
Hill, C. F., 59
Hitler, Adolf, 109–114, 116, 118, 121–122, 178
Hoare, Samuel, 152–153
Hodson, Ada, 61
Holland, 116, 118–119, 133, 162–166, 176
Holst, Wilhelm, 82, 89, 92, 94–96, 98–99, 101, 120, 140, 142–143, 146, 151, 154–155, 163–164, 166–171, 173, 175, 178
Hope Hospital, 5–6
Humphreys, Leslie, 169

IBA, 74, 83, 100, 176
Ibarruri, Dolores, 14, 26
International Brigade Association *see* IBA
International Brigades, 9–10, 20–23, 26, 29–30, 39, 41–43,

## Index

45–46, 54–56, 59–60, 62–63, 67, 71, 74, 106, 150, 183
Italy, 17, 23–24, 26, 31–33, 38, 41, 109–110

Jacobsen, Fernanda, 55
Japan, 109–110, 112
Jedburgh Teams, 133, 137
Jeger, George, 50–51, 91
Jews, 123, 125–129, 169
Jones, Jack, 39
Jones, Louise, 74–75, 83–84, 100
Joseph, Richard, 59

Kemp, Peter, 43

Labour Party, 28, 32–33, 35–40, 42
Langley, Jimmy, 151–152, 156, 161
Laval, Pierre, 122–124, 127
League of Nations, 109–111
Left Book Club, 10, 41, 45, 72
Liberal Party, 32
Lightfoot, Arthur, 7–10, 72, 94–95, 178
Lisbon *see* Portugal
London University Ambulance Unit, 55
Lorca, Federico Garcia, 44
Luft, Issy, 72

MacDonald, Ramsay, 38
McKenna, Bernard, 9
Machado, Antonio, 106
Malimson, Nat, 72–73, 80, 89, 93–94, 100, 176

Manchester Aid Spain/Medical Aid, 1–2, 10–11, 72–73, 80, 89, 93–94, 100, 176
Manchester and North West Spanish Civil War volunteers, 9–11
Manchuria, 110, 112
Manning, Leah, 50–52, 82
*Maquis*, 128–131, 133, 136–137, 149
March, Juan, 16
Marseille, 126, 139–140, 142–150, 152–154, 156–157, 159–161, 163–165, 168, 170–171, 173, 175
Matthews, Herbert L., 103
Mauthausen, 107, 162
Medical advances in Spanish Civil War, 55–60, 63–65, 68
Medical Aid to Spain, 1–2, 10–11, 29–30, 37, 39–43, 46, 48–51, 53–68
Mers-el-Kebir, 124
Mexico, 74, 104, 106
MI5, 130–131
MI6, 130–131, 140, 152–153
MI9, 130–132, 140–141, 145, 148, 150–153, 156, 158, 167, 169, 172, 178
*Milice*, 125, 128, 130
*Milicianas*, 18–19
Miranda de Ebro, 147, 153, 157–158
Mola, Emilio, 16
Montseny, Federica, 14–15
Morgan, Hyacinth, 50
Mosley, Oswald, 2, 31, 42
Mosside, 5, 7

Moulin, Jean, 127
MIS-X, 153
Munich Agreement, 113
Murphy, Molly, 11, 66–67
Murray, Annie, 66

National Government, 28–29, 31–32, 34–38
National Joint Committee for Spanish Relief *see* NJCSR
Nationalists, 29–30, 34–35, 43–44, 47
Neave, Airey, 148, 152, 157
Negrin, Juan, 23, 26–27, 108
Nelken, Margarita, 14
Neveu, Roger le, 158, 162
Nin, Andres, 22
NJCSR, 49, 51–52, 104
Non-Aggression Pact, 114, 117
Non-Intervention Agreement, 21, 32–38, 41, 46, 71
Norway, 107, 118, 132–133, 139, 142–143, 178
Nouveau, Louis, 146, 148, 151, 159
Nouveau, Renee, 146, 148, 151
Nurses (British), 61–68, 71, 73–75, 83–85, 90, 100
Nyon, 33

Odena, Lina, 18–19
O'Duffy, Eoin, 43
O'Leary, Patrick, 141, 145, 147, 153–162, 173
Oradour-Sur-Glane, 130
Orwell, George, 18, 45

PCE, 14, 16, 18, 20–22, 26, 106, 108
Pejot, France, 129

Pessac Power Station, 133
Petain, (Philippe) Marshal, 116, 121–124, 130, 178
Phelps, Penny, 63–65, 67
Picasso, Pablo, 11, 52
Pierre-Jacques Line, 141, 162, 164–168, 171–172, 176
Planel, Claude, 162, 164
Poland, 113–114, 116–117
Polenino Hospital, 54, 70, 83
Pollitt, Harry, 41
Portugal, 139–140, 152–154, 156, 159, 163, 167, 169, 172–173, 178
POUM, 17–19, 22–23
Powell, Margaret, 65–66
Praeger, Leslie, 11
Prassinos, Mario, 146–148
Primo de Rivera, Miguel, 12–13
PSOE, 13–17, 20
PSUC, 62
Purser, Joan, 63
Pye, Edith, 52

Quakers, 45, 49, 51–52, 55, 66, 96, 104–105, 142, 167–169, 171

Rathbone, Eleanor, 52
Ravensbruck, 129, 137, 166
*Retirada,* 27, 66, 71, 74, 102–105
Reynaud, Paul, 116, 119–120
Rhineland, 110–111
Robertson, Janet, 63
Rodocanachi, Fanny, 146–147
Rodocanachi, George, 146–147, 150–151
Roman Catholic Church (Spanish), 13
Ross, Rosaleen, 60

## Index

Rudellat, Yvonne, 137
Rusholme, 4
Ruys, Thomas, 59

Saarland, 110, 117
Safe Houses, 140, 143, 145, 153, 160, 165, 167
Sanchez, Rosario, 19
*Sanidad*, 56
Sanjurjo, Jose, 13
Saxton, Reg, 60
Scott-Ellis, Priscilla, 43
Scottish Ambulance Unit, 54–55
Second World War, 102, 104, 106–109, 114, 116–173
Secret Intelligence Service *see* SIS
Secret Services Bureau, 131
Silverthorne, Thora, 60, 63, 67–68
Sinclair-Loutit, Kenneth, 50, 53–54, 60, 68
SIS, 158, 172
Slater, Mary, 11, 63, 66
SMAC, 50–51, 53–57, 59, 62, 66, 68, 70–73, 75, 78, 80, 82, 85, 88–90, 93, 96, 99–100, 104
SOE, 126, 130–138, 140–141, 147, 151, 154–155, 158–160, 162, 165, 167, 169–172, 176, 178
Soviet Union, 21, 23, 33, 40, 106, 109–110, 113–114, 117, 124–125, 166
Spain, 12–13, 29, 32, 34, 46, 50–51, 53, 56–57, 63–65, 68–102, 126, 138, 140–141, 143, 145, 147, 150–153, 157–158, 161, 163–164, 171–173, 178
Spanish anarchists *see* CNT–FAI
Spanish army, 12–13, 16

Spanish Civil War, 17–101, 176–178
Spanish communists *see* PCE
Spanish Marxists *see* POUM
Spanish Medical Aid Committee *see* SMAC
Spanish Republic, 13–16, 28–47
Spanish Republican Exiles, 74, 102, 105–108, 116, 131, 142, 153, 162, 176
Spanish Revolution, 17–18, 22–23
Spanish socialists *see* PSOE
Special Operations Executive *see* SOE
Stalin, Joseph, 40, 114, 117
Steer, George, 44
Stewart, Frida, 104
Straight, Whitney, 161
Stretford, 1–2
Sudetenland, 113
Sullerot, Evelyne, 129
Sweden, 142
Switzerland, 126, 152, 157, 162, 164, 169

Tapsell, Walter, 43
Thomas, Frank, 43
Trueta Raspall, Josep, 58–59
Tudor-Hart, Alexander, 60, 84

Uclés Hospital, 56, 64, 69, 73–84, 86–88, 93, 97–99
United Nations, 108
Urmston, Lillian, 63, 66, 91, 105

Vassie, Ena, 83–84, 100, 104
Versailles Treaty, 109–112
Vichy France, 102, 107, 121–130, 138, 139–173

Wake (née Fiocca), Nancy, 140, 146, 148–150, 159, 161, 173
Wilkinson, Ellen, 38
Wilson, Francesca, 105
Wingate, Sybil, 37, 42
Withington, Pearl, 136
Women and Aid Spain, 30–31
Women French Resistance, 128–129
Women secret agents, 132, 135–138

YCL, 42
Yugoslavia, 133

Zafiri, George, 146–147
Zembsch-Schreve, Guido, 141, 162–167, 172–173, 176